POWER TOOLS

for
Logic Pro 9

Rick Silva

HAL LEONARD BOOKS

An Imprint of Hal Leonard Corporation | New York

Published in 2010 by Hal Leonard Books
An Imprint of Hal Leonard Corporation
7777 West Bluemound Road
Milwaukee, WI 53213

Trade Book Division Editorial Offices
19 West 21st Street, New York, NY 10010

www.halleonard.com

Book design by Kristina Rolander
Front cover design by Richard Slater

Library of Congress Cataloging-in-Publication Data is available upon request.

ISBN 978-1-4234-4345-2

Printed in the United States of America

Acknowledgments

When I was presented the opportunity to write books for the Hal Leonard Corporation, I was honored. It was not something I set out to do, but sometimes opportunities come by way of pure circumstance, and being at the right place at the right time. Being prepared, however, is something that allows one to take on unforeseen challenges with enthusiasm and confidence. When I found out I was to write books for Pro Tools and Logic Pro simultaneously, I must admit I was a bit nervous. Not only was this my first publishing deal, but also I was asked to write intermediate-to-advanced books for the two biggest digital-audio workstations on the market. Nevertheless, I was excited to take on the challenge.

While writing these books, both Apple and Digidesign released major software updates (Pro Tools 8 and Logic Pro 9), forcing me to revise both books extensively. There were other obstacles to overcome while writing this book, but it's finally finished, and I lived to tell about it!

Since writing two books at the same time was a tall order, I had to call in many favors, and for that I would like to thank the people that really came through for me and made the completion of both books possible. First and foremost, I would like to thank my entire family, especially my mother. She is unbelievably positive and supportive. Her confidence in my ability never wavers, and she still insists that I should never give up on my dreams—even if sometimes it is expensive advice for her to give. She's awesome. Thanks, Mom!

Many musicians have inspired me over the years. Ross Bolton and Gary Hoey are two of the most talented, motivated, and professional musicians I've ever had the pleasure of listening to and studying with. They both inspired and encouraged me in a big way. They showed me how it's possible to make a living in the music business, but only if you are dedicated, have a plan, and are willing to "go after it" to make it happen. I'm proud to say they both were incredible mentors to me. Thanks for the great advice.

Scott Pederson at Waves, you're awesome! I can't thank you enough for helping my studio (Mixed Emotions) become one of the first Waves Certification Training Facilities in Los Angeles. Ultimately you introduced me to Mike Lawson and made this book possible. Thanks so much for your enthusiasm and professionalism.

Mike Lawson, publisher extraordinaire, thank you so very much for giving me the opportunity to write these books and introducing me to the world as an author-instructor. I look forward to our future business endeavors, and many years of collaboration and friendship.

Roy Burns, thanks for all of your help. I appreciate all of the fact-finding and gathering of information that you did for the rough model of this book. It's a shame you weren't able to see this Logic Pro 9 revision to completion, but your efforts in the earlier stages of this book do not go unnoticed or unappreciated. You were a huge help.

A very special thanks must go to some of my former Musicians Institute (RIT) students who assisted me throughout various stages of production for this book. They are April Arroyo, Marius Rostad, Carolyn Ong, J.E. Stewart, Mackenzi Eddings, Ellie Mc Neil, and Jonathon Gusoff. I would recommend each of them to anyone looking for a dependable, dedicated, and talented audio engineer. I look forward to working with all of them again sometime in the future.

Finally, many thanks to Rusty Cutchin and the many people at Hal Leonard who helped with the production of this book. I appreciate all of you for seeing this book to completion. Thanks so much!

Table of Contents

CHAPTER 6
PRODUCING WITH LOGIC

CHAPTER 7

A LOGICAL APPROACH

CHAPTER 8
MIXING AND MASTERING ESSENTIALS

ON THE DVD-ROM
Instructors: Rick Silva, Roy Burns, Dave Hewitt

Introduction

Hello, and thank you for choosing *Power Tools for Logic Pro 9*. I approached writing this book by providing what I've always wanted to know about Logic, demonstrating how easy it is to use professionally, and answering the question "How do I learn all of the cool new stuff everyone says it does?" Apple's release of Logic Pro 9 in September 2009 was a surprise and a bold statement to many of the company's competitors. It was another powerful upgrade, with plenty of new guitar-oriented goodies included, and I am pleased to show off many of the program's new features in this book.

I was primarily a "Pro Tools guy," but after using Logic Pro 9 exclusively for the past few months, I agree with the thousands of users worldwide that that the program is incredibly powerful. I will definitely be spending a lot more time using it in professional situations. Almost all of my past complaints about Logic have been resolved, and speaking from a guitar player's point of view, I can assure you that Logic Pro 9 simply "kills" in the sounds and ease-of-use departments. The wide variety of tones you can create with the new Amp Designer and Pedalboard are so inspiring and of such high quality that Logic Pro 9 is a must for any guitar player's studio—not only for recording music, but for writing, producing, editing, mixing, and mastering it, too.

This book is intended for the intermediate-to-advanced-level Logic user, but it also includes the fundamentals—the essential ingredients to becoming a true "expert user." Knowing the fundamentals and using the software consistently and productively will bring out your full creative potential and motivate you to learn as much as you can about Logic Pro 9. Unfortunately, not everything about Logic Pro 9 could possibly be covered in one book. You'll find, however, that I've included enough information to challenge you regardless of your skill level, and the book will help you quickly learn what's new in version 9. You'll also pick up a few pro-audio engineering concepts and techniques that will take your projects to a new level.

Most important, learning the tools described in *Power Tools for Logic 9* will ensure that you are current with your Logic skill set and ready for future versions of the application. Logic software is continually evolving, and keeping up with its many updates is challenging, but the rewards will be obvious as you make your way through the book. Enjoy!

A Logical Choice

Apple's Logic Pro 8 was a landmark release that raised the bar for digital audio workstations (DAWs) and MIDI sequencing applications. With the release of Logic Pro 9, Apple has redesigned and redefined its music production software. Over the past few years, Logic has become a force to be reckoned with in the professional audio community, and this book was developed and written to show you why.

Logic was created in the 1980's, but began to become known when the German company Emagic released the program under the name Notation Logic. The application was written for the Atari computer system, but unfortunately for Emagic, Atari was nearing its end as a maker of personal computers. However, Logic's creators believed in the software's fundamental approach, and were convinced that the program could succeed with newer operating systems. Eventually, they decided to drop the "Notation" from the name, and the program reemergeed simply as Logic. New Logic software was designed for the Mac and Windows platforms, and its functionality improved quickly. With the release of Logic 3, the software evolved from a basic MIDI sequencer to a MIDI sequencer with the ability to mix audio. However, it required some processing help from sound cards or DSP cards made by companies such as Digidesign and MOTU. When Logic 4 introduced the ability to record audio and combine it with MIDI tracks without the use of additional hardware, it was an awesome concept, but the program was severely limited by the computing power of the day. Even though the computers at the time couldn't quite perform at an optimal level for most creative musicians and demanding audio engineers, Emagic realized that computers were getting faster and more powerful, so it continued to develop its software. Logic 5 featured an updated GUI (graphical user interface) and greater compatibility with the increasing choices of audio hardware. When Logic 6 was released, Emagic introduced software products that were optimized specifically for Logic, such as the EXS sampler, various software instruments, and the company's own plug-ins. Logic had become a top contender, at least among those musicians who compose or produce music on computers. Then Logic was acquired by Apple, whose engineers have worked to give the program the same functionality and simplicity as all of Apple's other products and to get the program recognized by the professional audio industry as a powerhouse audio application. Because of that effort, today Logic software has amazingly powerful production tools that are also intuitive and "logical."

Professional audio engineers and musicians have been divided for many years over which DAW or MIDI sequencer is superior. Because of steady improvements to these applications, however, it is more difficult than ever to declare one program as the best.

So the question is, Why would you choose one program over another? For its sonic quality? Because it is more "musical" than other programs? The answer depends upon the user's preference, the program's usability, and the purpose for which the program is being purchased. These days you will find that most applications do just about everything, but each one has a slight edge in specific areas. This is where personal preference comes into play. Logic was originally designed to be a powerful MIDI sequencer, and in recent years it has added comprehensive audio editing, mixing, and mastering tools. Pro Tools, on the other hand, was originally designed for audio editing, mixing, and mastering, but has since become a contender in the MIDI and virtual instrument departments. Cubase and Digital Performer are also excellent programs with their own unique advantages.

Today almost every digital audio application can perform any audio-related task. For those musicians and producers who want a really powerful program that is competitively priced, comes bundled with great plug-ins and software instruments, and is fully self-contained, Logic Pro 9 is just what the doctor ordered. And it has its own unique strengths, as we will see.

SO WHAT'S NEW?

Logic has always focused on music creation. This is what makes musicians feel at home in the program. Logic Pro 9 has added several new features, but more importantly, it has become even more intuitive and aesthetically pleasing. Apple has very strict standards for its products, and after acquiring Logic from Emagic, it was not interested in just re-branding the application with an Apple logo and calling it a day. Logic 7 saw many improvements from earlier versions, but it still didn't quite have the signature Apple look and feel. However, all that changed in Logic 8, and only a little over a year and a half later came the incredible new features of Logic 9.

In Logic Pro 9, you have the ability to make music extremely quickly. This is great for the musician who has an idea he is dying to get out. Inspiration can be a rarity, so when it strikes, you want to be ready. Nothing is more frustrating than having a computer or piece of software hinder your music-making ability; after all, it is supposed to help you make music. Logic's zero-to-music approach has been embraced and applauded by many users, and now with new features such as Flex Time, drum replacement and enhancement, the incredible-sounding Amp Designer, and the ability to make track content transfers from project to project, just to name a few, you'll have full control and total flexibility over your recording session. That's the beauty of it all. With Logic Pro 9 you can use professional audio engineering techniques, or get on with making music with just a few clicks. What's really nice is that as you become more of a Power Tools user and take a more advanced audio engineering approach to creating your final product, you will not necessarily abandon the "easy tools." Rather, you will learn to incorporate them into a new, more productive workflow.

The complete Logic Studio software package includes mastering software, a live performance enhancement feature, and a revolutionary audio editing and sound design application. This book will focus mainly on Logic Pro 9 as your main DAW, and how to choose and use the thousands of included loops and samples. It will also cover how to use the great software instruments and audio plug-ins that come bundled with the program, including the new Amp Designer and Pedalboard features that allow you to combine the sounds of different amps and speaker cabinets, with several classic-style stompbox pedals. Guitar players will be loving the fact that they now have an easy-to-use program that allows them to practice, write, record, and chart out their music so it can be printed and passed out to band mates. Oh yeah and let's not forget to point out that you will learn how you can expand Logic Pro 9 by using third-party virtual instruments and plug-ins.

Another thing about Logic Pro 9 is that it is scalable and more versatile than ever. This means it can be used by both an on-the-go producer who uses his or her laptop to inspire and capture writing sessions, and by a professional recording studio engineer who is using a "decked-out" tower to record and mix professional productions. Even the serious mobile engineer can use Logic Pro 9 to record an entire orchestra on a soundstage. While reading this book, you will learn how to scale Logic to suit your needs.

Apple's ultimate box set, Logic Studio is a complete beginning-to-end music creation and production package that includes some very powerful tools. Covering them all is not the goal of this book, but exploring and using them will be much more intuitive after reading it.

A LOOK UNDER THE HOOD

This book focuses on Logic, but here is a brief summary of the other software that comes bundled with Logic Studio. Check this software out; these great programs complement Logic perfectly.

Mainstage 2 is a cutting-edge, live performance tool that allows you to bring Logic's software instruments and effects to the stage.

Offering sound-on-sound recording with the Loopback plug-in as well as support for the Apogee GiO, it provides hands-free functionality. It also allows you to build your set list with all program changes ready to go. When used to its full potential, it is a an incredible power tool for any performing artist.

Soundtrack Pro 2 is a powerful audio editor that completes the bridge between sound and picture. It allows artists to take their music to the screen with easy-to-use editing tools, surround mixing, and seamless integration with Final Cut Pro to make audio post-production a snap.

WaveBurner is a pro-level mastering application that gives you ultimate control over your final mixes and comes with standard authoring tools for delivering professional premasters and Red Book standard CDs. Armed with these tools and some help from the inspiration gods, there is no limit on what you will be able to create.

Recording, editing, mixing, mastering, and sharing your music has never been easier or more fun. In this book, we will be focusing on Logic Pro 9's user-friendly functionality and its professional audio engineering tools, increasing your creative power and artistic control, and improving the sonic quality of your productions. Because, with Logic Pro 9 you really *can* do just about anything you can think of.

A LOOK AHEAD

These days many people neglect to read software manuals, so luckily Apple has made a "don't make me think" application for making music.

The goal of this book is to cut to the chase and show you the practical power tools that will help you create music quickly and effectively in Logic. You will learn to use standard audio engineering techniques that professionals have been using for decades, while at the same time learning the most efficient ways to get from point A to point B. If you are an aspiring engineer or a modern musician–audio engineer hybrid, this book will help you develop good engineering habits that will eventually become second nature to you. The result will allow you to easily capture the ideas and sounds you hear in your head, without your having to put much thought into the technical aspects of audio engineering. It really doesn't get better than that for musicians.

Since every person learns differently, this book also provides you with QuickTime video demonstrations, end-of-chapter Tune Up questions, a summary of Power Tips, and important keyboard shortcuts. Using all of these tools is the best way to get the most out of this instructional book.

GETTING A GOOD START

Nothing is more exciting than opening a shiny new piece of gear or launching a new program for the first time. All too often we find ourselves just diving in without reading the manual, because that's no fun, and almost everyone wants to start making music right away. Since software installation and configuration has become much easier over the years, it's definitely possible for you to point and click your way around and manage to make many things work. However, it's still a good idea to learn a little about the application you are about to run. If you are coming from another DAW, you might hate the Logic interface at first; you may even go so far as to call it counterintuitive. This reaction will more than likely be because things are different, and no one likes to leave their comfort zone. On the other hand, if you embrace "change" and accept the challenge of learning a new program for what it is, many times you will find new ways to accomplish common pro audio tasks using methods you never knew were possible.

My job as a professional audio engineer and pro audio instructor is to keep abreast of the multitude of software programs, virtual instruments, and plug-ins currently on the market. I also have to have the ability to use any one of them at a moment's notice. I have the confidence to do this because I know the fundamentals of audio engineering and digital audio recording, and am extremely familiar with Pro Tools, one of the most widely used programs on the planet. With those three things, I believe anyone can work in just about any software program with some level of proficiency.

It's no secret that Pro Tools has dominated the pro audio industry for years, and is considered the "industry standard" for professional audio and post-production. It is also quite clear that Logic Pro 9 is finally a true competitor that has now commanded the attention of everyone in the pro audio industry.

Using this book will help you become a better Logic user quickly, and along the way you will learn some nice Power Tools "tips and tricks" for instant gratification. As the book progresses, you will learn effective and efficient practices for setting up your DAW and using it properly. These setup tips may not be as fun as instantly creating music, but they are essential knowledge to acquire. This book is geared toward giving you a method of working that will allow you to quickly achieve a respectable level of proficiency. Even if you were to read the Logic manuals cover to cover, where would you begin? The Logic manuals contain so many pages of information, that it can be intimidating to even open them.

Your software comes with a "Readme" file, and I highly suggest you read it. A Readme file is usually just a bare-bones collection of what you need to know before you install your software. Get into the habit of actually reading the Readme files to save yourself time and trouble in the long run. Readme files often contain information regarding system compatibility, known issues, and new features. If you need to have the latest and greatest at all times, it is important to read these files to ensure that the associated software won't conflict with your system. Furthermore, you may not know about any new features unless you read about them first.

WHAT YOU SHOULD EXPECT

Logic 9 is the culmination of years of development. With each release the program has grown and added more features, and Logic 9 is no exception. It would be too overwhelming to go over each individual feature in Logic, so we are going to be concentrating on some of the more exciting tools and the program's newest features. We will also build on the fundamentals of Logic. My advice to you is to be patient. The advanced concepts, techniques, and Power Tools covered in the later chapters of this book will make much more sense after you have a solid grasp of the fundamentals. These foundational elements generally remain unchanged with software updates, as they are usually deeply embedded in earlier versions.

Those who have been using Logic or other DAWs have seen this evolution firsthand. The versatility and portability of Logic allows us to create works of art on the go with very little hardware. Please take note of the following categories, which will be the major areas of focus in this book.

Recording with Logic

The evolution of recording has jumped by leaps and bounds in recent years. What used to require a massive console and a refrigerator-size tape machine can now be done with a laptop and a small recording interface. Even though there are ongoing debates over the quality of analog vs. digital recording, this is not the place to discuss such things. However, it is worth noting that there was a time when digital recording was not considered a serious threat to old-school analog recording. Now digital recording is well on its way to holding its own and being equal in quality to analog recording. Remember, it's not always about which is better. Oftentimes it is more of a preference issue, not a quality issue.

Logic is expandable and can be used in conjunction with high-end consoles and TDM systems. Having the ability in Logic to record a solo acoustic performance track or a symphony orchestra on a soundstage is a realistic example of how scalable the program is. Whether you use Logic for fun or professionally, you need to have a decent understanding of music and audio engineering as well as a decent amount of practice with both. You will learn how to select microphones, how to set good mic pre levels, some basic signal-flow, and how to use the proper record mode. You'll also learn about latency and how to minimize it, how to record multiple takes, and how to easily execute playback and recording functions.

Editing with Logic

I have spent many waking hours editing in DAWs—everything from full-length multitrack CD projects to simple radio edits. Non-linear editing is an art form that has been in existence since the first time we could capture audio on a computer. The basic editing tools used in DAWs evolve with each new update to a program, and the ways in which they are used are constantly being improved with shortcuts and new techniques that optimize workflow. While you can get by with using only one tool one way, it isn't a very efficient strategy. Many people are reluctant to try the latest methods because it can seem like overkill to learn every new technique that comes around, but it is important to learn various ways of editing your audio files. Modern editing techniques will not only increase your speed and efficiency, but will help you better manage your sessions.

Logic bridges the gap between professional audio engineers and the musician-engineer hybrid we are seeing more and more of these days. It gives the everyday musician access to tools that are normally reserved for audio engineers, and engineers the flexibility of editing musically instead of just conforming to a sample-based timeline. With the simultaneous advances in computers and software, editing with DAWs has outpaced analog editing big time! Destructive editing that once took hours is now nondestructive and takes mere minutes in the digital domain.

Creating with Logic

The process of recording, programming, and editing MIDI tracks has also been vastly improved in Logic 9. MIDI is considered ancient by technology standards, yet it is still used nearly every day in all levels of music production in home and pro studios alike. Not long ago we relied on external MIDI interfaces and sound modules to generate our MIDI data and desired sounds.

There was a time when everyone needed certain sound engines and keyboards for professional production. Now we rely on our computers to do all the heavy lifting with MIDI and sound production. MIDI controllers are still employed, but now they trigger internal sounds and events in the computer, showing us that "vintage" technology still has a few tricks up its sleeve.

Instrument tracks are a huge part of the creation process in Logic. The program includes several studio-quality instruments that cover a wide range of sounds. We'll be using Ultrabeat to create drumbeats and the EXS24 sampler for our sample-based patches—Logic Pro 9 comes with over 1,300 EXS instruments and plenty of other really nice new features that we will be covering in the later chapters of this book. We'll also use Sculpture to shape sounds and create luscious, atmospheric elements and pads. The vintage instruments included in Logic are very impressive and feature some classic clavs, organs, and electric pianos. Rounding out the collection is a large variety of synths. All of these instruments have several editable parameters that allow you to take your creations to new sonic heights.

Working with virtual instruments and MIDI generally requires some kind of controller. Any keyboard with a MIDI port will work with Logic; however, modern-day controllers come with a USB port in addition to MIDI. USB provides a true plug-and-play experience. Modern controllers also employ more controls to help you shape your sound. Knobs, sliders, trigger pads, and buttons galore are all assignable so that tweaking your sound can be done in a more organic fashion.

Mixing with Logic

Creating music, choosing new sounds, and editing and arranging is an art. Yet mixing is an art form as well. It may be much harder to see mixing as part of the creative process, yet it plays a very important role in the overall sound of your creation. There is a big reason mixing engineers are paid far more than tracking and editing engineers in the recording industry. Thankfully, Logic gives us some very powerful tools to help us mix the music we create. Unfortunately, it can't give us the years of experience a great mix engineer has, nor can it develop our ears instantaneously.

Mixing "in the box" refers to a style of mixing where all of the dynamic and time-based effects routing is done inside of the computer, and then continues on to your audio interface, and finally to your speakers. There are various benefits and a few disadvantages to mixing in the box, and we'll go over some of them as this book progresses. What is important now is to know that the amount of RAM and processing power your system has will directly affect how many tracks you can effectively mix in Logic. We'll go over some tips to help you free up power and use your computer to its maximum potential. For example, you can use Logic in conjunction with a Pro Tools HD system to add more DSP to your system, and you can also network multiple computers to distribute the processor load to other Macs.

You'll quickly learn that there is no "magic bullet" solution to mixing. While presets can't guarantee a great-sounding mix, they can provide a nice starting point. Compression, EQ, and time-based effects are all variables in mixing. We'll see how fader levels and panning also play a big role in how well your mixes turn out.

Mastering

Mastering is the final step in the process before your music is sent to the duplication labs for mass reproduction. Just like mixing, there is no magical solution or preset method for mastering, so it can be challenging. The main goals are to ensure that your mix is playing at an acceptable broadcast level and that the overall frequency curve of your project is somewhat consistent. Remember, your CD has to have a certain level of continuity from song to song, so that it is comparable to other professional CDs on the market. I suppose you could easily throw on a multi-band compressor followed by an EQ, then perhaps a nice limiter to maximize your overall level, but it won't maximize your sound. Understanding that a mix needs room to breathe may sound very abstract now, but it will make more sense as you start to learn about and experiment with the mastering process. Mastering is relatively subjective: what sounds good to one person might not sound good to someone else. It is important to keep in mind the style of music you are going for when mastering, and to listen to similar CDs as a reference. It is often difficult for musicians to differentiate between the sonic quality of their music versus its tonality and rhythmic qualities. Training your ear to listen to different frequencies is not easy, and cannot be done overnight. We'll go over some fundamental ear training tips for mixing, as well as basic mastering within Logic Pro, so that all of your projects will be ready for mass duplication when you are finished with them.

WHAT YOU SHOULD KNOW

The Power Tools series is geared toward users who have a solid grasp of the application and would like to learn some new techniques and "Power Tools" used by professionals. What are power tools in general? They are motorized tools that generally make your work easier. A powered screwdriver saves you tons of time and energy, right? Likewise, the tips and techniques used in this book will act as power tools that you can add to your recording toolbox. There are always several ways to do various things, but the trick to working smarter and not harder is to know which tool is the right one for the job. Now imagine that tool is a power tool—even better!

Power Tools books are not for beginners, nor are they necessarily for advanced professionals, although seasoned pros may pick up a few handy tips along the way. You should already know the fundamentals of Logic, or a similar recording platform. Many of these fundamentals apply to all DAW applications. You should also have a decent amount of music theory under your belt, or at least know the basics well enough to let Logic do the rest for you. You should also have some sequencing experience with piano roll–based MIDI editing. Knowing the fundamentals of audio engineering, musicianship, and signal flow will also be of great value when reading this book.

If you do not already possess this knowledge, you may find some of the terminology and examples in this book to be a bit challenging, yet understandable. On the other hand, if you have a solid background in Logic and audio engineering, this book may seem a little slow at first. However, keep in mind that there will be Power Tip summaries and questions at the end of each chapter that will allow you to find out quickly what this book can add to your skill set. While both amateur and pro users will still find this book useful, it is essentially geared toward the intermediate-level Logic user who would like to step up their game substantially.

Back to DAW Basics

ESSENTIAL ELEMENTS

This chapter will provide you with the essential elements required to use Logic Pro 9 effectively. What is presented here is general recording theory that applies to the overall art of recording sound, not just to Logic. While Logic caters to the musician, there are still elements of recording engineering you must be familiar with in order to get the most out of your recordings. You don't have to be a professional audio engineer to achieve high-quality results from a program such as Logic these days. However, having a firm grasp of the basics of audio engineering and knowing the fundamental process of digitizing audio for recording, editing, and mixing will increase the quality of your recordings dramatically. Understanding the visual representation of your sound will also give you an edge when it comes time to edit. Furthermore, understanding the key elements that comprise your sound will help you make better recordings in the long run. Over the next few pages, we will dive into some different subjects that should make you think of sound in a new way. Awareness of how we perceive sound may be something you've never thought about, but a little bit of theory goes a long way.

OVERNIGHT SUCCESS?
I DON'T THINK SO!

The art of recording has undergone many radical changes in the past 15 years or so. Skeptics and recording engineers alike swore that computers would never replace analog tape machines. While computer-based recording has not killed analog tape recording entirely, it has certainly proved to be a viable option. Today, many artists and bands record their music with computers. This is the result of a couple of things. The first and most likely reason is that the cost of recording digitally and mixing "in the box" is far less expensive than booking a professional recording studio and high-priced engineers to run large recording consoles costing several hundreds of thousands of dollars. Since the cost of digital recording hardware and software has gone down considerably over the past few years, musicians can now afford recording tools that were not previously available to them. In addition to the decrease in cost, quality has risen. In the past, recording with computers wasn't taken very seriously because the quality of the recordings simply couldn't compete with their analog counterparts. Nowadays, affordable hardware and software is capable of recreating the analog sound to the point that even the most discerning ears cannot tell the two apart.

Understanding some basic audio engineering fundamentals is a key factor in capturing quality sound. If you feel you already know most of the following information, I suggest you take the time to go over the Logic 9 Tune-Up questions at the end of this chapter. These questions will serve as a good gauge of your knowledge if you are considering skipping over this chapter. They will either inspire you to move on, or prompt you to go back and gather the information you need before continuing with this book. Without further ado, let's get right to it and start with the source.

SOUND ADVICE

Many of us take for granted the sounds we hear around us every day. Right now, you may be hearing birds chirping, phones ringing, cars going by in the distance, or the hum of the refrigerator, air conditioner, or other electrical appliances within earshot of wherever you are reading this book. More than likely you are so used to these sounds that you probably just tune them out without even realizing it. If you want to get better at capturing audio with any recording medium, start by simply listening to every sound you hear and realize how each sound has its own distinct character. If you are wondering how that can help you, try thinking about it this way. Let's say you have four pets—two cats and two dogs. When one of them makes a sound, it is easy to tell whether it is one of your dogs barking or one of your cats meowing. Simple enough—a dog sounds like a dog and a cat sounds like a cat, right? The exciting thing about this simple analogy is not that dogs sound like dogs and cats sound like cats. The exciting part is how easily we can tell exactly which one of our pets has just made a sound. Do you ever wonder why? Knowing how sounds are created and why we perceive each sound as unique provides invaluable insight into how to go about recording. The more you know about sound, the better you will get at recording audio. The better you get at recording audio, the more you'll understand how to mix it within the context of other instruments. The cycle is endless, and one always feeds the other. Therefore, knowing as much as you can about the sounds you are working with is sound advice.

The Source

When we hear a sound, we are experiencing a change in pressure in the air around us. These changes in pressure are created by vibrations in a given object. When an object vibrates and completes a single back-and-forth motion, it is referred to as a *cycle*. This cycle of vibration creates an audio event. The event is perceived as sound to the human ear if it falls within our range of hearing. Humans generally can perceive sound between 20 cycles per second and 20,000 cycles per second. If an object vibrates outside of that range it doesn't mean it doesn't make a sound, it just means humans cannot hear it. It is safer to say we may *feel* it instead of hear it.

The cycles produced by any given source have other variables that give that source a unique sound. Let's go back to the earlier question, "How can we determine which of our pets made a sound?" Well, this depends on three factors contained in the vibrations created by the animal's "voice box." These factors are the sound's amplitude, frequency, and waveform. Simply put, *amplitude* is the volume or strength of the sound. *Frequency* is the pitch of the sound in terms of high and low. The *waveform* is the shape of the vibrations that caused the sound. When all three of these factors are combined, we can identify it as its own unique sound. One of the goals of this chapter is to break down the science of sound into a more digestible concept. This will also help you understand why you should have an overall awareness of the basics of sound as it applies to recording and mixing audio.

For example, when you are tuning your guitar, you might use a tuner set to A 440. This means the sound is vibrating at 440 cycles per second, but what you are hearing is a computer-generated sine wave (see **Fig. 2.1**). This obviously sounds different from a guitar or piano playing an A note at 440 Hz. Even though an A 440 in each source can be measured at 440 cycles per second, each source still sounds very different. Let's break this down further so you can better understand the variables that make a sound unique.

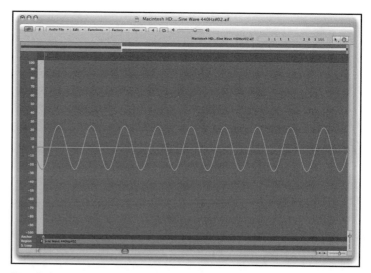

Fig. 2.1: A Sample Editor view of a simple sine wave at 440 kHz.

Amplitude

Our ears perceive the magnitude or strength of the variations in sound pressure as overall volume or loudness. Amplitude is also commonly referred to as *sound pressure level*, or SPL. The sound pressure level is measured in decibels. A *decibel*, as its name implies, is one tenth of a bel (a seldom-used unit). A decibel is based on a logarithmic scale that indicates the ratio between the amplitude of a sound and a standard reference. This standard reference is the threshold of hearing, which has been assigned the value of 0 dB. Most people can perceive sound at this level. Therefore, all other sound is measured relative to this value. To give you an idea of the measurement, see **Table 2.1**. Remember, this is a logarithmic scale, so the higher the number, the greater the SPL on an exponential scale.

TABLE 2.1: COMMON SOUNDS IN DECIBELS

SOUND	AMPLITUDE
Threshold of hearing	0 dB
Rustling of leaves	10 dB
Average recording studio	20 dB
A quiet bedroom at night	30 dB
A library	40 dB
An average home	50 dB
A normal conversation	60 dB
A vacuum cleaner	70 dB
Heavy traffic	85 dB
Average club before the band starts playing	100 dB
Chainsaw at around five feet away	110 dB
Threshold of pain or discomfort	120 dB
Average rock concert	125 dB
Jet engine	160 dB
Rocket engine	195 dB

Frequency

The term *frequency* refers to the number of cycles that pass a fixed location over a period of one second. Knowing that a sound is perceived when an object completes one vibration cycle, we can determine that the pitch of that sound is a reflection of how many cycles pass our ears (or a microphone) in one second. Frequencies are measured in units called *Hertz* (abbreviated Hz). One thousand cycles per second is equal to one kilohertz (kHz). Earlier, it was mentioned that the range of human hearing is between 20 cycles per second and 20,000 cycles per second. Therefore, we can also say that the range of human hearing is 20 Hz to 20 kHz.

How does frequency relate to music? As a sound's frequency increases, so does its pitch; conversely, as its frequency decreases, so does its pitch. A 440 is our standard tuning note: if we were to play an A note one octave higher, the frequency would be 880 Hz (see **Fig. 2.2**). An A note played an octave below 440 Hz would be 220 Hz. Hopefully this example illustrates how knowing the fundamental frequencies, and the range of frequencies,

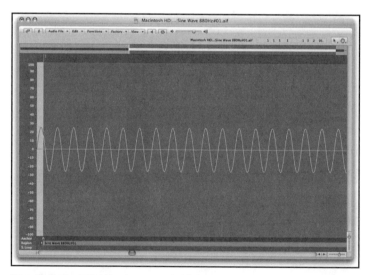

Fig. 2.2: An 880 kHz sine wave is higher in pitch and cycles twice as fast.

of various instruments is important to know when you are recording or mixing audio. Understanding the fundamental frequencies of a given instrument will help you in the mixing process, as instrument frequencies can overlap and occupy the same frequency range. Placing instruments in different areas of the stereo field and properly tweaking the EQ will help you create space for each instrument in your mix, which is why a basic understanding of frequencies is essential.

Waveform

A waveform is a visual representation of a sound's vibration cycle and amplitude. A simple waveform, such as a sine wave, is a great depiction of what a sound looks like. A sine wave is a smooth curve that repeats and maintains a consistent pitch and amplitude.

A sine wave is often used to calibrate a digital interface or professional recording console. Also, when you are using it as a tuner, you are essentially calibrating your instrument. Because it is a simple waveform, it lacks character in its sound. The sounds we hear in everyday life are typically complex waveforms. Complex waveforms look very different from a basic sine wave. They are jagged in appearance, and not nearly as symmetrical as our simple sine wave. However, complex waveforms allow us to differentiate between the sound of a piano and the sound of a guitar even if they are playing the same note in the same octave. Although these complex waveforms are identical in pitch, they look very different. Like humans, each source has its own set of auditory and visual fingerprints, thus giving them their own unique complex waveform. Let's compare our same 440 Hz sine wave signal to 440 Hz played by a piano. Despite the complex waveform having much more going on, it is still the same note (see **Fig. 2.3**).

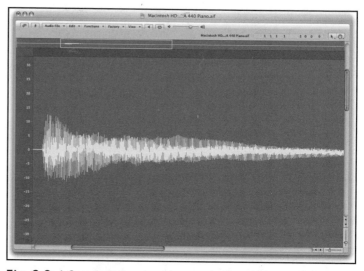

Fig. 2.3: A Sample Editor view of a complex waveform (440 kHz) from an A note played on a piano.

SIGNAL FLOW

Recording workflows can be very diverse; however, they all follow the same basic signal flow. This theory applies to both analog and digital recording to a certain extent. Here's an example of basic signal flow before it gets to the multitrack recorder:

Source ⟶ Microphone ⟶ Cable ⟶ Preamp ⟶

This is just the beginning of a long signal-flow chain. The source in this scenario is analog and represents infinite resolution. For instance, a sine wave has a smooth, round curve. For the sake of this example, let's imagine our source is an oscillator generating a sine wave. This could be your tuner set to A 440. The source is oscillating at 440 times per second. Oscillation (a complete vibration cycle) is what is producing our sound source. As the oscillator generates sound, this sound causes air molecules to be pushed outward, and as they push outward, they compress against each other. This is known as *compression*. As the oscillation moves to the other extreme of its fixed value, the air molecules are in a state of *rarefaction*. This compression and rarefaction is the basis of all sound (see **Fig. 2.4**).

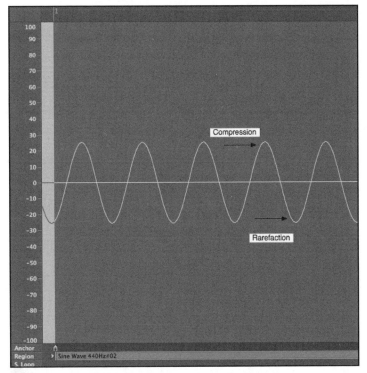

Fig. 2.4: The compression and rarefaction of a waveform.

As the source is oscillating at 440 times per second, the job of the microphone is to pick up that sound and convert the acoustical energy into electrical energy. Converting one form of energy into another is called *transduction*. Therefore, a microphone is a *transducer*. Our ears are also transducers. Our ears convert acoustical energy into electrical energy to be interpreted by our brains. In order for a microphone to convert energy, it uses a diaphragm that is connected to an electromagnet via a small induction. When a microphone picks up acoustical energy, the coil moves in the magnetic field, producing a varying current in the coil through electromagnetic induction. Although this is a very small amount of electricity, it is enough to travel through the microphone cable and into a preamp, where it can be amplified to a usable level. This is a brief explanation of how microphones work as transducers. (For more information on this topic, feel free to explore Faraday's law of induction or any book specifically related to microphones.) Below are a couple of important characteristics you should know about different types of microphones.

Dynamic Microphones

A dynamic microphone is equipped for handling loud sound pressure levels. Dynamic mics generally have a darker, less-defined sound, but are also very durable, resistant to moisture, and usually more affordable. They are very versatile, and great for guitar and bass amps as well as the kick, snare, and toms of a drum kit.

Condenser Microphones

Condenser microphones are very common in many recording situations. The most important characteristics to know regarding these microphones are that they typically require 48 volts of *phantom power* (usually supplied by the mixer or an external power supply) and have an extremely fast transient response for extended sensitivity and detailed sound reproduction. Some have multiple polar pattern selections, various high-pass filters, and a decibel pad to protect the microphone from damage caused by very high sound pressure levels. High-quality condenser microphones reproduce a very accurate "top end" of any source. They are great for acoustic instruments and are especially known for capturing vocal performances.

FREQUENCY RESPONSE AND FREQUENCY CURVE

All microphones have a *frequency response*, meaning the lowest and highest frequency they are able to capture. Many microphones manipulate the frequency curve and have bumps or dips at set frequencies either by design or as the result of the manufacturer trying to keep costs down. When using or selecting a microphone, it is wise to keep in mind the fundamental frequencies of the source and what kind of representation of the sound you are trying to achieve. It is equally important to know the limitations of any given microphone. Knowing these things will help you achieve acceptable results, even on the most modest budget. Always try to use the right tool for the job if you can. In most cases, that is very subjective, but when cost is an issue, understanding the microphones you have to choose from and the source you are trying to capture will allow you to make better decisions.

Preamplification

A preamplifier's job is to boost the incoming signal of the source. Since the amount of electricity generated by a microphone is weak, the level is very low. A preamp boosts the signal until it is at an acceptable level for analog-to-digital conversion. The best preamps are usually referred to as being "transparent," meaning they do not "color" or alter the source of the sound too much. Certain preamplifiers are known to have a "coloration" that is desirable. A professional-grade "preamp" will greatly increase the quality of your sound, but if you apply proper recording techniques, you can generally achieve acceptable results without the hefty price tag of a high-end preamp.

These are the first steps in signal flow. Our analog source has been converted from acoustical energy to electrical energy and boosted to a workable level. At this point our signal is still analog. Sticking with a very basic workflow, let's assume we would like to record the signal we have coming into our preamp. This takes us to the last few steps in signal flow before our source can be used by Logic, or any other software program.

ANALOG-TO-DIGITAL CONVERSION

Analog-to-digital conversion (or A/D conversion) is the final stage before your analog source becomes digitized, or converted to digital bits or binary numerical information (also known as ones and zeros) that can then be archived and ultimately read and manipulated by a computer. Regardless of what platform or operating system you are using, the sound source must be converted from acoustical energy to electrical energy by way of a microphone, a guitar pickup, or other input device and then translated into ones and zeros so that the information can be used by the computer's software. The limitations of this process are defined by sample rate and quantization. Let's take a closer look.

Sample Rate

Sampling occurs when the electrical signal enters an electronic circuit known as a *sample-and-hold circuit*. This circuit suspends the incoming signal, takes a "snapshot" or "sample," and analyzes the voltage level at that instant. Once analyzed, it is then sent to the A/D converter to be converted into a digital number. This digital number represents the voltage level or amplitude at that specific instant. The *sample rate* is how many times this process happens in one second. The sample rate required for digital audio is based on the fundamental law of A/D conversion known as the Nyquist Theorem.

The Nyquist Theorem states that in order to properly translate the frequency of a sound, the digital recorder must have a sampling rate at least two times greater than the rate of the source's highest frequency. If the sampling rate is any lower than that, an audio anomaly known as *aliasing*, caused by frequency distortion, will occur. This is definitely an unwanted artifact in digital recording. However, since we have already established that the range of human hearing is 20 Hz to 20 kHz, then it should be safe to say that since the highest rate of vibrations we can perceive is 20,000 cycles per second, any sampling rate over twice that amount (40 kHz) is acceptable and can capture full-frequency audio.

Almost all digital recorders have a sampling rate of at least 44.1 kHz, and usually 48 kHz. These days, it is common to have an interface that offers sampling rates of 88.2 kHz, 96 kHz, and often as high as 192 kHz. If you are using a higher sampling rate, be aware that these rates take up much more hard drive space and greatly decrease the number of audio tracks that can be recorded and played back simultaneously. When choosing a higher sampling rate, you should choose one that is divisible by the standard rate used for audio CDs (44.1 kHz). The mathematical equation is easier on your computer's processor and can actually result in better sound quality. Professional compact discs (CDs) that we buy off the shelf are stored at a standard sampling rate of 44.1 kHz.

Bit Depth and Amplitude Resolution

The dynamic range of any given sound is the difference between its lowest and highest amplitude. The useful range of dynamics for music and speech is considered to be from 40 to 105 dB. To successfully capture this range, an A/D converter needs to be able to accurately represent differences in amplitude of at least 65 dB. The relative loudness of a sample is captured by a process known as *quantization*. In simple terms, this means that each sample is quantified, or assigned to the nearest amplitude value available. Computers use bits to quantify each sample that is taken. The number of bits used to define a value is referred to as the *binary word length*, or "bit depth." What this means is that the range of values represented by a word length is defined by a binary word length and is the equivalent of 2^n. Here's an example using this mathematical equation: A 4-bit recording is equal to two to the fourth power (2^4). This is equivalent to saying $2 \times 2 \times 2 \times 2 = 16$. This word length (bit depth) would be able to capture and define 16 levels of amplitude to represent your recording's dynamic range. That is not so good. On the other hand, a 16-bit recording is equal to 2^{16}, and would be able to define 65,536 amplitude levels. This will obviously result in a huge jump in the accuracy of your recordings. If you do the math on 24-bit resolution, you'll figure out that a 24-bit digital word length can define 16,777,216 discrete amplitude levels, and is clearly the most obvious choice when recording any sound source. For many years, a 16-bit digital recorder was considered the standard for recording digital audio and was widely accepted, but was definitely subject to criticism. It was constantly debated as far as how accurately it was able to reproduce the original sound source. Today, a 24-bit recording crushes the accuracy of its 16-bit counterpart. Analog vs. digital recordings are still fiercely debated, but current-day 24-bit digital recordings are getting so much better at maintaining the integrity of the original sound source that it is becoming more a matter of taste than audible quality.

Dynamic Range and Headroom

An important thing to understand about all of this information is that for each additional bit of information recorded, the dynamic range of your system will increase by 6 dB. Therefore, if an 8-bit recording has a dynamic range of 48 dB, a 16-bit recording will have a dynamic range of 96 dB. Consequently, a 24-bit recording has a dynamic range of 144 dB. This is more than enough to accurately reproduce the dynamic range of the original sound source, and is better than many high-end analog multitrack recorders. When a system is capable of capturing such a large dynamic range, it means that the signal-to-noise ratio is exceptionally good. Please keep in mind that just like using a higher sampling rate, using a larger word length or bit depth takes up more hard drive space. Therefore, a 24-bit recording generally uses approximately one-and-a-half times the space of a 16-bit recording. If you can spare the hard drive space, a higher bit resolution is well worth it.

DIGITAL RECORDING THEORY

Remember how we used a preamp to boost the level of our analog source signal? This is important, because it will ultimately affect the quality of the digital waveform. Getting a good recording level is essential. If you try to boost a quiet signal too much you will introduce noise. The more you boost a weak signal, the more you boost the noise. If you simply make certain that your source is relatively loud or close enough to the microphone, you should be okay. The amount of noise introduced into a signal is known as the *signal-to-noise ratio*, often abbreviated SNR. It is exactly what it sounds like: the ratio of signal versus the amount of noise "corrupting" the signal. The higher the signal-to-noise ratio, the higher the quality of the signal. It is always easy to turn the volume down on something once it has been recorded, with little or no loss in sonic quality, but turning up a poorly recorded signal will raise the noise floor and almost always make your mixes harder to tame.

Maximizing your bit depth works on the same principle as maximizing your SNR using microphones and preamps. Recording at a "hot" level without peaking is how we maximize bit depth and maintain the highest quality. The system by which we record digitally is known as Linear Pulse Code Modulation, or LPCM. This has been the standard for many years. The only trouble is dynamic range. The quieter a signal is, the fewer bits it is using, and thus the poorer the quality. However, music is supposed to be dynamic, to get loud and soft, to "breathe." By constantly being recorded at the maximum level in combination with overcompression (which we'll go over later), music has suffered, and we are now in what's referred to as the "Loudness War." Remember to maximize your bit depth, but not at the expense of your music.

THE VIRTUAL CONSOLE AND MULTITRACK RECORDER

After a source passes through a microphone and the signal goes through the A/D conversion process, the music is in the computer and ready to be manipulated in any way our creativity and DAW knowledge allow. At this point, you should understand the basic concept of how an analog signal is recorded by a microphone or any other transducer, translated to electric energy, and then digitized to be Logic ready.

Before we get into using Logic, there are still a few more things to know about what is waiting for you inside the digital domain. In the scheme of DAW signal flow, Logic acts as a virtual recording console, which makes professional recording easier than ever. Logic software and hardware combinations have all of the elements of high-end recording consoles. Once a source travels through the interface and is recorded onto a hard drive for storage and manipulation, we have the same basic signal-processing and routing options we would if we were using an analog board. One of the main differences is that the internal dynamic processing and time-based effects used in Logic are primarily nondestructive. This means you can change the parameters of these processors anytime you choose, save them at any stage of the session, and recall the settings as you wish within a matter of seconds.

In order to better understand how to use all the features that Logic has to offer, it is vital to be aware of some common terminology and some of the limitations you may encounter with your computer. Not everyone has the same computer; therefore, it is impossible to tell you the best way to set up your particular system. It is your responsibility to know the specifications of your computer. This will really help you understand its capabilities and recognize its limitations. It is always wise to purchase as much RAM as your computer can accommodate. Doing so will allow you to use Logic at your computer's full potential.

ESSENTIAL TERMS

Below are some key terms you should know. Throughout the rest of this book, we'll be sure to add more terms and their definitions to your vocabulary. One thing you should realize as you go through this book is that audio engineering isn't just about twisting some knobs and letting the computer fix it. The computer doesn't think; therefore, it is up to you to tell the computer what to do. What you tell it to do is directly related to the amount of knowledge you have about digital audio workstations and their capabilities. Knowing the following terms will help you get the most out of Logic and your computer.

AMS (Audio MIDI Setup): Bundled with OS X, this is an application that lets you tell the computer what audio and MIDI devices you have connected to it. From here you can select what inputs and outputs you would like your computer to use, and graphically connect various MIDI devices to your system.

AU (Audio Units): These are system-wide plug-ins for use with Core Audio. Plug-ins that have an AU component must be validated for use with Logic using the AU Scan utility in Logic.

Core Audio: This is Apple's system for managing audio. Core Audio is part of the OS X core services. Core services require very few instructions from the application to the CPU, cutting down on latency while maintaining quality.

CPU (Central Processing Unit): This is the main chip in your computer that makes everything run. It is the brain that communicates and gives instructions to the other hardware attached to your computer. A fast CPU will give you more power to run more overall tracks, virtual instruments, and plug-ins in Logic. Newer computers generally have multiple CPUs or CPU cores. Logic takes advantage of having multiple cores at its disposal.

Digital Audio Workstation (DAW): A term used to refer to a system that has audio and sequencing software as well as hardware that adds functionality to the system.

External Hard Drive: A storage medium for data. External drives and/or dedicated internal drives are recommended for professional audio and video workflows. A drive with an rpm of 7200 or more and a seek time of less than 10 ms is preferred. Despite claims that USB 2.0 is faster than FireWire, it is not recommended for professional applications, as USB drives take their toll on your CPU. FireWire 400, 800, and eSATA are all great solutions for fast and reliable drives.

Interface: The device used for the analog-to-digital conversion process. Interfaces vary in quality and number of potential inputs and outputs. The interface routes audio into and out of your computer; some also integrate MIDI as a means to get MIDI data into and out of your computer.

Latency: A delay in audio throughput caused by a given process. Latency is most noticeable when working in a multitrack session with many plug-ins. The amount of latency varies depending on your system configuration and the amount of tracks and plug-ins you have. We'll go over ways to help eliminate latency when recording in the upcoming chapters.

Plug-ins: A plug-in is a software add-on that enhances a program's capabilities. Think of it as a software accessory that provides extra tools for shaping the sound of any source. Plug-ins usually do not function as stand-alone applications; they are accessed from within the host software (Logic) and use your computer's CPU for processing power (Native).

Random Access Memory (RAM): This is the amount of memory your computer has instant access to. The more RAM your computer has, the quicker your computer can pull data at a moment's notice. RAM acts like an extremely fast hard drive. It has a cache that fills with data, and when that cache is filled your computer has to make more calls on your hard drive, so having a large amount of RAM cuts down on the amount of time your computer needs to pull data from the hard drive. Virtual instruments and plug-ins require large amounts of RAM. For example, when loading a piano sample, your sampler is loading hundreds of samples into RAM so you can have quick access to them.

Time Division Multiplexing (TDM): Dedicated DSP hardware. Originally designed for Pro Tools, Logic is able to take advantage of the hardware DSP provided by Pro Tools HD systems.

OPTIMIZING YOUR COMPUTER FOR LOGIC

You may have already installed the application and content, which is fine. However, in this section I am going to go over a few ways to optimize your system for Logic, starting with the installation type and location of the program.

If you have nightmares recalling the four-hour process of installing Logic Studio and you do not wish to uninstall/ reinstall, I can't blame you. However, should you reach a point where computer performance becomes an issue, come back to this chapter and give this a try.

Logic is a hefty install, weighing in at nearly 45 GB of content. Luckily, you can choose where some of this content goes, but not all of it. The applications must always be installed on your system's main hard drive in the Applications folder. The content, however, can be installed elsewhere.

Partitioning Your Hard Drive

Let's take a step even further back before we even touch on Logic installation. We are going to start with OS installation. I am not going to go in depth as to how to perform a clean system install. However, when configuring your computer for audio there are a few things to keep in mind.

If possible, you should have more than one internal hard drive. Having a fast internal drive that is separate from your main system is ideal for audio. Sadly, laptops, iMacs, and Mac Minis cannot accommodate extra internal drives. But don't worry. If you are limited to one hard drive, you can partition it into two drives.

Warning: You cannot partition a drive if your system is already up and running. Partitioning a drive erases everything permanently.

Back up everything from your system onto another computer or external hard drive. You can drag-and-drop files and folders as you please, but I recommend using a backup utility. Time Machine is a built-in utility in OS X Leopard that provides a one-touch solution, giving you the ability to save and restore your backup with just a few clicks. You can also use programs such as Carbon Copy Cloner, Super Duper, or Disk Utility.

Next, boot your system to the OS you are installing. Go to the Utilities menu and launch Disk Utility. From here, you will see your computer's hard drive. By selecting it you will be able to create partitions: two, three, four, or more. I recommend creating two or three partitions, and keeping them equal. With drives exceeding 250 GB in size, it is more viable to partition in equal halves or thirds.

Once you've partitioned the hard drive, you can exit Disk Utility and resume installation. The OS X installer will prompt you to choose a location to install to, and then you may choose any of your partitions.

How Should I Install My Content?

Install the sample libraries, bonus content, loops, and so on onto your second drive or onto one of your partitions. Putting this material on a separate drive allows the main system drive to spin and run the OS without having to focus on pulling audio files from the same drive. This can be very taxing on a single hard drive. It is also good to run your sessions from another drive. This may be a FireWire drive, a second internal drive, or a partition. USB drives have dipped in price and often boast faster speeds than FireWire 400, but stay away from them. USB data transfer rates are based on packet bursts and not sustained speed. FireWire was designed with pro audio and video users in mind. Music happens in real time, and we can't afford to have any of the hiccups that USB may introduce.

Run Only What You Need

Computers can do amazing things these days, but all of these amazing things require system resources. Chances are you will want your computer to dedicate all of its processing power to Logic so you can get a higher track count and run more plug-ins.

Make Sure You Are Compatible

This requires a bit of research. Oftentimes system updates are pushed out and users install them without a second thought. Sometimes these updates are incompatible with existing hardware or software. Luckily, Apple makes Logic, so it is generally safe to install Logic updates as they are released, although as a rule of thumb do not update your system if you are in the middle of a project. Updates aren't necessarily a bad thing—in fact, they often make vast improvements. Many users saw a significant increase in the amount of tracks they could run with the 10.5.2 update. Naturally, your mileage may vary. For example, as I am writing this book, the newest operating system for Macs is Snow Leopard, or OS 10.6. It is fully compatible with Logic Pro 9, but other peripheral devices I am using may not be compatible yet. It is good to keep your OS current, but it is always wise to check its compatibility with all of your DAW's hardware and software before you commit to a new OS.

General Housekeeping

Keeping your files and folders organized not only helps you, it helps your computer. Be sure to keep your system organized. Clear out any unnecessary startup items from your system preferences. Don't use Dashboard. If you don't launch Dashboard after a restart, then it is not running. However, if you launch Dashboard after your computer is restarted, it will run continuously in the background. It can be harmless if only a few widgets are used, although some audio professionals prefer to "kill" Dashboard altogether and not risk it at all. You can disable Dashboard if you have some command-line expertise, or you can install a small free app to do it. Remember to keep 20 percent or more of your hard drive free at all times. There is no magic number of gigabytes you need to keep free; this is merely a suggested percentage. Hard drives tend to run better if they have a bit of breathing room. Also, although it may seem annoying, restarting your system before you launch Logic can be rewarding. If you launch Logic from a clean restart, you can be sure nothing else is hogging resources. Even when you quit applications, processes often continue to run in the background; the only way to ensure they don't is to restart. Again, this only works if your startup items are cleared out. It is not absolutely necessary to do this, but for some users, every bit of extra horsepower helps.

LOGIC 9 TUNE-UP

1. When any source vibrates, that vibration is made up of three primary components that allow us to interpret them as sound. Those three elements are _____, _____, and _____.

2. Amplitude is the sound-pressure level or volume of a particular sound. Sound-pressure levels are measured in _____ and are commonly abbreviated as "dB."

3. The threshold of pain usually occurs when the amplitude of a source reaches _____ dB.

4. The number of vibrations that a source produces in one second is referred to as cycles per second. The term *cycles per second* is referred to as _____.

5. Frequencies are measured in _____ (abbreviated "Hz").

6. When there are more than 1,000 frequencies in one second, the frequency is measured in _____ (abbreviated "kHz").

7. The frequency range of human hearing is _____.

8. Higher frequencies represent sounds that are high in pitch, and lower frequencies represent sounds that are _____ in pitch.

9. Each time a frequency doubles, it goes up in pitch by one octave. Each time a frequency is cut in half, the pitch of the frequency goes down by _____.

10. A visual representation of a sound's vibration cycle and amplitude is called a _____.

11. There are two main categories of waveforms; they are _____ and _____.

12. A _____ waveform provides us with an audio fingerprint that allows us to distinguish one sound from another sound.

13. The terms *dynamic* and *condenser* refer to typical types of _____.

14. A _____ microphone requires the use of phantom power.

15. The lowest frequency and the highest frequency that a microphone can capture is called its _____.

16. Bumps and dips in the _____ of a microphone can cause a misrepresentation of the pure sound source once it has been recorded. This is neither good nor bad. Simply being aware of this fact will help you make better microphone selections when you are trying to capture a particular sound.

17. The final stage before your analog source becomes digitized is referred to as _____.

18. Currently, the most common sampling rate for audio in the music industry is _____. The highest sampling rate available in a Pro Tools LE system is 96 kHz, and the highest sampling rate in an HD system is 192 kHz.

19. The Nyquist Theorem is the fundamental law stating that in order to properly translate the frequency of a sound, a digital recorder must have a sampling rate at least _____ greater than the rate of the highest frequency produced by the source. If the sampling rate is too low, you can expect frequency distortion known as *aliasing* to cause strange artifacts in your audio.

20. One of the most important things to take into consideration when choosing a bit depth is that each bit represents 6 dB of dynamic range. Therefore, a 16-bit recording has _____ dB of dynamic range, and a 24-bit recording has _____ dB of dynamic range.

21. A software add-on that enhances a software program's (host application's) capabilities is called a _____.

22. Native applications such as Logic Pro 8 use plug-ins that utilize the host computer's CPU. These types of plug-in are referred to as _____ plug-ins.

23. *Latency* is a fancy term for _____. It is most noticeable when tracking live instruments and when the system's hardware buffer size is set to a high number.

Trimming the Fat 3

A LOGICAL MENTAL WORKOUT

Over the next few chapters, we will be diving right into Logic. This chapter will cover the essential tools you need to get things going quickly, allowing you to create music end-to-end without many "bells and whistles" getting in the way. While these bells and whistles are often what make Logic so great, if we were to cover all of them at once you would be reading 1,000 pages of theory before you touched the mouse. The average engineer should possess these basic skills or habits in Logic. Taking time to learn proper session management and workflow is a valuable asset for musicians and engineers alike.

When Apple revamped Logic with version 8, the idea was to add GarageBand-like simplicity to a professional audio application. (For those of you unfamiliar with GarageBand, it is part of the iLife suite of applications that Apple bundles into all new Macs. GarageBand was designed for the casual musician and features a simpler interface than most pro audio applications.) Apple has continued adding powerful new features to Logic Pro 9 using this approach.

By taking such a simple approach, musicians and engineers feel at home almost immediately. Logic still offers all of its amazing floating windows, but the default layout in Logic Pro 9 is very simple and combines aspects of various windows into one workspace. We will spend the next few chapters working with the interface and getting very comfortable with it. You'll be creating entire projects from beginning to end without ever leaving this environment.

I am hoping you are already familiar with many of the following features and that this next section will merely serve as a refresher for you while showing you how these features apply in the relatively new interface of Logic 9.

Creating a New Session

All right, first we must launch the Logic Pro 9 application. This can be found in the Applications folder on your system's hard drive by default. If you haven't already, I recommend putting the Logic Pro application in your dock for quick and easy access.

Fig. 3.1: Mac OS X dock at the bottom of the screen.

Fig. 3.2: The dock positioned at the left.

Once you open Logic, you see the icon bounce a few times, and if the program is being launched for the first time, Logic performs an Audio Units (AU) scan. This takes a few minutes to complete and will vary based on how many third-party plug-ins you have installed. Immediately following the Audio Units scan Logic will show you the Audio Units Manager. From here you can see which plug-ins have been validated. If a plug-in is not compatible, the AU Manager will notify you, and you will have the option to disable the selected plug-in. Once Logic performs this initial Audio Units scan it caches (stores) the Audio Units so that the application will open much faster on subsequent launches. You will still see Logic scanning the Audio Units as it opens, but it will take much less time after the initial scan.

When Logic is opening, it also makes a few calls on the operating system and initializes any connected audio and MIDI hardware. Once Logic opens you will be presented with the template browser. From here we will create our session.

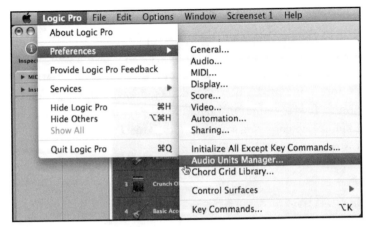

Fig. 3.3: A Marker example.

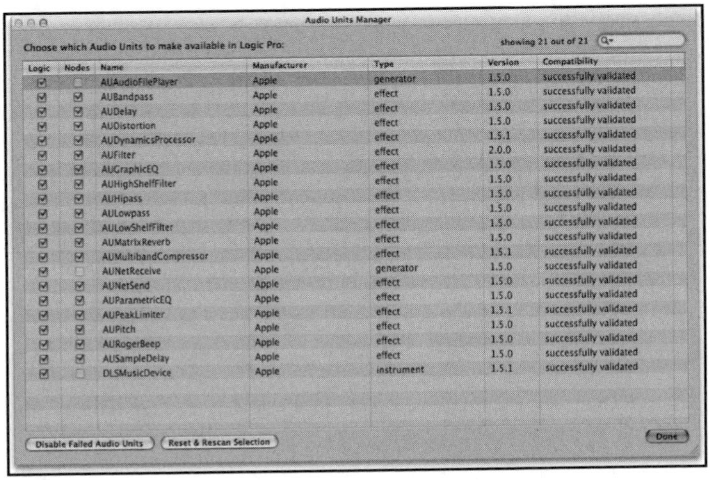

Fig. 3.4: List and status of plug-ins in the AU Manager window.

New Session and Template Browser

Logic provides various templates as a starting place for different workflows. Apple has designed each template to cater specifically to a particular type of project. These templates are just suggestions; later on, we'll go over how to create your own custom templates.

Here is a breakdown of the templates offered in Logic. In the Collection window, there are three categories: Explore, Compose, and Produce.

EXPLORE

The Explore category allows you to explore various instruments and settings in a project. I wouldn't recommend using these templates for actual recording, but they are a great way to explore some of the best sounds Logic has to offer. There are quite a few new ones in Logic Pro 9, especially for guitar. The Explore category consists of Empty Project, Guitar Tones, and Instruments (see **Fig. 3.5**).

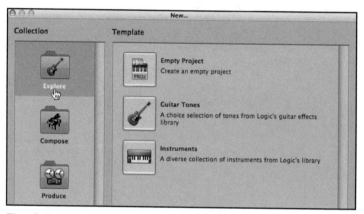

Fig. 3.5: The Explore folder from the Template Browser.

COMPOSE

The Compose templates are geared toward writing and producing tracks. These preset templates will open projects that have an assortment of songwriting tools broken down into various genres. Each project template caters to a specific genre of music. These templates are great for capturing your musical ideas when inspiration strikes. The Compose category consists of Empty Project, Electronic, Hip Hop, Orchestral, R&B, Rock, and Songwriter (see **Fig. 3.6**).

PRODUCE

This last category of project templates is laid out for various mixing and production scenarios. Here you will find templates for mixing in stereo and surround, as well as templates for mastering, and even utilizing a Digidesign TDM system (see **Fig. 3.7**).

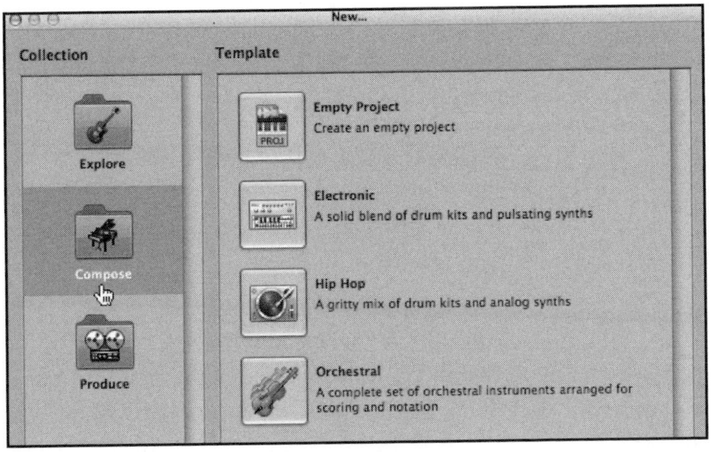

Fig. 3.6: The Compose folder from the Template Browser.

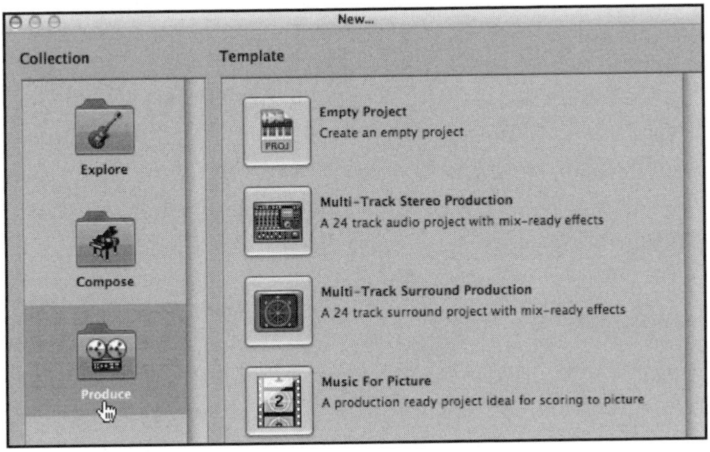

Fig. 3.7: The Produce folder from the Template Browser.

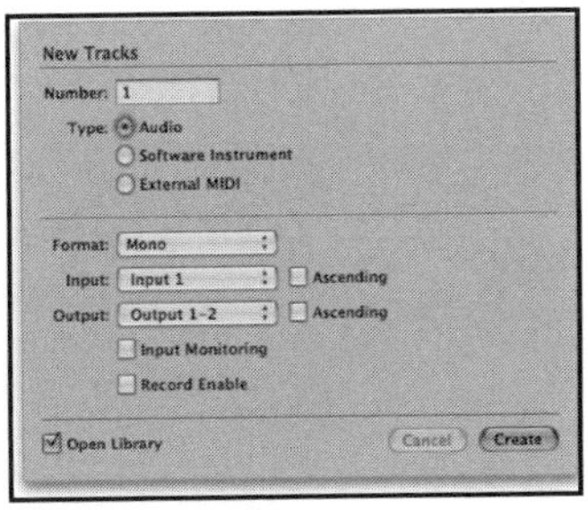

Fig. 3.8: New Audio Tracks options menu.

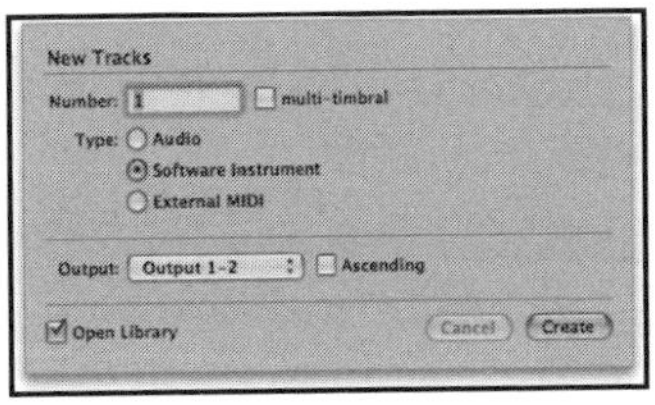

Fig. 3.9: New Software Instrument Tracks options menu.

All of these templates are great starting points, but you should know how to create the very same elements for your own custom project, which is why we are going to start with the Explore category and create an Empty Project. Once you create an Empty Project, you are immediately presented with a pop-up window and prompted to create one of three types of tracks: Audio, Software Instrument, or External MIDI (see **Figs. 3.8** and **3.9**).

You have the option to create as many tracks as you like from this window. Also, the dialog box expands to show various details based on which type of track you have selected. When selecting

Audio, Logic will ask you for the format (mono or stereo), the input, and the output, as well as input monitoring and the option to record-enable the track.

Notice that once you select Create, another dialog comes up. This window asks you where you want to save your project. Oftentimes eager users are so excited to dive in headfirst to a project that they fall into some bad habits with project management. Please keep in mind that proper project management is very important. You must know where your files are saved, and what is saved and not saved. Step one is to name your session something appropriate. Try to avoid very long file names and unnecessary characters like parentheses, dashes, and underscores. By default Logic will want to place your sessions in a folder it has created for you. That folder is located in: Mac HD > Users > username > Music > Logic.

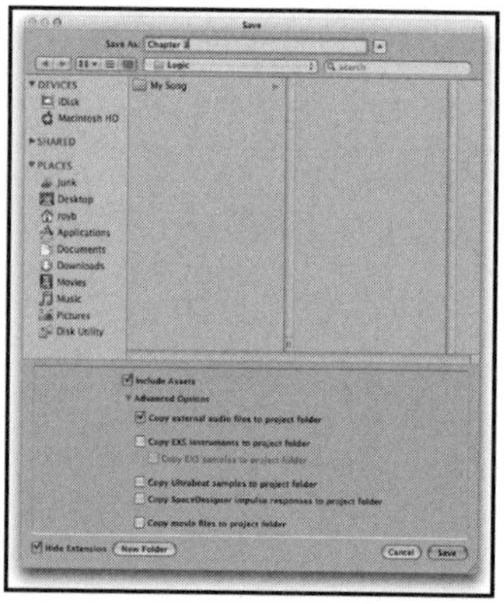

It's nice and convenient that Logic has created a place to store these projects in the same relative location as your other music. However, whenever possible you should change the destination to your dedicated audio drive, if you have one. Remember, storing your project to a drive dedicated to audio has enormous performance benefits (see **Fig. 3.10**).

Fig. 3.10: File menu/Save As options window.

Choose the exact location where you would like to store your project and try to remain consistent with a naming scheme and structure when creating new sessions. This will help you find them later on. One omission from these dialog windows is the ever-important Sampling Rate and Bit Depth. Please be aware that the sampling rate of your projects will default to 44.1 kHz. This can be changed from the Audio pane of the Project settings window.

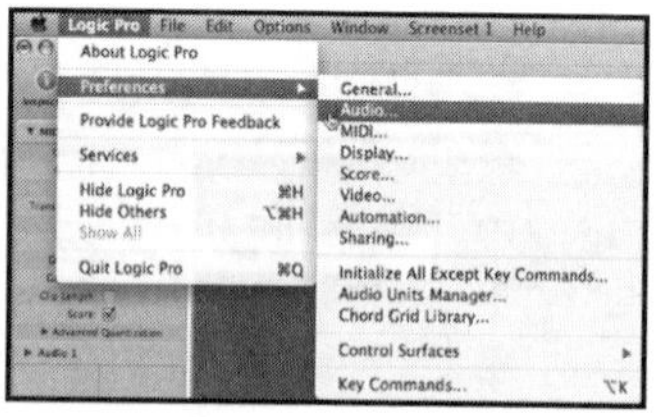

Although bit depth is tightly correlated with sampling rate, it is located in a different place. Bit depth is a global setting that affects how all of your Logic sessions are tracked. The bit-depth settings can be found in the Audio pane of the Preferences window (see **Fig. 3.11**). Turning on 24-bit recording enables all recordings to track at 24-bit resolution (see **Fig. 3.12**). Turning this off means recordings will come in at 16 bits.

Fig. 3.11: Navigation to Audio Preferences.

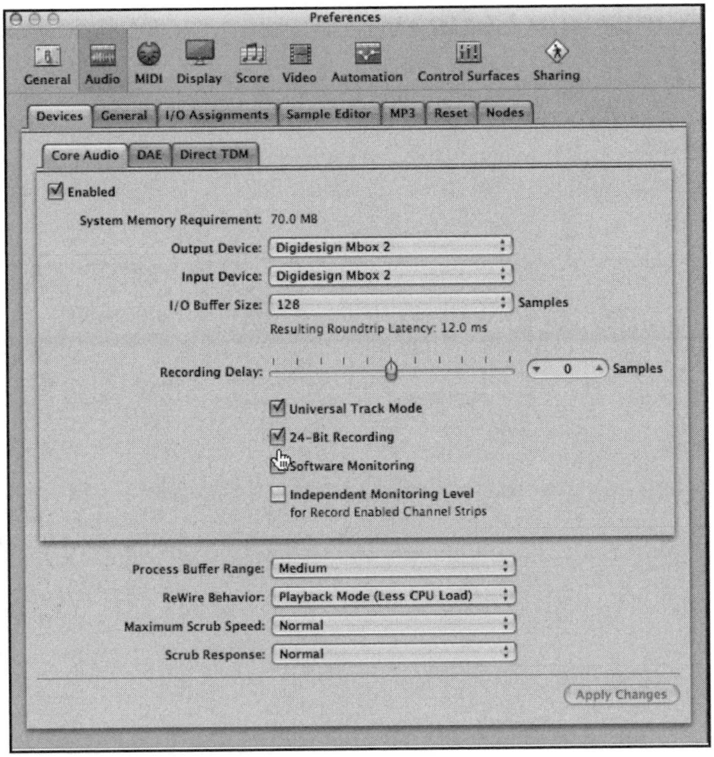

Fig. 3.12: Selecting 24-Bit Recording from the Audio Preferences.

In keeping with good session management, it is important that you remember the settings of your project. If you are working on a project that is going to DVD, you should be working in 24-bit, 48 kHz. Logic won't prompt you to set your bit depth and sampling rate, so it is imperative to be deliberate in your choices from the beginning of your project.

The available sampling rates will be determined by your hardware. Remember from the previous chapter that sampling rates will differ based on your project. Broadcast and DVD-based music should remain divisible by 48 kHz, while music that will end up on CDs should use sampling rates divisible by 44.1 kHz.

Broadcast and film standards are 24-bit resolution, and even though consumer audio CDs are 16-bit resolution, it is still preferable to record using 24 bit. It gives your music more dynamic range, and overall it just sounds much better.

Audio File Formats

The default file format is a global setting. If you need to change it for a particular project you can do so in the Settings window (see **Fig. 3.13**) by navigating to Preferences > Audio > General > Recording File Type.

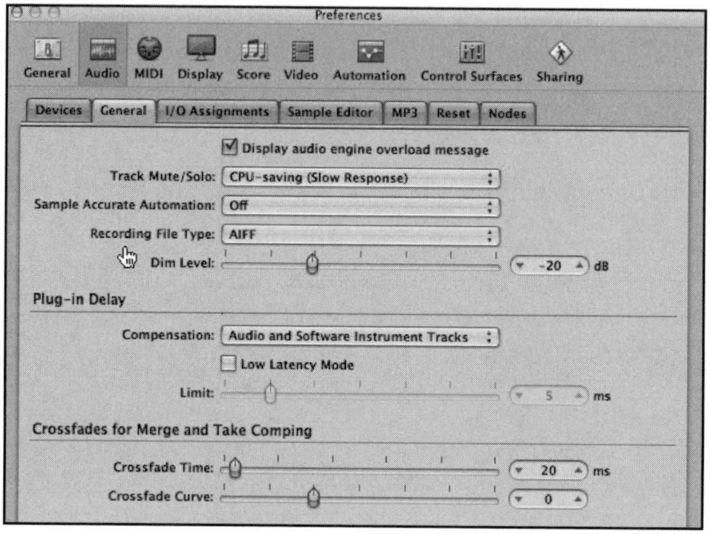

Fig. 3.13: Selecting the overall project file type in Audio Preferences.

Logic records audio using the AIFF format; however, it also recognizes the following audio formats.

AIFF

AIFF, or Audio Interchange File Format, was developed by Apple, and is commonly used on various DAW platforms. This format stores uncompressed Pulse Code Modulation (PCM) data.

WAV

Short for Waveform Audio, and developed by IBM and Microsoft, this format is very similar to AIFF in terms of quality, and it also stores uncompressed PCM data. It is more commonly used on Windows-based platforms.

SDII

SDII, or Sound Designer II, is a proprietary audio format developed by Digidesign that also stores uncompressed PCM data. SDII also stores session-specific metadata. Due to its closed format, SDII can often cause compatibility issues and is no longer a commonly used file format.

CAF

Core Audio Format (CAF) was developed by Apple for use with OS X 10.4 and later. While it is not an open standard that works on Windows, it does overcome the limitations of previous file formats. CAF also holds metadata similar to SDII, and is not limited to the 4 GB file size that WAV, AIFF, and SDII are restricted to. Developers say that a single CAF file can theoretically hold hundreds of years worth of audio.

Chances are the AIFF format will be exactly what you need and you won't have to change it. At the risk of sounding redundant, remember that there may come a time when someone will need to know the specs of your session, and you should be able to tell them immediately that your project is a 24-bit, 44.1 kHz AIFF file.

When importing audio from a previous session, you ideally want to avoid file conversion. Modern DAWs will convert just about any audio file into your current project's format, but you want to avoid file conversion whenever possible. To do this, you should change your session's audio format to the specified format you are importing. Also set your sampling rate and bit depth accordingly. If these three options are set properly, your audio will be imported with zero conversion.

What's Saved and Where Did It Go?

After you create a project, you will probably want to click around and start making music. Before we dive into making music though, let's take a quick look at what happened when we created our project.

Navigate to where your project was saved. You will notice that Logic has created a folder named after your project (see **Fig. 3.14**). Within this folder you will find everything associated with your project. All of your audio files are placed in the Audio Files folder, and other folders are automatically created as you progress through your session. You will also notice your project file with the name of your session. This document stores all the info about your project, from the placement and arrangement of tracks to the levels and panning you have assigned. Your project file is generally pretty small but very important; it acts like an index of a book. Without it you would have no idea where your content is.

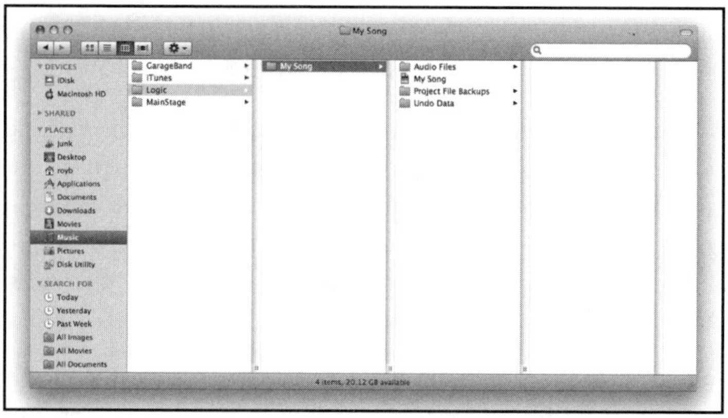

Fig. 3.14: Default project-save destination.

If you are making drastic changes to your project, you may want to select Save As under the file menu instead of just using Save or using the keyboard shortcut (Command + S). When you "Save As," you create a new project file. This project file still points to the same content as your original project; however, you can completely rearrange and remix your song without fear of losing your original work. Because project files are so small it is a great idea to save multiple versions of a single project at various stages of production so that you can revert to any one of them if necessary. The Save Copy As option will create a new folder that will mirror the contents of the existing folder, including all of its assets.

The Audio Files folder contains the audio pertaining to your project. Keeping all of your audio in this location is great project management and makes portability much easier.

The Project File Backups folder contains incremental backups of your projects. If you need to revert to a previous project, you can check this folder, although I recommend creating your own backups using the Save As command so you have more control over your project. Should your project file become corrupt midstream, and your system fails, then it may be convenient to reopen your project from one of these backups, as they all reference the same content.

An Undo folder will appear if you have made destructive edits to your audio from the Sample Editor. The level of undo depends on your settings and available hard drive space. Be careful—these undos will add up quickly and eat up lots of space.

Be sure to save early and save often; it only takes a moment. Remember, you can find Save and Save As in the File menu, but you should get in the habit of quickly pressing Command + S to save and Shift + Command + S to "Save As."

What's on the Menu

Once your project is open you will see the menu bar change to represent the different menus available in Logic. There are often multiple ways to accomplish the same task in Logic, and you will often find commands located in more than one place. Understanding the layout and placement of these tools will help you optimize your workflow. As we go on you will learn keyboard shortcuts, or shortcuts to the various commands you will be accessing frequently, but first, let's get familiar with Logic's main menu bar.

The main menus are broken down similarly to many other applications. First is always the application menu; in this case, it says Logic Pro (see **Fig. 3.15**).

Fig. 3.15: The Logic menu bar.

LOGIC PRO

From this menu you will find tools that deal with global preferences. As is typical of most applications, you can find out the exact version of Logic you have and hide and show the application.

FILE MENU

The File menu is for creating, opening, closing, and saving projects. The File menu also deals with individual project settings and file-import and -export functions.

EDIT MENU

Next we have the Edit window, where we see the basic tools for editing. Cut, Copy, Paste, and Undo are the big players in this menu, and a few selection tools are at your disposal here as well.

OPTIONS MENU

The Options menu lives up to its name, basically giving you access to various options based on your selection. Here is where you will set markers, tempos, and key signatures.

WINDOW MENU

The Window menu gives you access to the individual floating windows within Logic. While Logic was redesigned with a consolidated single-window look, from time to time you will find it necessary to open individual windows. We'll go over what each window is in detail later on.

SCREENSET MENU

The Screenset menu is very similar to the Window menu. Screensets are snapshots of what windows and setups you have open. Screensets help you manage multiple windows. Different screensets are geared toward different activities. This is another place where Logic shows its versatility and can speed up your workflow.

HELP MENU

Last but not least, we have our wonderful new Help menu. Here you will find guides that help expedite your troubleshooting needs. The guides are searchable, and having quick and easy access to all of the written material that shipped with Logic is a great tool. Also, if what you are looking for can't be found, there are options that will take you to the Internet to help you in your search.

Preferences and Settings

Now that we have gone over a few of the menus in Logic, let's dive into one of them so we can set a very important preference. Not all computers are created equal, and many computer components affect the ability of Logic to render audio. The default settings may work fine for you, but there will come a time when you absolutely must change these settings, so we're going to have a look at that now.

Under the Logic menu, we are going to go to the Audio preference. As soon as we open that preference, we are inundated with more menus and options, but don't let that confuse you. From here you can select any of the options from the toolbar and go to the associated preferences. If you accidentally clicked on General instead of Audio, you are just one click away. You'll notice that all of the menu items are displayed across the top of the Preferences dialog box.

Within the Audio preferences, you will see a few tabs. "Devices" is what we will be dealing with for now; we'll touch on the others later.

You will notice three tabs within the Devices tab. These are given below.

CORE AUDIO

Core Audio is the way OS X–based computers communicate with your audio hardware. Core Audio is a very-low-latency service and uses the fewest instructions possible to "talk" to your equipment (see **Fig. 3.16**). This is where most users will make their audio hardware I/O settings.

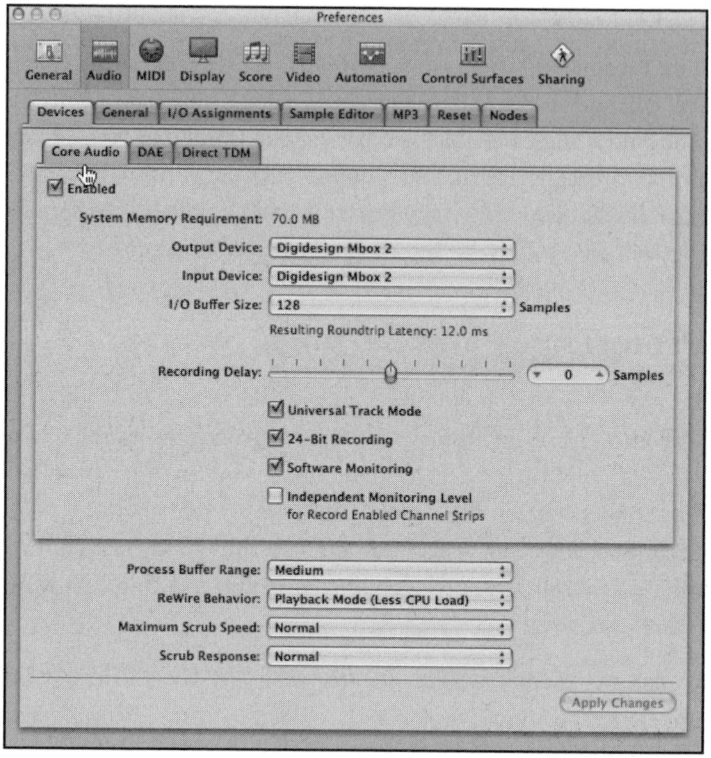

Fig. 3.16: Core Audio Preferences.

DAE

DAE, or Digidesign Audio Engine, is the Digidesign version of Core Audio. Built upon the same ideas as Apple's Core Audio, DAE uses a few more instructions to communicate with its own proprietary hardware.

DIRECT TDM

TDM is another Digidesign acronym. It stands for Time Division Multiplexing. All that really means is that you are using additional hardware to accelerate your system. A Pro Tools HD system uses TDM, and Logic Pro can take advantage of the extra horsepower in a TDM system.

For this book, we will stick with Core Audio. In the Core Audio tab you will see your recording interface listed under "Device," and will also see the I/O Buffer Size. The I/O Buffer Size is what we are mostly concerned about for now. Using a lower buffer will greatly reduce latency when tracking live instruments. While this puts more strain on your computer, as you are forcing it to process audio "on the fly," when you are tracking, latency is your worst enemy. Yet when it comes time to mix and add some plug-ins to your recorded tracks, your system will require more horsepower. Since latency isn't an issue when mixing, we can raise the buffer size and have the ability to use more real-time plug-ins and higher track counts.

Below are explained the other settings found in this window.

RECORDING DELAY

This parameter allows you to compensate for any latency introduced by the audio driver. You should not have to touch this; it defaults to 0 samples.

UNIVERSAL TRACK MODE

This parameter is on by default and should be left on. It allows us to play back mono and stereo regions on a single track. It should only be turned off when using TDM or DAE, as they are processed differently.

24-BIT RECORDING

As we talked about earlier, this is where we set our bit depth. If your recording interface supports 24-bit recording, it is suggested that you turn this on, as you will hear a difference in audio quality and dynamic range.

SOFTWARE MONITORING

This allows you to monitor audio "in the box," letting you listen to the software using your computer's built-in speakers. If your outputs are connected to an external mixer (not a control surface) or you are using a third-party audio interface for monitoring, then you should turn this feature off.

INDEPENDENT MONITORING LEVEL
FOR RECORD-ENABLED CHANNEL STRIPS

This setting allows you to change the monitoring level of a record-enabled track; when record-enable is off, the track's monitoring returns to its previous position. Note that this only affects monitoring level, not recording level.

PROCESS BUFFER RANGE

This goes hand in hand with your buffer size. A larger buffer will give you more horsepower and allow for more real-time effects. A lower buffer range decreases latency.

REWIRE BEHAVIOR

If you are using an application such as Reason, you will use a protocol called ReWire to get the audio from that third-party application into Logic. Running more than one music application at a time is CPU and RAM intensive; therefore, we have some settings for this scenario. Luckily, they are easy to figure out. Playback Mode and Live Mode translate the same way as buffer sizes, so go ahead and switch them accordingly.

MAXIMUM SCRUB SPEED

From this pull-down menu we can change our default scrubbing speed. You can preview audio or MIDI by pressing the pause button in the Transport. You can click and drag the playhead across your arrangement and listen as you drag; you can also use the fast-forward and rewind keys on the transport. This activity is known as "scrubbing." By default the maximum scrub speed is set to Normal, which means when you are scrubbing at full speed you will hear the audio play back as it would if you were to hit Play. Changing this to Double will allow you to scrub twice as fast.

SCRUB RESPONSE

This last option adjusts the reaction time before scrubbing occurs. Performance will vary based on the power of your computer; however there is little difference between the various settings.

THE TOOLBAR

Now that we have seen what's on the menu, we are going to have a look at what is in the toolbar (see **Fig. 3.17**).

Fig. 3.17: The Logic toolbar at the top of the Arrange window.

The toolbar is designed to give you quick access to tools you use frequently, and it can be customized to your heart's content. We are going to go over the default settings right now. The default tools by no means cover every tool available, just the ones you will probably use most frequently. You will also notice a few things on the toolbar that are new to Logic 9, such as the Flex and Crop options.

The Inspector

This button hides and shows the Inspector, which is shown by default. Should you need to free up some screen real estate, feel free to click it to hide it to gain a little more workspace in your Arrange window. The Inspector is dynamic, and changes based upon which track is selected. Everything in the Inspector can be found elsewhere, but the most important commonly used tools for any given channel are readily available here.

Preferences

This button is identical to the Preferences we saw in the Logic window, except it is about a half-inch closer, with a nifty icon on your toolbar for easy access.

Settings

This button shows you your project settings, which you can access from the File menu too.

Auto Zoom

This tool will zoom a selected track to a preset value. With this feature on, you can increase the height of the selected track to make it easier to spot and edit. You can always adjust the amount of zoom by hovering your cursor over the lower left-hand corner of a track until the cursor turns into a hand with a finger. You can use this tool to drag and resize a track. Resizing works with this tool on or off, but when Auto Zoom is on, whatever you choose as your track height will be the default for the selected track.

Automation

This button toggles your track view to show the automation lanes.

The next four tools are ones you will probably use the most from the toolbar. They are the essential editing tools.

Flex

This button will show and hide the new Flex Time features just underneath all of the track names in the Global Tracks list. When this is turned on, you can quickly choose the type of Elastic Audio properties you want to use for each track.

Set Locators

Set Locators is a tool designed for looping sections. You can set locators yourself by dragging above the ruler where the bars are shown. The selection will loop if it is lit green; click once to turn it off (notice it turns gray). The selection is remembered if you need to toggle it back on. The Set Locator button will turn on locators if they are off and set locators based on your selection. With a region selected, locators will be placed at the exact beginning and end of your region. If you need to tighten up the loop without editing the region, you can use the marquee tool to make a selection within a region. Then selecting "Set Locators" will reflect your selection.

Repeat Section

This button does just what it says. It will copy every track and parameter in a given section, determined by the locators. If you have a 16-bar chorus that you wish to repeat, set your locators around the 16-bar region and press the Repeat Section button.

Crop

This new addition to the toolbar allows you to trim or "crop" a region based on your cycle range. For instance, if you have an eight-bar region, and you would like to keep only the middle four bars, set your cycle range from bar 3 to bar 7 and select the Crop button. You will notice that the beginning and the end of the region have been cropped based on the selected cycle range. If there is no specific cycle range selected, but the whole file or region is selected and you click on the Crop button, you will be asked if you would like to delete the file from the disk. This permanently deletes the file from your hard drive, so be careful!

Insert Section

This feature is no longer part of the toolbar by default in version 9, but it can still be found under the Edit menu by choosing the Cut/Insert Time options, or it can be added to the toolbar when you are customizing it. This feature works in conjunction with the Cut Section tool. The Insert Section tool will insert the region that was cut. It is not the same as pasting, as it will shuffle your existing regions to allow the cut region to fit. The insert point is based on the location of the playhead. Using these two tools together is a quick way to do rough editing and arranging.

The next set of tools also deals with editing.

Split by Locators

This is another feature that is no longer a default item, but can be added when customizing your toolbar. This tool follows the locator and will split a region based on the locator selection. It can be accessed from the Region menu under "Split/Demix" or by using the quick key \

Split by Playhead

Split by Playhead places an edit in a region based on the location of the playhead. It essentially cuts the region in two. This is also located in the Region menu under Split/Demix. The quick key is simply Command + \.

To mend edited regions into a single audio file, select the edits you wish to combine, and from the Region menu go to Merge and select Regions.

NOTE

If there is space between audio files, a dialogue will notify you that you have selected non-contiguous audio files and that a single audio file will be created from this selection. In place of the space between the files will be silence.

These are just a few of the editing tools at our disposal. Apple put these tools in the toolbar for easy access. You might find as you go along that you prefer other tools and methods. We'll also go over quick access to tools using the contextual menu and mouse, but should you choose to customize the toolbar to suit your tastes, you can right-click (or Control-click) anywhere in the toolbar and select "Customize Toolbar."

THE TRANSPORT

The Transport (see **Fig. 3.18**) is located at the bottom of your screen and encompasses the entire bottom row of buttons and displays. The first set of buttons are the universal transport buttons that can be found just about anywhere. First, the Go to Beginning button does exactly what it says and will return the playhead to the top of the arrangement. Next, the Play from Selection button will play the arrangement from the beginning of a highlighted selection. Some more common buttons are the Rewind and Fast Forward buttons, which move the playhead

Fig. 3.18: The transport and all of its functions at the bottom of the Arrange Window.

forward or back a bar with each press. Pressing and holding these buttons allows you to jump multiple bars quickly. Command-clicking these buttons will move you to the nearest marker.

The Stop button will stop recording or playback. Pressing it a second time will return the playhead to the beginning of the song, or the left locator position if Cycle mode is active. New to Logic 9 are the Jump modes. They allow you to "jump" back and forth between different locations and Project Start positions. To choose between the various Stop-button functions, simply right-click on the Stop button. The keyboard shortcut for Stop is the number 0 (numeric keypad only), or you can simply hit the spacebar.

The Play button starts playback from the playhead position, or from the left locator if Cycle mode is active. The play button also has some new options. You can choose Play Marquee Selections, Cycle, From Selected Region, or Last Locate Position for your playback start location. As usual, to access these options, simply right-click on the Play button. The standard keyboard command for playback is Spacebar or Enter (not Return).

The Pause button will pause playback or recording until you click either Pause or Play again.

The Record button begins recording when it is clicked, and all record-enabled tracks will begin recording. You can also use the keyboard shortcut * (keypad only).

You will quickly find that using the spacebar is the most effective way to start and stop your song.

As you might have noticed, the position of the playhead determines the location of playback and recording in most cases. To change the position of the playhead you can click in the ruler area or set the location manually in the Transport's playhead position display. You will notice that the time is shown in two different formats. The upper display is SMPTE time, which is shown in the format hours:minutes:seconds:frames: subframes. The format below it is a little easier to understand for musicians, as it displays time in musical divisions, with the numbers corresponding to bars:beats:division:ticks.

The beat corresponds to the denominator of the time signature, which you will also notice in the Transport display. The absolute smallest denomination Logic can handle is a tick, which is equal to 1/3,840th of a note.

By double-clicking in the Transport display, in either SMPTE time or musical time, you can enter values by typing them in. For example, in musical time, typing in a value of 3 will take you to bar three, beat one, division one, tick one.

Immediately to the right of the playhead locator you will see two additional sets of location tools. These represent the locator's position in musical time. Locators can be set by dragging from left to right above the ruler; the display will show the current value. You can also set Cycle length by dragging above the ruler or by typing the length into the Transport. These numbers will remain even if Cycling is turned off. Similar to a Cycle is the Skip Cycle function; this skips over the selection you set with your region locators. To set a Skip Cycle, drag your locators from right to left. Instead of being solid green like a Cycle region, a Skip Cycle appears striped. Moving further to the right along the Transport display you will notice the tempo, which can be changed by double-clicking or by clicking and dragging. The number shown underneath the tempo is not to be confused with tempo or time signature. This number represents the number of bars in your song. When you begin a song it is often hard to tell exactly how many bars your song will be. By default, Logic assumes your song will be 130 bars long. If you didn't change this and are tracking a band that is ready to launch into a 15-minute extended jam, don't worry. Logic will ignore the song length when you are recording. When you bounce your song, the end is whatever bar number this is set to.

Up next is our time signature. Setting this in advance is critical. If your song is in 3/4 time, you may find that tracking in 4/4 isn't so bad, but when it comes time to edit and arrange it won't be so much fun. Double-click to edit, or click and drag as with the other Transport parameters. The number below the time signature represents the division. This is set to 16 by default, meaning your grid's resolution will be accurate up to a 16th note.

The MIDI In and Out display is extremely convenient: it lets you know that your system is properly configured and MIDI is flowing in and out correctly. From a musical perspective, it also analyzes your playing on the fly. For example, if you play a chord and aren't sure what it is named, look at the MIDI display window and it will show you.

Lastly in the Transport display is a small visual representation of the load you are placing on your system. If this spikes into the red during playback or recording, you will be interrupted by an error message. It is our goal to avoid such messages. We'll go over later how to do that. It's a good idea to keep an eye on this as you add tracks and plug-ins. You will also see the performance on any nodes you might have attached; we'll go over that later as well.

Past the Transport display is another useful set of buttons for playback, recording, and editing. First up is the Low-Latency mode button. This magical little button will work wonders for you. It allows you to bypass plug-ins and set a maximum latency time (determined in the Preferences). Plug-ins with the highest latency will be bypassed first. This is a very important mode to use when tracking with a virtual instrument. You want to get the most out of your performance, and this is a quick and efficient way to get around any latency issues without having to jump through hoops to figure out what is causing the delay.

Remember when we talked about locators and cycle length above? This next button toggles Cycle mode on and off. You can also toggle Cycle/skip on and off by clicking once on the Cycle button. If you right-click on this button, you will notice the new modes for the Cycle button. Now you can cycle by Marquee, Region, or Note selection.

Next is the Autopunch mode button. Turning this on gives you a new set of locators (in red) representing the region to be recorded. Hitting Record will start playback from the playhead, and Logic will start recording when it hits the red recording region, and stop recording when the playhead leaves the recording region. We'll cover punch recording in-depth later on.

Next is Replace mode, another recording-related button. With Replace turned on new recordings are saved normally; however, any overwritten regions will be deleted. This is a dangerous mode in that you can lose data, yet you will notice various performance gains and your hard drive won't be bogged down with extraneous files. When used in conjunction with Cycle mode, only the first recording is discarded, but all subsequent passes are still safely recorded, allowing you to record multiple passes of a take and keep all of them.

The next button on the Transport bar is the Solo button. Pressing it will do nothing more than highlight your ruler in yellow unless you have a selection. If you have a selection, pressing this button will solo that selection; however, this button is more convenient for notifying you if any track is currently soloed. In the event you have tracks soloed and you wish to un-solo them, press this button.

The last button on the Transport bar is the handy Metronome. The Metronome will turn on by default when you start recording. This is Apple's not-so-subtle way of encouraging you to make the best choices while recording. The Metronome derives its tempo from the song tempo, which is set in the Transport. If you have tempo changes throughout your song, the Metronome will follow them. The Metronome's sound is actually an instrument called a Klopfgeist, a remnant from Logic's German origins as the company Emagic. You won't see the Metronome in the Mixer by default, but if you select "All" from the Mix window, you will see that the click track has its own channel strip and fader. This allows you to get a little creative and throw a few inserts on the channel if the right situation presents itself.

The last little tool, located in the lower right of the Transport bar, is the master volume control. The master volume control is conveniently accessible at all times from any window. I am old-fashioned and still use the master fader in the Mixer. But if you run into feedback or something crazy, the master volume control acts as a pretty nice kill switch.

Transport	Display	Modes and Functions
☑ Go to Beginning	☑ Positions (SMPTE/Bar)	☐ Software Monitoring
☐ Go to Position	☑ Locators (Left/Right)	☐ Auto Input Monitoring
☐ Go to Left Locator	☐ Sample Rate or Punch Locators	☐ Pre Fader Metering
☐ Go to Right Locator	☐ Varispeed	☑ Low Latency Mode
☐ Go to Selection Start	☑ Tempo/Project End	☐ Set Left Locator by Playhead
☐ Play from Beginning	☑ Signature/Division	☐ Set Right Locator by Playhead
☐ Play from Left Window Edge	☑ MIDI Activity (In/Out)	☐ Set Left Locator Numerically
☐ Play from Left Locator	☑ Load Meters (CPU/HD)	☐ Set Right Locator Numerically
☐ Play from Right Locator		☐ Swap Left and Right Locators
☑ Play from Selection		☐ Move Locators Backwards by Cycle Length
☑ Rewind/Fast Rewind		☐ Move Locators Forward by Cycle Length
☑ Forward/Fast Forward		☑ Cycle
☑ Stop		☑ Autopunch
☑ Play		☐ Set Punch In Locator by Playhead

Fig. 3.19: Customize Transport menu.

A TOUR OF THE ARRANGE WINDOW

We have already gone over much of the Arrange window, but let's take a step back from the trees so we can see the forest. The Arrange window was redesigned in Logic 8 to give you the ability to accomplish everything you need, without leaving this one window (see **Fig. 3.20**). That sounds a bit ambitious and too good to be true, and I suppose it is, but for basic music production, you really won't *have* to leave this window. There are only a few changes to the Arrange window in Logic Pro 9; the most important ones will be pointed out to you throughout the book.

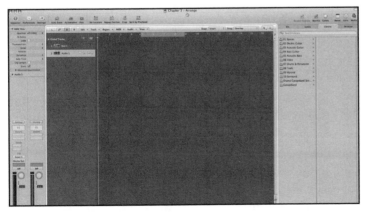

Fig. 3.20: The Arrange window.

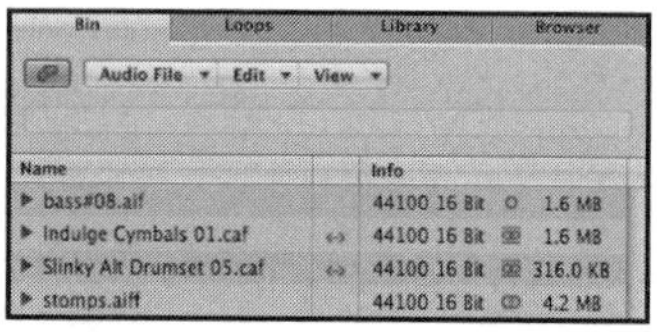

Fig. 3.21: The Bin browser.

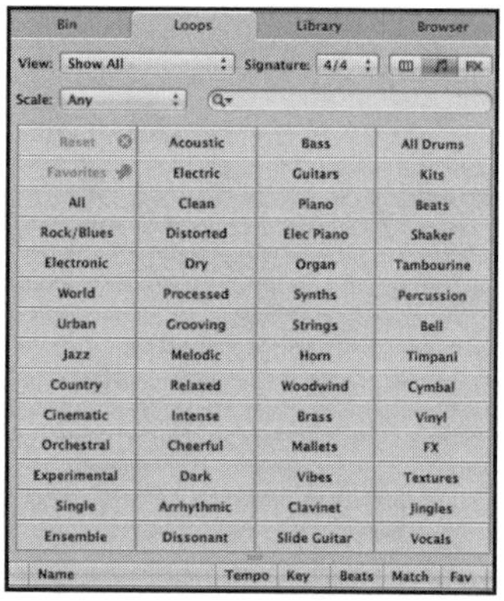

Fig. 3.22: The Loop browser.

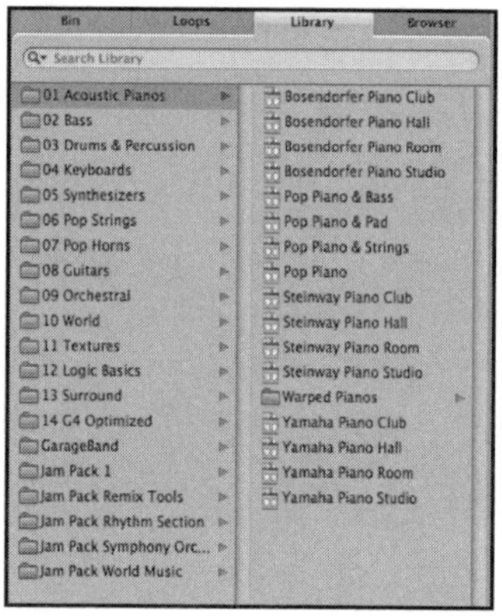

Fig. 3.23: The Library browser.

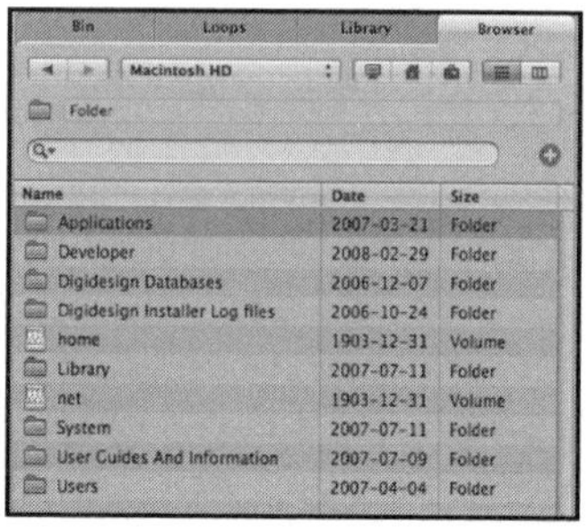

Fig. 3.24: The System browser.

To sum it up, the arrange area is where you record your audio and instrument parts as regions. It is also where you quite literally arrange them into a song structure.

The Media, Lists, and new Notes buttons on the right-hand side give you various tabs to navigate. This is your one-stop shopping area for selecting effects, instruments, and various settings. You also have access to the various events and lists generated by MIDI, tempo changes, and more.

Under Media you have access to your Audio Bin (see **Fig. 3.21**), which shows you all of the audio in the current session and important information about the files, such as their sample rate, bit depth, length, file size, and whether they are mono or stereo. The Loops browser is also part of the Media tab (see **Fig. 3.22**). From here you can dynamically search in various ways for loops. Having quick access to loops is great when you are brainstorming song ideas. The Library tab (see **Fig. 3.23**) allows you to browse effects, instruments, and settings. Having this tab open within the Arrange window is very nice. Last is the Browser (see **Fig. 3.24**), another shortcut to browse for files on your computer without having to switch to the Finder. Logic supports dragging-and-dropping from the Finder, but it is much more elegant to be able to navigate to any directory within this single window interface.

The Lists button gives you more tabs pertaining to your song. Events shows the location of various changes. You can filter this list dynamically—a visual representation of the names and location of events helps you better arrange and edit your song. The Marker tab allows you to create and edit existing markers. Viewing markers as a list can help you see the linear flow of your song as opposed to viewing the markers in the timeline. The Tempo tab allows you to create or modify tempo changes; viewing these changes as a list is also helpful. Along the same lines as the Tempo tab is the Signature tab. You can change the key of a song and/or the time signature within this tab. Automating these changes with lists is much better than trying to guess without a metronome. Another benefit to conforming your song to these tools is that all of your effects will lock to the tempos and keys as they change. It is especially convenient to have the ability to make changes to the various features, once your parts have been recorded. Taking advantage of these creative tools can really help your song come together.

The five buttons along the bottom of the Arrange window comprise the editing area (see **Fig. 3.25**). Clicking on any of these edit windows will keep you in the same space but will expand to show you more. Opening the Mixer shows you all of the tracks and inserts; we'll go into much more detail about the Mixer later. The Sample Editor allows you to edit audio regions. This window has its own contextual menus to help trim the fat—the menu items here only pertain to editing a region. It is also important to note that this window has a separate level of undo. You can make a few mistakes in this window and undo them without affecting the undo tree from your Arrange window. The last three edit windows are for MIDI editing. Piano Roll, Score, and Hyper Editor are all just different ways to get MIDI to do what you need it to do. Selecting which MIDI editor is right for you is a matter of preference, and we'll learn more about that later.

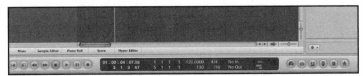

Fig. 3.25: Arrange window buttons.

Finally, on the left side of the Arrange window is the Inspector (see **Fig. 3.26**). The Inspector gives you pertinent information about the selected track. Selecting a track in the Arrange window will bring it into focus in the Inspector. By default the Inspector shows two channel strips. This is because the Inspector shows you all the tracks that are relevant to the track you have selected. By selecting one track, you will see it come into focus; the second track shown is the master fader, because they are related. If you create a bus, you will notice the Inspector instantly switches the second channel strip to be the newly created bus. If you want to view any related channel strip, simply click once on any of the buses, and the associated channel strip will come into focus.

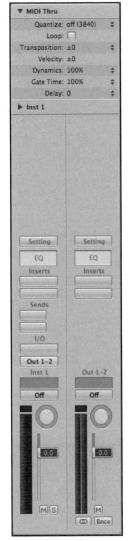

Fig. 3.26: The Inspector on the left of the Arrange window.

BACK TO THE MIXER

While the Mixer (see **Fig. 3.27**) is only one of five edit window buttons, it deserves its own little section because of how important it is and how often we will use it. This window is most familiar to audio engineers because of its mixer-and-multitrack-combination environment. The tracks are displayed from left to right, and look like traditional channel strips with options such as inserts for dynamics processing, auxiliary sends for time-based effects, as well as output routing, automation status controls, group assignments, and of course fader level and panning controls—all the tools of a professional console in software form. Additionally, we have access to solos, mutes, record-enable, input monitor, mono/stereo selection, and voice assignment. You can even color-code and add notes to your mixer channels from this area too. This helps organize your session even further.

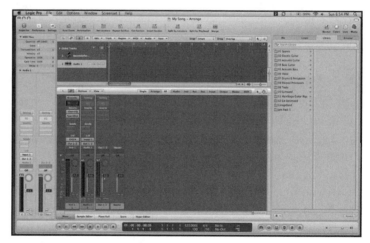

Fig. 3.27: The Mixer view.

The Channel Strip

Within the Mixer window you will see channel strips (see **Fig. 3.28**). Each of these channel strips has the aforementioned tools, which we will now go over in depth. Starting at the top of our channel strip, you will notice a button labeled Setting. This is basically a "Channel Strips for Dummies" button. Don't get me wrong; I love it. Clicking Setting will open a cascading menu that will allow you to select from an amazing array of presets for the entire channel strip. Everything is included in these settings—they are a quick and easy way to get a great sound with little to no effort. I am not ashamed to say I use them very frequently when I'm writing new songs for quick and easy inspiration. If you feel like playing around, knock yourself out and mess with a bunch of these channel-strip settings, you'll be amazed at how inspiring some of them can be. When you are ready to dive back into the theory, come back to the book and learn some more.

INSERTS

Just under the Setting button is an EQ button that is slightly grayed out, meaning it is not enabled. Double-clicking it will instantly turn on the Channel EQ and place it as your first insert. You will notice the grayed-out EQ has turned into a visual representation of the associated EQ. You can add more than one EQ to a channel, but only the topmost Channel EQ will be displayed graphically.

To help keep Mixer window clutter to a minimum, you are only shown two inserts per channel strip. However, as soon as you start to add inserts, you will see that Logic will add more accordingly. And you won't be disappointed, either—Logic can handle up to 15 inserts per channel. Should that not be enough, we'll go over how to add more. In general you should use inserts for dynamics, EQ, and gating. There are many variations of these plug-ins. In general, dynamic processing is for tone shaping; these are not the "fun plug-ins."

By fun plug-ins, I of course mean time-based effects—delays, reverbs, a nice chorus, a cool flanger, and so on. These effects can be inserted into your channel strip, and you may have noticed that by playing around with some of the channel strip settings. You'll learn, however, that while it's not necessarily wrong to do so, it isn't quite right either. More on these best practices for time-based effects later on in the book.

SENDS

After the inserts come the sends. Much like the inserts, Logic only displays two auxiliary sends by default; however, it can support several sends per channel strip. Sends are typically used

Fig. 3.28: A channel strip close up.

for busing (sending) an extra output of a dry signal on a channel into the input of an aux track that is set up to receive the input on the same bus. If you have a bunch of tracks and you want to create some ambience or depth, you might add a little reverb. However, adding reverb to each channel will really bog your computer down. Even if you have a powerful computer capable of handling multiple reverbs, you may be disappointed in the results if you use this method when working on your final mix.

When mixing your final product, you would more than likely create an aux send assigned to bus 1 on all of the desired channels. Then, on a separate aux channel strip, you would add a reverb plug-in. You can then adjust the amount of signal being sent to that reverb with the knob in each channel strip. Furthermore, you might need to bus the dry signal to separate outputs for different routing assignments. Using sends is how you create separate mixes when creating individual headphone mixes and the like.

INPUT/OUTPUT SELECTORS

The input/output selectors allow you to choose the path by which the signal comes into or out of a channel strip. On an audio channel, you can select various inputs depending on your interface. If you have eight inputs you will have eight choices in this menu; the same goes for the output. When mixing in the box, you will probably stick to using Out 1-2; you may take advantage of other outputs if you are using headphone mixes, though. The input/output selectors also affect instrument channels. Their input will show a list of available instruments. If you set up an instrument channel with a "channel strip setting," this is all taken care of for you.

GROUPS

Underneath the input/output selectors is an empty gray box. Here you can assign multiple channels to a group. By doing so you can control the various settings of all the members of that group, depending on the group settings. We'll go over groups in detail later, including the new Group Hide and Solo features from the Arrange windows, as they will help us streamline our workflow.

AUTOMATION STATUS SELECTORS

Underneath the Groups box is another gray box labeled "Off." This is referring to the status of the channel strip's automation mode. It is set to off by default because there is no automation data. As soon as data is written you will see this box change. Later in this book we will have examples of how to use different forms of automation. For now we'll leave this set to "Off."

PANNING KNOB

The panning knob affects the output positioning of the channel strip. Panning places the audio in the stereo (or surround) field. A value of 0 is the default setting, meaning equal power is being sent to both speakers. A value of -64 is referred to as "hard-panned left," and a value of +64 is referred to as "hard-panned right." Placing instruments in different locations in the stereo field will open up your mix and help create a "fuller"-sounding mix.

FADER

The fader position determines how much of the signal in the channel is being sent to its selected outputs. By default the output is set to 0 dB, or unity gain.

STATUS BUTTONS

The Record-enable (R) button at the bottom of the channel strip allows you to arm the track. Doing so means you can monitor the input, and the track will be recorded if recording is started. Input (I) is another way to monitor your input source while the track is playing, without having to record the source instrument. It is ideal for setting the correct input levels prior to actually recording. Rounding out the button selections are the tried-and-true Mute (M) and Solo (S) buttons. When the Mute button on the selected track is engaged, all other tracks play back normally. Conversely, engaging the Solo button will isolate the selected track so only it will play back. Multiple tracks can be soloed and muted, and these parameters can be assigned to groups for more convenience.

PUTTING IT TOGETHER

Now that we have gone over the major components of the main Arrange window in Logic, we'll finish up by touching on a few more key items to ensure you are off to a good start. If you feel comfortable and are already familiar with everything described so far, that's great. If you feel a little bit behind, then feel free to reread this chapter until you better understand what you have read and can answer all of the Logic 9 Tune-Up questions at the end of this chapter. You should know the information in these chapters inside and out. It may seem like a tall order, but keep in mind that we are trimming the fat from more than 1,000 pages of information in the manual. What is left is very important.

Creating New Tracks

When we first launched a new session, Logic prompted us to create at least one track. When you open a template, many tracks are provided for you, and I encourage you to familiarize yourself with the templates to get a better feel for how they work. To create new tracks, click on the Track menu within the Arrange window, and select New. You will notice a whole slew of options for new tracks in the drop-down menu, including a few new Bounce features that have been added to Logic Pro 9. You can get by if you simply select New Track, but let's say, for instance, that you would like a new track with the same settings as the previous track. You can save a few steps by selecting that option from the menu, or by pressing Command + D, as in "duplicate." Later on, as you create more and more tracks, you will find uses for all of these menu items. For now, select New Track.

You can also create a new track in the Arrange window right next to Global Tracks, by the timeline ruler. You'll notice two icons (see **Fig. 3.29**). The first brings up the New Track dialog, and the second creates a track with identical settings to the previously selected track. If that's not fast enough, you can always use the keyboard shortcut Command + Option + N.

Fig. 3.29: The "add track" (+) buttons.

When the New Track dialog comes up, you are prompted to choose how many of which kind of track you would like to create: Audio, Software Instrument, or External MIDI (see **Fig. 3.30**).

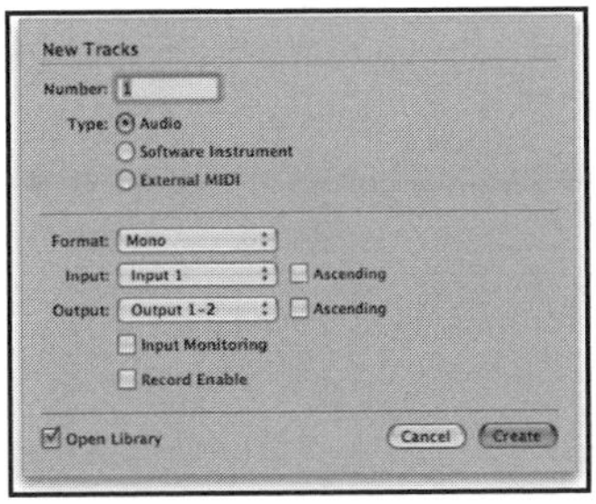

Selecting Audio will create audio tracks, and you are prompted to set the format to mono, stereo, or surround, as well as choose the input and output. If you are creating more than one track you can select "ascending," and each corresponding track's input and output will populate the available inputs and outputs of your interface. From here you may also indicate whether you would like to monitor the input of the track or record-enable it as soon as it is created. Lastly, you can tell Logic to open the Library so you can choose from the many different channel strip settings.

By selecting Software Instrument (see **Fig. 3.31**), you are choosing to create tracks that will have an input from one of Logic's 40 instruments. Because the input is derived from Logic and not your recording interface, an audio input is not an option; however, output still is. If you choose to open the library for a software instrument, you will be able to browse the nearly infinite channel-strip settings available for the software instruments.

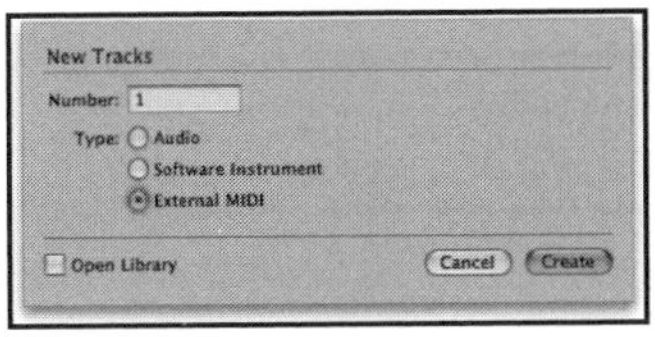

Lastly, you can select External MIDI (see **Fig. 3.32**). This is rarely used, but if you would like to use an external MIDI module or a keyboard workstation such as a Korg Triton, you can choose this option. This will create a track in the Environment window; we'll go over the Environment in more detail later on.

There are also the typical tracks that exist in every session that do not appear as options when creating new tracks. These tracks

Fig. 3.30: The New Audio Track options menu.

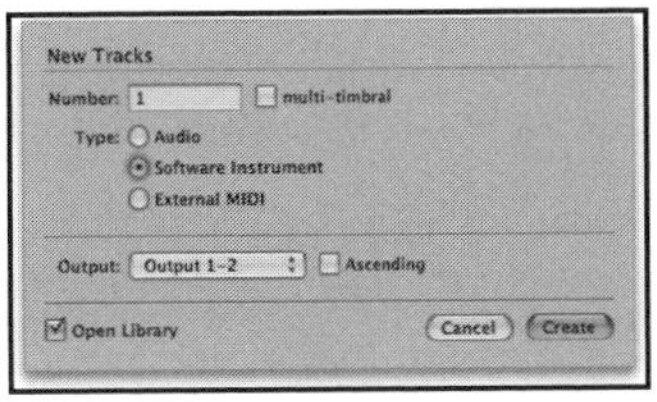

Fig. 3.31: The New Software Instrument options menu.

Fig. 3.32: The New External MIDI options menu.

include the master fader and the click track. By default, these are not shown in the Arrange window, but you can view them in the Mixer. If you can't see a track that you know exists, open the Mixer and select "All" from the buttons along the top. If you wish to view a track you see here that's not in the Arrange window, right-click and select "Create/Select Arrange Track."

Markers

Markers serve as a visual aid for laying out your song graphically. You can view markers from the Global Tracks marker track, and from the marker list. You can also view additional text and info pertaining to the markers from this list view. You can create markers at any project position. Markers round to the nearest bar for convenience; it makes them more manageable. You can always create a marker without rounding by using the shortcut Shift + Command + '. Creating a regular marker is done with the shortcut Command + '. Markers also can be created by moving the playhead to the selected position and pressing the Create button in the marker list. To see a list of your markers, simply press the letter K. This is the shortcut that brings up the markers list.

By default, markers have a start location, but continue through the end of the song unless another marker is created. You can create a marker to be the length of a cycle region by dragging the cycle region down onto the marker track (see **Fig. 3.33**). Another small addition to Logic 9 is the ability to import and export marker information, from the Options menu.

Fig. 3.33: A Marker example.

Scrolling

By default in Logic the playhead will scroll from left to right in the Arrange window, and when it nears the rightmost edge the playhead will reset itself back to the left of the screen and the scrolling will jump to the following information in the timeline. There is also another option called "scroll in play." With this turned on, the playhead will play until it reaches the center of the screen; from there it stays locked and the arrangement moves underneath the now-stationary playhead. Some engineers prefer this method of scrolling; it is a matter of personal taste.

POWER TIPS FOR CHAPTER 3

1. The placement of your dock as well as the auto-hide settings will vary from user to user. By default, the dock is placed on the bottom of your screen. If you set it to auto-hide, you free up some screen real estate, and if you move the cursor along the bottom, it will pop up. This can sometimes get in your way. The solution is to make the dock smaller, or to move it to one side of your screen. This is not absolutely necessary, but it can help when you feel like you are dodging the dock to click a certain button or window within Logic.

2. You can always relaunch the Audio Units Manager from within Logic. It is located under Preferences > Audio Units Manager. You may need to check this if you add third-party plug-ins. Deselecting failed Audio Units will allow Logic to launch more quickly. If a plug-in is not successfully validated, you should check its compatibility and version. Also, be sure the plug-in is properly authorized for use on your machine.

3. Be sure to save early and save often; it only takes a moment. You can find "Save" and "Save As" in the File menu, but you should get in the habit of quickly pressing Command + S to "Save" and Shift + Command + S to "Save As."

4. Various file formats exist because standards have changed over the years. SDII was the preferred format from Digidesign's Pro Tools 5 and earlier. BWF is the broadcast version

of the WAV format. AIFF is similar to WAV and BWF with the exception that it is generally more "Apple friendly." There is little difference between these standards, and no audible difference. However, you will notice the benefit of the metadata stored in CAF files while browsing for loops. Logic can read the extra data in these files, which makes searching much easier. Recent audio and video file formats have begun to adopt metadata.

5. If you find yourself not being able to turn the click up loud enough, try adding a Gain plug-in to the channel strip and boost the gain until you hear the click. Also, keep in mind that the volume of the click may be just fine; it just isn't cutting through your mix. Sometimes boosting certain frequencies with EQ will solve your problem.

6. Despite the vast amount of controls found on the Transport, you can also customize the Transport bar to add more controls or take away functions you don't use. You can also create an additional transport as a floating window and customize each transport individually. This may come in handy for displaying a large bar counter that you can place anywhere on the screen. To access the custom Transport setup, right-click on the Transport and click "Customize Transport Bar." To add a floating transport, press Command + 7 or select it from the Windows menu. Also note that customizing one transport will not affect another; you can always revert to the original transport settings by pressing the "Restore Defaults" button.

7. If you'd like to know what your song sounds like in a different key or at a different tempo, adjust the Key Signature and Tempo. For best results use this only as a pre-production tool. If you decide you like your song in a different key or tempo, you should retrack any audio in that key and tempo.

8. Holding down Option while clicking any parameter will return it to its default setting. Panning knobs return to 0, faders and aux sends return to unity.

KEYBOARD SHORTCUT SUMMARY

KEYBOARD SHORTCUT	FUNCTION
Command + S	Save
Shift + Command + S	Save As
\	Split By Locators
Command + \	Split By Playhead
Spacebar	Start/Stop Playback
*	Start Recording
Option + Command + N	New Track
Command + D	Duplicate Track and Track Settings
Command + '	Create Marker
Shift + Command + '	Create Marker without Rounding

LOGIC 9 TUNE-UP

1. Logic offers some great templates to get you started. These are broken into three different collections; the categories are _____, _____, and _____.

2. The default save location for Logic projects is located in: Mac HD/Users/username/_____ / _____

3. Broadcast and film standards are ___-bit resolution. CDs use a ___-bit standard.

4. Using 24-bit resolution in place of a 16-bit resolution will give your music more _____ _____.

5. Although the various audio format standards have no audible difference, Apple's CAF format is superior because the file size is not restricted to _____.

6. If you are making drastic changes to your project you should probably use _____ in place of "Save" when saving your project.

7. _____ _____ is the way OS X–based computers communicate with your audio hardware. It is a very-low-latency service and uses the fewest instructions possible to "talk" to or communicate with your equipment.

8. The _____ is located along the bottom of the main Arrange window. It houses controls for playback and recording, it also displays useful information in real time.

9. The Metronome's sound is actually an instrument called _____.

10. There are many ways to create new tracks without using a mouse. One way is by pressing: _____ + _____ + _____.

11. The three types of tracks available when creating a new track in Logic are: _____, _____, and _____ _____.

12. To prevent the playhead from jumping from the right-most edge of the screen back to the left during playback, use the _____ _____ _____ option to create a stationary playhead.

13. All of your work is important, and it only takes something as simple as a power failure to lose your work, so be sure to save _____ and save _____.

Exploring Logic

ONCE AROUND THE BLOCK

In the last chapter, we took a look at the main interface of Logic. We also took an in-depth look at the Transport and all of the essential tools you will need to use in an average music project. It is important that you understand what you have read up to this point. Answering the Logic Tune-Up questions and reviewing the Power Tips at the end of each chapter will help you retain and better understand the essential information contained in this book. In this chapter we will open up a session, create several different track types, and do an overall system check. We'll be taking your system "once around the block" to ensure that all of the connections are made properly, and that your computer and peripherals are all responding with maximum efficiency.

Logic is designed for you to make music quickly and easily; however, nothing can halt the creative process faster than having to stop and troubleshoot your system every five minutes. Even when your system is running smoothly, you'll soon learn that having an unorganized session will slow down your workflow and cramp your creativity.

System configurations will vary from studio to studio, but fortunately, Apple has some control of these variables. Logic Pro is only available on the Macintosh platform, and Version 9 has some stiff system requirements. By enforcing these requirements,

Apple is able to make an extensible product that will run smoothly and consistently from studio to studio.

During the production of this book, Logic Pro 9 was used on three different systems: a MacBook Pro, an iMac, and a Mac Pro with TDM. These represent the mobile, home, and professional studio environments. Logic can use any external Core Audio hardware interface, and mobile users can mix and edit in Logic without an external interface. An Apogee Duet and an Mbox 2 were used for the majority of the exercises in this book, so the screenshots and examples will reference them both.

As we go through this chapter, you will learn more ways to navigate within Logic using keyboard shortcuts, as well as develop troubleshooting skills and good organizational habits. Remember that wearing the dual hats of both a creative musician and a professional audio engineer is not as easy as it seems. Many artists do not realize that pro audio engineers are not merely "knob twisters" hired by recording studios to run expensive equipment. True audio engineers have years of experience in all areas of multi-track recording, and have spent countless hours of trial and error becoming great "knob twisters." A good engineer will always make it look easy because they have a solid understanding of audio engineering fundamentals and years of experience. This book is designed to teach you the fundamental elements that will allow you to record your music effortlessly as well as tips on how to streamline your overall workflow as a Logic Pro 9 operator, but nothing can take the place of years of experience.

Luckily, it is becoming much easier for the average musician to achieve high-quality results by using software such as Logic. Logic has always been known for being "musician friendly." Version 9 makes this very clear with its easy-to-use GUI, robust sound library, and high-quality channel strip presets to help musicians get great results right out of the box. Apple has taken some of the technical elements of audio engineering out of the equation for you with its Logic Pro 9 software, but it is still very important to realize that audio engineering skills are an extension of an artist's creativity. This is something that cannot be built into any software.

For instance, if you are setting up to record an artist or band, you should be ready when they are, even if they don't know they are.

If the band decides to rehearse a take before "actually recording for real," you should be there to capture the performance "just in case." Sometimes music happens when it happens, and the rehearsal should be captured in case it was one of those "I wish we recorded that" moments. An experienced audio engineer is ready to record at a moment's notice to capture "the take" that the artist wishes they had recorded. Your ability to recognize this type of thing, and having the skills and awareness to do this quickly and effectively will set you apart from the average hobbyist engineer. Having knowledge of all the tools available to you, maintaining an optimized system, and being able to run a well-organized project will not only keep your studio running like a well-oiled machine, but you will be known as one of the "go-to" engineers that gets the job done efficiently, and better than most.

Chapter Objectives

- Optimizing session settings

- Understanding the timeline

- Creating and using various track types

- Setting up MIDI keyboards using AMS

- Setting up USB MIDI controllers

- Using sounds with Logic's instrument collection

- Using Loops

OPTIMIZING YOUR SESSION/SYSTEM CHECK

When you are setting up a session, try going through a simple routine to help get a nice, productive workflow going. The templates that Logic provides are good starting points for a well-laid-out session; however, they only show you how a typical session should be set up. For this exercise, we'll be starting from scratch. This will help reenforce the fundamentals of DAW signal flow and proper session management. After building this session, you will learn how to save it, and use it to create your own custom template.

Okay; go ahead and open up Logic Pro 9 if it isn't open already. When you launch Logic, by default it will open your most recent project. You can change what Logic does on startup by selecting Preferences > General > Project Handling. On the pull-down menu for Startup Action, you can tell Logic to do a multitude of things. I prefer to set this to "Create New Project From Template," as it allows me to be creative instantly with a pre-made template, to select one of my own templates, or to launch an empty session.

We're going to create a new session, so if the New Session dialog is not on your screen, make sure that Logic is the active program. To do this, press Command + Tab until Logic Pro is the selected application, or click on its icon in the Dock. When Logic is active the top menu bar will have "Logic Pro" on the far left. Press Command + N to create a new session. The "New" dialog appears and allows you to choose from various templates. For this exercise, we are going to choose "Empty Project" (see **Fig. 4.1**).

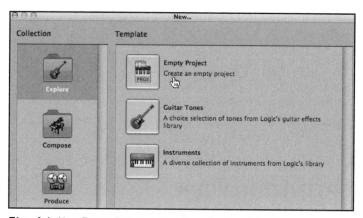

Fig. 4.1: New Empty Project option from the Template Browser.

As soon as you select this option, Logic will ask you to create at least one track. You can tell they really want you to start recording right away. Yet it is often hard to tell what you need right away, so to start we'll just create a single mono audio track (see **Fig. 4.2**).

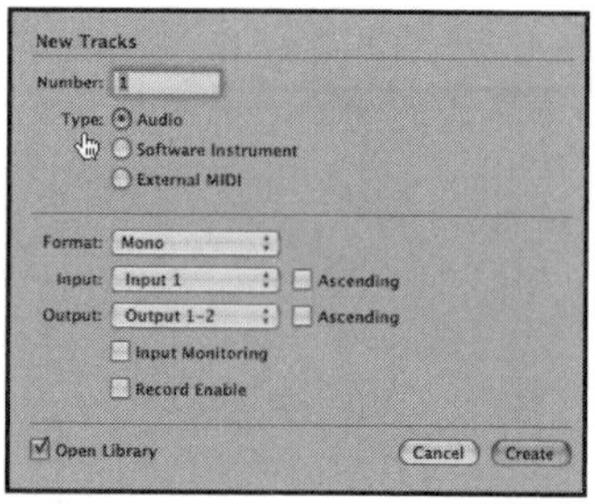

Fig. 4.2: New Audio Track menu.

Before you go any further it is important to save your session. You can often get on a roll loading settings and patches, and not notice that Logic hasn't prompted you to name your session yet or where to save it. Luckily, when you first record-enable an audio track, Logic will immediately prompt you to name and save your project.

It's nice that Logic will prompt you to save and name your projects properly, but you should take the initiative to name and save your project, prior to being prompted by the software. This is just a good habit to get into. Poor file management will come back to haunt you.

Okay, let's name this session "Chapter 4." Remember to try to store all of your projects on an external FireWire drive, or a fast hard disk separate from your main system drive. Once you save your session, open the Preferences window, click on the Audio tab, select Devices, and make sure that your preferred recording interface is selected. Also, set your buffer size to something like 128 samples. Using a small buffer size when recording will minimize latency, which will usually inspire a better performance from the artist you are recording. Next, select 24-bit recording (see **Fig. 4.3**). If 24-bit recording is not selected, Logic will record at 16-bit resolution, greatly reducing the quality of your final product.

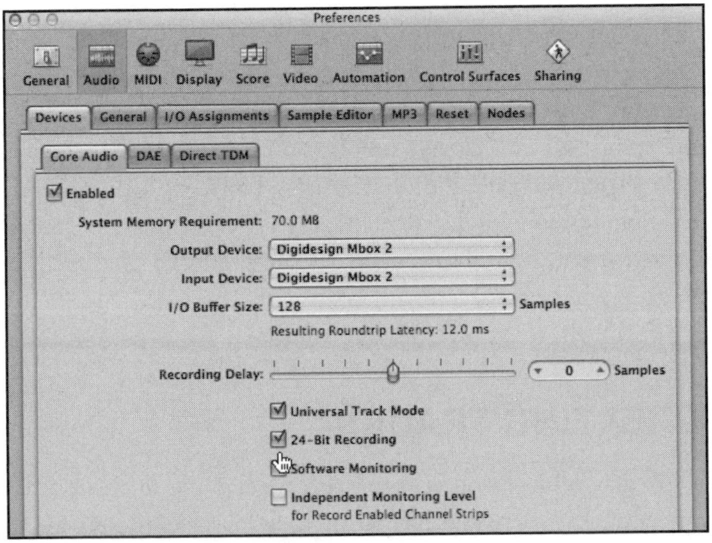

Fig. 4.3: Selecting 24-bit recording.

We're almost set up; but lastly, we need to verify our sampling rate. Go to the Project Settings window (Option + *) and select the Audio tab. For music production, remember that you want to stick with numbers evenly divisible by 44.1. Depending on your interface, you will have multiple sample rates from which to choose. Keep in mind, that using higher sampling rates will take their toll on your CPU and available disk space. Since this is a music example, let's stick with 44.1 kHz for this session (see **Fig. 4.4**).

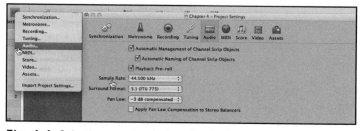

Fig. 4.4: Selecting sample rate from the Audio Project Settings menu.

We're now set up to record audio: we have named and saved our session, set up our buffer size, bit depth, and sampling rate. This may have seemed like a hassle, and doesn't quite fall in line with the zero-to-music mentality that Apple is going for. However, it is important to remember that this is a power user book. While a generic Logic user may never change his or her sample rate or bit depth and still make some amazing music, being armed with this knowledge will help you make better technical decisions when recording, and take full advantage of all of the professional features that Logic Pro 9 has to offer. Furthermore, these preferences do not change unless you change them. Creating a new session will yield the same settings. However, opening a pre-existing session with different settings *will* cause them to change. In any event, it is always good to know how to change these settings when working on any session, new or old.

CREATING TRACKS

Now that your session is optimized, we're going to create a few more tracks to ensure that all of their basic functions are in working order. To create new tracks, use the keyboard shortcut

(Command + Option + N). You can always add new tracks from the File menu, or from the + buttons, or the Tracks tab just beneath the Toolbar, but get into the habit of using shortcuts. The fewer times you have to reach for the mouse, the better.

The New Track dialog we saw when we first made a new session appears again. Notice that you can change the number of tracks you wish to create, so if you want six audio tracks you don't have to repeat this process six times. We already have one mono audio track, so let's add four software instrument tracks. Make sure multi-timbral is not selected; we'll go over that later. This time, make sure Open Library is selected so the Media tab opens automatically and exposes the Library of sounds to choose from without your having to remember how to navigate to it.

Naming and Organizing Your Tracks

After you create your new tracks, it is a good idea to name and arrange them. Right now, you should see what is shown in **Fig. 4.5**.

Fig. 4.5: Arrange window with new tracks and their default names.

If you open the Mixer tab from the Arrange window, and select the All button, you will see a few additional tracks that we did not create. These tracks are automatically created in each Logic session. In addition to our four instrument tracks and single audio track you will see a Prelisten channel strip, a Click channel strip, an Out 1-2, and a Master fader (see **Fig. 4.6**).

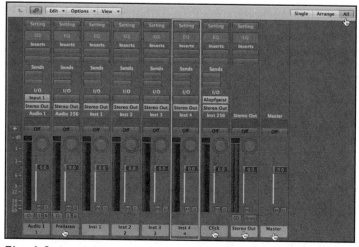

Fig. 4.6: Automatic channels created in the Mixer with every new project.

The Prelisten channel strip is hidden from view by default. This strip is used to monitor playback from the Sample Editor, Loop Browser, Audio Bin, and the browser. Its basic function is to let you audition audio. When browsing for loops this fader provides control over the volume at which the loop will play back. Although it is hidden from view normally, remember you can easily see it by selecting the All tab button in the Mixer window. You can also adjust the Prelisten volume by using the volume slider in the lower left side of the Loop Browser. The volume slider will correspond to the Prelisten fader.

The Click channel strip is also hidden from the standard arrange view. As previously mentioned, you may feel the need to change the settings of your click track, so once again, choosing the All button in the Mixer window will help you out by showing all of the channels that are being used in the project, including the click.

The Out 1-2 and Master faders are the last remaining channel strips. They are present in the Mixer window without selecting the All tab, yet neither of them actually appear in the Arrange window. The Stereo Out 1-2 channel strip is the final summing bus for all of your tracks. If you want to put some compression or EQ on your entire mix, this is where to apply it. This channel strip's meter is also very important; be sure to constantly reference its level to avoid distortion. Do not confuse this with the Master fader, which only affects the output to your speakers. It is important to understand the fundamental difference between levels and relative volume. Your mix could be very low, but your speakers could be cranked. This is a common mistake that has probably happened to all of us at one time or another.

Similarly, when adding track after track to the mix, people tend to forget that the sum of many tracks is greater than just one track alone, and there is the possibility that the Stereo Out 1-2 channels may peak, and the mix will begin to distort. Some of my colleagues and I chuckle when we see our students doing this, and we often refer to it as "add-it-on-itus." Turning down the headphones or speakers will not help this problem. Only bringing down the individual channel faders will resolve this issue, so make sure you understand the difference. Should you want any track in the Mixer window to show up in the Arrange window that isn't there by default, simply right-click on the desired track and select Create/Select Arrange Track.

Okay, back to naming and organizing. To name or rename a track, simply double-click the name and you will be able to edit the text. This works in both the Arrange and Mixer windows, so changing it in one place will change it in both places. Naming is very important because the recorded track and audio files will inherit the name of the channel. So let's select Inst 1. Make sure the Library is open, and select Acoustic Pianos > Bosendorfer Piano Club. Notice that once the desired piano patch loads, there are a few inserts automatically added to the channel strip, and the channel is now named Bosendorfer Piano Club. Press the Record button on the Transport. Assuming you already have a USB controller connected properly, go ahead and play something, and listen for the sound. If you don't have sound, quickly look at the Transport area where it says "No in and No out" and verify that your controller information is being received by Logic. If you don't see any activity coming into the program, try going to the preferences, choose the MIDI option, then click on the General tab, and select Reset All MIDI Drivers. Sometimes this re-recognizes any controllers that are hooked up. If you don't have a USB controller hooked up, you can still work through this exercise by using the computer keyboard as a musical keyboard. To do this, simply turn on the Caps Lock key on your standard keyboard. This is also a great option for laptop users. Once the piano keyboard appears on your screen, press some keys and you will hear the piano we selected earlier. Press the Record button on the Transport, then play the piano and record a few bars of something, then press Stop on the Transport or stop the recording by pressing the spacebar.

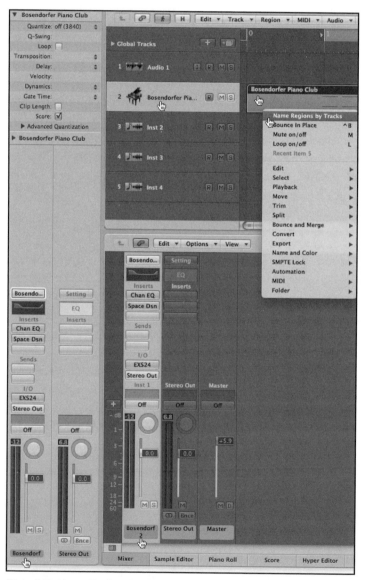

Fig. 4.7: Name Regions by Tracks option.

Notice that the name of the file is now "Classical Piano." That's a little weird, right? So let's change the generic instrument name that was pre-selected by holding down the control key, left-clicking the mouse and selecting Name Regions by Tracks (Command + Option + N). This will name the selected region after the channel. Now the regions, Arrange window, Mixer window, and Inspector windows match (see **Fig. 4.7**).

If you followed along in your own session, go ahead and delete this track by selecting it from the Arrange window, and pressing the Delete button. If there are any regions in the Arrange window associated with the track, Logic will warn you, but you can disregard that for now. So let's do this again, starting with Inst 2. Select an instrument from the Library, and it will load and name the Arrange channel accordingly like before. It's fine to load and play around with a few different channel strip settings before deciding; however, before you record, double-click and name your track accordingly as shown above. We want a piano track, so after auditioning a few acoustic pianos, I have decided I like Steinway Piano Hall. Before recording, double-click the track in the Arrange window and rename this track Piano. Notice the change takes place in the Mixer window. Now go ahead and press Record again on the Transport, let it run for a few bars, and stop it. Notice the region is still named whatever Logic sees fit; in this case "Steinway Piano," which isn't too confusing, but I still highly recommend you use the Name Regions by Tracks option for consistency.

Audio tracks are a little more consistent out of the gate, so by making sure to name your audio tracks before you record, the recorded audio will automatically inherit the name of the channel. Nice!

Now let's continue to set up and name our tracks. For the audio track, open the Library and select Voice > Female Voice > Female Ambient Lead Vocal. Double-click the track to name it Vocals. Next, select Inst 2; if you didn't already rename this and load the Library channel strip, please do so. We are using Steinway Piano Hall, and the track is labeled Piano. For Inst 3 select Bass > Electric Bass > Liverpool Bass. Rename the track Bass. Rounding out our quartet, Inst 4 will be our drum track. Select Drums and

Percussion > Acoustic Drum Kits > Studio Tight Kit, and be sure to rename the track Drums. Your session should look something like this (see **Fig. 4.8**).

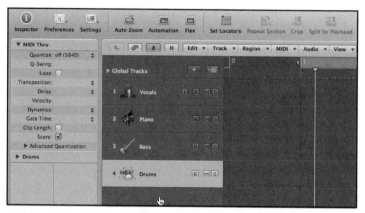

Fig. 4.8: Quartet arrangement.

To rearrange the order of the tracks, simply click and drag on the track in the Arrange window. Let's go ahead and move our Vocal track to the bottom. Click on the Mixer and notice the change is reflected there as well. While in the Mixer window, also take note of a few other things. Notice that because we loaded presets from the library, we already have inserts for each of our four tracks. Remember that these are mere starting points; we'll go over more advanced options when we delve into sound shaping, creation, and mixing later on. Also, notice the colors. By default, all instrument tracks are green, all audio tracks are blue, and all auxiliary and master faders are yellow. These can all be changed, but for now let's keep them as they are as it will help you to learn the difference between tracks at a glance.

Back in the Arrange window, we're going to go over a quick tip to help your visual workflow. We only have four tracks, so this session isn't cluttered and everything is in plain view. However, you will find that sessions can get out of hand with tons of tracks. For example, let's say your singer hasn't arrived at the studio yet and you want to start working. No problem; you can start auditioning and recording some parts right away. If you don't wish to see the vocal track, you can simply hide it. Click on the H just below the toolbar to enable track hiding. Once this is selected, you will notice an additional button show up next to your existing Record, Mute, and Solo buttons. An H now appears on all tracks. On the vocal track, turn on the H. The button will turn green, indicating it is on (see **Fig. 4.9**). Now return to the big H below the menu bar, and press it again. Notice it turns orange, and the vocal track is hidden (see **Fig. 4.10**). To unhide, simply toggle the H again. This will come in handy later when dealing with high track counts.

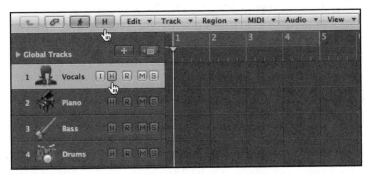

Fig. 4.9: Show/Hide Tracks button with green indicator.

Fig. 4.10: Indicator that there are hidden tracks is orange.

NOTE

It is important to realize that a track is still active and will play back even when hidden, unless it is muted. Hiding tracks will not free up resources—it is purely for visual aesthetics and organization.

AMS SETUP

Audio MIDI Setup is the standard setup tool for audio and MIDI devices to interface with OS X. We are going to open AMS in the Finder. Go to Applications > Utilities > Audio MIDI Setup. There are two tabs in AMS: one for audio devices and one for MIDI devices. First we are going to ensure we have a MIDI connection. I am using an Apogee Duet as my recording interface, and while the rotary encoder can act as a MIDI controller, the Duet does not have a MIDI input. I use an Edirol PCR-49 as my mobile MIDI controller. It can connect via MIDI or USB; in my case I connect it through USB and it shows up automatically in AMS. In my studio setup I use a Korg Triton Pro X. To get a MIDI signal from this to Logic I need to use a USB-to-MIDI interface. I am currently using M-Audio's Uno USB interface. This requires an extra step. AMS will recognize the Uno, but I must add the Triton manually. You will have to do the same if your controller does not support USB. Click Add Device. A new external device will show up. Double-click it to edit the parameters. Under Device Name you can name it whatever you please, but I generally stick with what the device is actually called, in my case Triton Pro X. Under Manufacturer I select Korg, and under Model I select Pro X. This setup ensures that the patches on your external keyboard will match whatever your host platform is. You can use the icon browser to select the icon that best suits your keyboard. There happens to be a picture of a Triton, so I have selected that for mine. Your device will transmit and receive on all channels; when finished, press Apply. Notice that your device now shows up in AMS, but you need to connect it to your MIDI interface. First make sure you have physically connected your keyboard to the MIDI interface: plug the MIDI Out of your keyboard to the MIDI In of your interface. Then in AMS, drag from the up arrow on the Devices icon, and a patch cable will appear. Drag this to the down arrow of your MIDI interface to make the connection (see **Fig. 4.11**). Test the setup by pressing Test Setup, hit a few notes, and you should hear a bell ting. This tells you that you are sending and receiving MIDI.

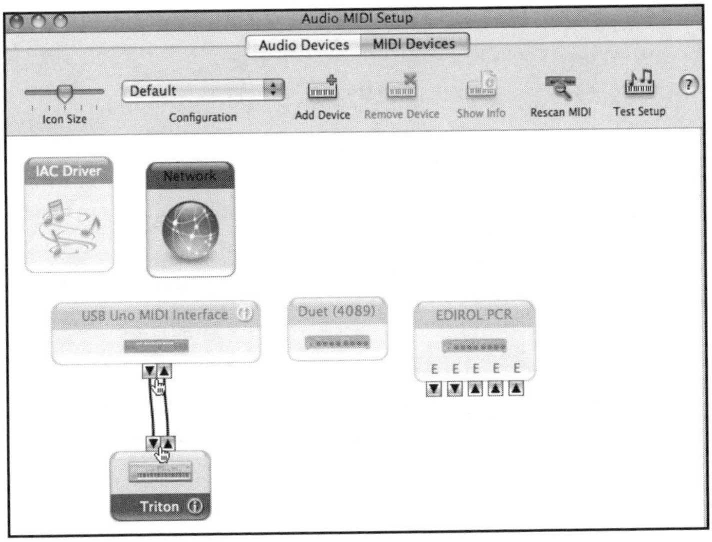

Fig. 4.11: Mac OS X AMS MIDI Setup Window.

If setup was unsuccessful, delete your devices and rescan, then add and reconnect them. If problems persist, refer to the owner's manual for your keyboard or go to the Web site of the company that makes your controller, and look for information there. Often, you will find the answers to your troubles using this method.

MAKING THE CONNECTION

Now we have our devices physically connected and virtually connected. To verify that we have MIDI coming into Logic, all we have to do is bang on some keys or move a knob or button on our controller. The visual display is on the Transport; you should see a change as you play the controller. This display will tell you which MIDI controller number you are using or what chord you happen to be playing (see **Fig. 4.12**). If you arm one of the instrument tracks we have created, you should instantly hear beautiful music. If you don't hear anything, or you don't see anything coming in on the visual display, you need to check your connections and refer back to AMS setup. Be sure to only arm one instrument at a time. Sometimes it can be cool to layer instruments by arming multiple tracks at once, but that time is not now. Start by arming just the Piano track.

Fig. 4.12: The MIDI In/Out indicator shows if any MIDI activity occurs.

Go ahead and start recording by pressing the Record button on the Transport. The metronome will automatically play and give you a two-bar count-in. We didn't set a key, tempo, or time signature for this song, so by default Logic gives us C Major, 120 bpm, 4/4. We'll go over changing this in a bit, but for now record your part and stop the Transport. If you aren't used to recording to a metronome, you will certainly learn quickly. We'll go over more advanced recording in later chapters, but if you want to review what we have gone over in this chapter and keep playing, you can work on your timing by "jamming" over a drum loop.

The quick-and-easy way to play over a loop is to click on the Media option in the upper right corner of the screen, select the Loops tab, select All Drums, and choose a loop by clicking it (see **Fig. 4.13**). Keep your instrument track armed and review the various drum beats. Change the tempo on the Transport, and cycle through various channel strip settings if you want to experiment with different instruments.

Fig. 4.13: Media browser with Loops > All Drums selected to audition various loops.

FINAL THOUGHTS

We are getting to the point where you can start experimenting with sounds and having some fun. Make sure you are comfortable browsing through the Library for channel strip settings. Also, be sure you have a solid grasp on how to name, arrange, and delete tracks and regions. Watch the QuickTime tutorials that are included with this book to further reinforce what we have gone over. Also, don't forget to see how you measure up by trying to answer the Logic Tune-Up questions at the end of the chapter. After you feel comfortable with everything up to this point in the book, it's time to move on to more advanced techniques to help you shape your sound.

POWER TIPS FOR CHAPTER 4

1. Try to get in the habit of always recording, even rehearsal takes. Many times you'll capture the best performance when the band, musician, or you are merely rehearsing.

2. When being creative and looking for inspiration, you can use a pre-made template, but when it comes to serious recording you should build your own project from scratch, or create your own templates so that you are more deliberate with the choices you make.

3. You can change what Logic does on startup from Preferences > General > Project Handling. On the pull-down menu for Startup Action, you can tell Logic to do a multitude of things. By default Logic is set to open your last project.

4. If 24-bit recording is not selected, the default bit depth is 16 bits. If you have enough hard drive space, be sure to enable 24-bit recording; the audio quality is definitely much better.

5. In the Mixer select the All button, and you will see a Prelisten channel strip, a Click channel strip, an Out 1-2, and a Master fader in addition to the tracks you have created.

6. To rearrange the order of the tracks, simply click-and-drag on the track in the Arrange window; the changes are also reflected in the Mixer window.

7. Click on the H just below the toolbar in the Arrange window to enable track hiding. The H button will now show up on every track in the Arrange window. Turning this button on will toggle it between show and hide.

8. Audio MIDI Setup is the standard setup tool for audio and MIDI devices to interface with OS X. AMS is located here: Applications > Utilities > Audio MIDI Setup.

9. You can check your MIDI signal flow without any tracks armed. All you need to do is press a key or turn a knob on your MIDI controller, and the Transport should show the incoming MIDI signal.

KEYBOARD SHORTCUT SUMMARY

KEYBOARD SHORTCUT	FUNCTION
Command + Tab	Change Applications
Command + N	Create New Project
Command + Option + N	Name Regions by Track
Option + *	Open Project Settings

LOGIC 9 TUNE-UP

1. Creating a project from scratch helps re-enforce the fundamental decision of DAW _____ _____.

2. For music production sampling rates, remember that you want to stick with numbers evenly divisible by _____.

3. To help stay organized it is a good idea to _____ and _____ your tracks immediately after creating them.

4. To rearrange the order of your tracks, you need to move them in the _____ window.

5. Selecting Create/Select Arrange Track will put a track that is in the _____ window into the _____ window as well.

6. To keep your region's names the same as your track names, right-click and select _____ _____ _____ _____.

7. By default, all instrument tracks are _____ all audio tracks are _____, and all auxiliary and master faders are _____.

8. Click on the _____ just below the toolbar to enable track hiding.

9. There are two tabs in AMS: one for _____ devices and one for _____ devices.

10. The default key signature in all Logic projects is the key of _____, the default tempo is _____ bpm, and the default time signature is ____/____.

A Logic Creation

5

In the last chapter, we took our Logic system "once around the block" to make sure everything was connected and working properly. Learning the theory and technical side of Logic, or any DAW, can feel like a never-ending task at times, but it's important to dedicate a good amount of time to studying and understanding the system you are working with. Having command of your system will let your creativity flow with very few obstacles along the way. As we move forward, you will continue to learn fundamental techniques that will help you a great deal with your Logic creations. Once you are armed with this knowledge, you will be ready for any creative situation. As always, valuable Power Tips, a Keyboard Shortcut Summary and Logic Tune-Up questions are included at the end of the chapter to ensure you retain the most important information.

ARMED AND READY

Record Modes

There are a few different ways to record audio and MIDI in Logic (see **Fig. 5.1**). Each recording mode is unique and designed for a specific purpose. By default, you will be recording in "Standard" record mode. In this mode you simply record-enable or "arm" a track, press the Record button on the Transport, and start recording. What is important to remember is that all of Logic's record modes take advantage of a few global parameters. For example, all record modes work in conjunction with the region-cycling function, which will allow you to loop a particular section until you get your recording right. Also, count-in or pre-roll is universal.

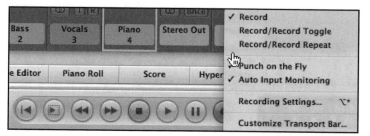

Fig. 5.1: Select Record Mode by right-clicking on the Record button in the Transport.

To change the count-in or pre-roll, we need to go to our recording preferences. There are a few ways to get there, but for convenience's sake, right-click on the Record button on the Transport, and select Recording Preferences. You can also use the keyboard shortcut Option + *.

From this window, we can set the default count-in or pre-roll duration. What's the difference? A count-in uses the tempo of the song to count you in before recording. Pre-roll allows you to adjust the same parameter, only using seconds as your time duration. Because we are working with a song that has a predetermined tempo, we will stick with the count-in and set it to two bars. If this is too long or too short, you can simply change it to suite your needs.

When recording with pre-roll or a count-in, the audio is recorded as soon as you hit Record; therefore, you can trim back to recover a few pickup notes if your "in point" was a little late.

You can start a recording by pressing the Record button on the Transport, or by pressing the asterisk (*) key on the number pad. Pressing the Record button starts a recording; pressing it again (in Standard mode) will do nothing. To stop recording you must press the Stop button on the Transport, or simply press the spacebar. You can also pause a recording with the Pause button.

Pressing Record again after pausing will resume recording from the playhead's current position.

Another mode is Record/Record Toggle. Select this by Control-clicking the Record button and choosing it. In this mode the Record button initiates a recording; when pressed again it stops recording and playback continues; pressing a third time resumes recording; and so on.

Next on our list is Record/Record Repeat. This mode allows us to delete the current recording and start recording over again from the playhead position. This is very similar to our next mode, which isn't so much a mode as a relatively standard key command: Discard Recording and Return to Last Play Position. The keyboard shortcut for this is (Command + .). Using this command during a recording will stop the current recording pass and erase it, and then the playhead will return to the last play position. This is different from the prior modes because both recording and playback stop, allowing you to communicate with the artist if necessary before recording again.

Record Repeat mode is for those who wish to record their part over, and over until they are happy with it. Using Record Repeat and Discard Recording are good ways to keep your regions and hard drive uncluttered. If you know you have several takes that are unusable, there is no need to keep them, and your system will thank you with better performance. Please keep in mind that discarding a recording is different from the undo command. You can always undo a recording by pressing Command + Z. This is less destructive, as you can always redo by pressing Shift + Command + Z. These undo and redo commands are global.

The way Logic deletes audio files depends on how the file was created. For instance, to delete a region that you just recorded, select it and press Delete or Backspace. Immediately, a dialog box appears and asks you if you would like to erase the corresponding audio file. This helps save hard drive space and keeps your Audio Bin less cluttered. However, using the same method with an audio file that was imported into the session will not yield the same result. When you delete the region, no dialog box appears, and the region is simply removed. If you would like to delete the region and the audio file associated with it, you can do so manually by selecting it from the Audio Bin and then deleting it from there.

Recording with Logic makes it easy to get the perfect take. Sometimes the perfect take is the first take, but most of us must make a few attempts before capturing what we really want. A "take" is a part that has been performed and recorded multiple times. It is often referred to as a "pass." When recording audio or MIDI files in Logic, these multiple takes are automatically recorded, and nothing is deleted. This means if you record "over" an existing pass, your first pass is still in the project and still accessible.

This method of recording takes the pressure off the musician to play flawlessly, and makes the recording process less tedious. However, if you, or someone you are working with only accepts flawless, "one-take" passes, you might want to consider Replace mode. With the Replace button turned on from the Transport, any existing audio or MIDI in the recorded region is overwritten and deleted. This can be undone to a certain degree, but this mode is definitely much more destructive than other record modes. Replace mode's main benefit is that your session and hard drive isn't cluttered with miscellaneous files. It is generally safer not to use Replace mode, which is why it is not on by default.

As mentioned earlier, when you use Standard record mode, if you record over an audio region, a new take is automatically created. To view all of your takes, click the triangle on the track for an expanded view of all of them, or double-click on the region to expand and collapse your takes (see **Fig. 5.2**). Please note that while the different takes are shown in what appears to be multiple tracks, it is important to realize that they are all still only on one track. The "tracks" populated with your multiple takes are called lanes. You can record multiple takes and they will all show up here. Logic Pro 9 also allows you to Auto-Colorize Takes. Turn this function on by selecting the Auto-Colorize Takes option from the Recording tab in the Settings drop-down menu. You also have the option of importing audio into one of the lanes as a take. You can do this by dragging audio onto the track, and it will appear as a take.

Fig. 5.2: Disclosure triangle for showing multiple takes and take options.

To audition the various takes, click on the downturned triangle at the right edge of an audio region, or simply right-click on the region and select the take number you would like to hear (see **Fig. 5.3**). You will also notice that there are a few new choices on this menu. If you don't know which ones were added, don't worry. They will be pointed out as this book continues.

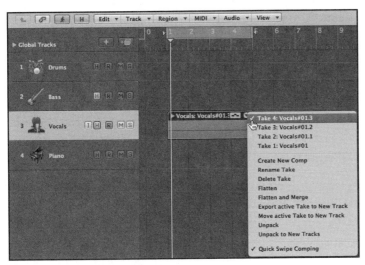

Fig. 5.3: Takes list and take options.

This method of take management is great, but what about when you are recording multiple tracks? Let's say you are recording a guitar with two microphones. When you change the take on one track, it will not change on the other. Sure, it's not hard to manually change both, but if you aren't careful, you may forget to do that—for example, if you are tracking a full drum kit with 12 microphones and you want to record several passes. I'm sure you can imagine how this might get annoying and tedious real fast. Yet if you aren't careful, it is also a pretty good way to get lost in the land of multiple tracks and takes, too.

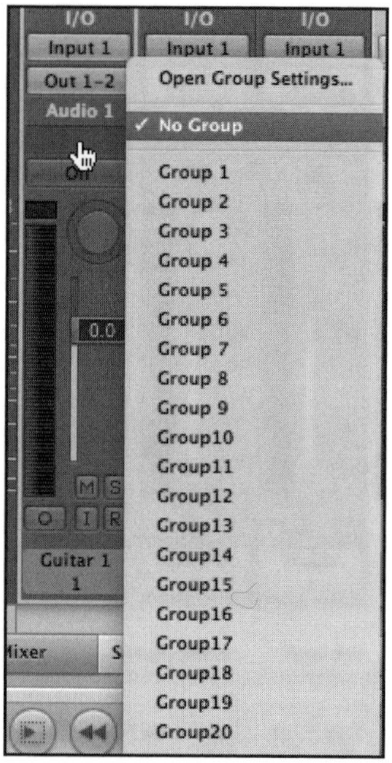

The simple solution for this is to use groups. By linking tracks and parameters to groups, we can make a single change that will affect all the members of the group. We'll go into more advanced grouping configurations later. For now, let's use a simple group to help us with our take management.

To create a group, open the Mixer window and select the first track that you would like to be part of the group. Now, hold down Shift and click on the other track to select both tracks (you can also click-and-drag to highlight desired tracks). Once the desired tracks are selected, click on the gray box that is just below the output selector. Clicking in this box will show a drop-down menu for groups (see **Fig. 5.4**). From here, select Group 1 to quickly create your group.

Fig. 5.4: Group list located just below the channel-output selector.

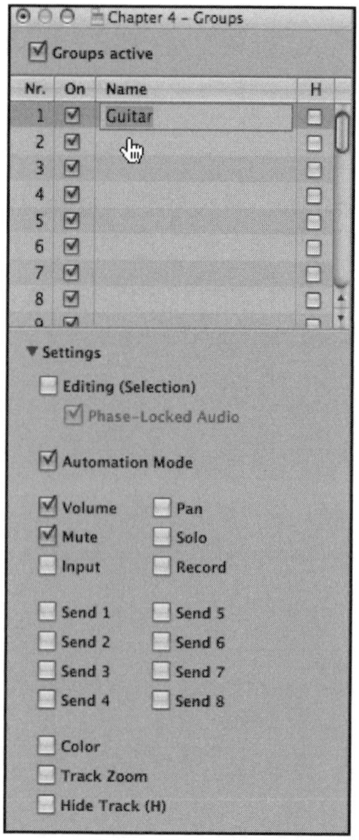

To name the group, click on the gray box again and select the "Open Group Settings" option. Here, you can see the many options you have for the grouped tracks. If you are a longtime Logic user, you'll notice some changes. Some of the more significant changes are the ability to group soloed tracks, record-enabled tracks, and inputs, but for now click the Settings arrow and select the "Editing (Selection)" box.

You could also choose the Phase-Locked Audio option if you were editing multiple tracks at once. The Phase-Locked Audio option is perfect for editing drums, or on any source recorded with multiple microphones. Before you close this window, click in the area under the Name column to open up the "name" field for the desired group, and then type in the name of your group (see **Fig. 5.5**).

Punching

Punch recording allows us to get in and out of a recording. It is often used to fix a mistake. The concept is to "punch in" just

Fig. 5.5: Group Settings menu.

before the mistake, record and fix the mistake, then "punch out," and playback continues. When punching in and out, it is good to hear the section in context. It can be hard to correct a mistake if you have no frame of reference. There are a few ways to punch record with Logic.

Punch on the Fly

You "punch on the fly" when you are in playback mode and want to manually punch in to start and stop recording. This can be rough on your system because your hard drive is busy reading data until you decide to punch in, so naturally there will be a slight delay between when you punch in and when the drive starts recording. Logic adjusts for this delay with a "Punch on the Fly" option that you can select from the recording preferences. This means that Logic is ready to record at any moment. However, you may notice a performance loss with this turned on.

While you can still punch on the fly with this mode off, you will notice a delay. To punch in and out during playback, simply press the Record button. Start playback, hit Record to punch in, record, and then punch out by pressing Record again. Playback will continue until stopped. That's not so bad, is it? Well, it can be if you are the engineer *and* the musician. For this reason modern systems have adopted an autopunch system.

Autopunch

You will find the Autopunch button next to the Cycle button on the Transport (see **Fig. 5.6**). If you press Record with Cycle mode off, recording will start from the playback head. With Cycle mode on, your recording will start with a pre-roll/count-in, record at the cycle region's start point, and go through to the end of the cycle, at which point it will loop back and record another take. Autopunch is designed to work in conjunction with Cycle mode or on its own.

Fig. 5.6: The Autopunch button in the Transport.

On its own, Autopunch creates a red range similar to the green Cycle range, but it is important to note that they are independent of each other. Turn on Autopunch from the Transport and change the Autopunch length (range) by clicking and dragging, or selecting a specific region and then turning it on. It works the same way your Cycle range works (see **Fig 5.7**).

Fig. 5.7: The Autopunch range is red and just underneath the green Cycle range indicators.

After you set the Autopunch range, you can quickly set your playback cycle range by clicking-and-dragging the red Autopunch range upward. Similarly, dragging the Autopunch range down will create a marker of the same length.

Once your Autopunch range is selected, you can start recording. Remember that recording will start from the last position of the playhead with no count-in or pre-roll: playback starts, the playhead crosses the punch-in point and recording starts, recording continues until the out point is reached, recording stops, and playback continues.

For advanced Autopunch, use it in conjunction with the cycle range. This way you can set up a cycle to loop and only punch in a few notes; for example, if you have a solo that is near-perfect and you just need to punch in on a bad note. It's nice to get in there real tight with the Autopunch feature alone; however, you will be constantly stopping the recording and playback. If you set a cycle range and an Autopunch range, you will be able to loop record over your mistake and hear the solo in context.

Even though you may be very accurate in setting in and out points for autopunching, sometimes you may forget to take certain things into consideration, such as pickup notes leading into the punch-in point. This can affect how clean your in and out punch points are. Luckily, Logic starts the recording about a bar before the punch, in case you need to trim the region back from the start of the punch-in to retrieve the pickup notes that were played but were not part of the original Autopunch range.

You can manually type in the length of the cycle region in the Transport. If you click-and-drag to change the length and location, you will see these numbers change dynamically. You can also have this functionality with the Autopunch feature, but it must be added to the Transport by customizing it. Right-click the Transport and select Customize. Check the box for "Sample Rate or Punch Locators," and you will see a second set of numbers similar to those of the cycle region. When Autopunch is off, this extra box will display the sample rate of the song (see **Figs. 5.8** and **5.9**).

Fig. 5.8: Punch locaters display in the main transport.

Fig. 5.9: Sample rate display in the main transport.

HEADPHONE MIXES

Once you have a solid grasp of all of the different ways to record, you must have a good understanding of how to create and use headphone mixes. Headphone mixes are an essential part of the recording process. It's generally easy to record yourself and other artists using direct recording while listening through your monitors. However, we don't have this luxury when recording parts with a microphone. When the music from the speakers is used to let the artist record their new part, there is a good chance it will bleed into the microphone and will be recorded onto the newly recorded track. Also, you might accidentally run into feedback, which could damage your ears and your equipment. To get around this, we are going to give the artist a headphone mix. Let's take a look at some of the ways to accomplish this.

Stereo Bus Mix

A stereo bus mix is the same mix you hear coming from the speakers. Depending on the interface you are using, there are a few ways to send this type of mix to the artist. I am using an Apogee Duet, which sends the main output to my studio monitors. There is also a ¼-inch headphone jack on the front of the interface. Simply plugging in a pair of headphones will allow the artist to hear the same mix that is going to the monitors. The drawback to this method when using the Duet is that the volume control for the headphones is tied directly to the volume of the monitors. This can prove to be a problem in a couple of ways. Your artist may need more volume, but you are being blown away by the volume coming out of your studio monitors. One solution would be to disconnect the studio monitors, but then you will be unable to monitor the mix yourself. That doesn't make a lot of sense. A better option is to turn down the volume on your monitors to compensate. If for some reason you cannot turn your speakers down, you can also connect a Y-cable to the output of the headphone jack on the Duet and connect two pairs of headphones, allowing you and the artist to hear the same mix. Most interfaces have a dedicated headphone output. Some even have two. Use the appropriate option from what you have available to you.

Independent Headphone Mixes

While recording using the stereo bus (Stereo Out) as your headphone mix you'll recall that the artist hears in their headphones what the engineer hears in their main monitors. This means that if the engineer makes a change in the level of an instrument while the artist is recording, the artist will hear this change too. This can be very distracting to the artist. However, if we send the artist a mix that is separate from the monitor mix, then the engineer is free to change the volume and panning of various instruments as they please, without affecting the mix being sent to the artist.

To send independent headphone mixes, your interface must have more than two outputs. In the case of the Duet, you are out of luck. However, many interfaces have four or more outputs. Find one that works best for your particular needs. Headphone sends are limited by the number of auxiliary sends and available outputs you have. Logic has eight available buses per channel strip. By clicking on one of the empty sends and assigning it to a free bus, Logic will automatically create a corresponding auxiliary track to monitor the input and output of that send. You can select an output separate from Out 1-2; for example, Out 3-4. The outputs from your interface should be plugged into a headphone amplifier or a mixer so that the signal can be distributed to multiple sets of headphones, and the overall volume can be controlled from there too. It's generally not a good idea to send a headphone mix to someone without having physical control over the volume level you are sending. Having a mixer or headphone amp gives you and the artist more immediate control.

To create a headphone mix from the aux send, you must assign the same send to all of the channels the artist wishes to hear in their mix. Once this is done, you can adjust the level being sent to the headphones using the circular send volume control icon just to the right of the send. Simply click and drag it up or down to change the level. One very important step to take before setting all of the send levels for the headphone mix is to change the status of where the auxiliary is in the signal path. By default, the auxiliaries are post-fader sends, which is ideal for effects-based sending. However, in case you want a completely independent mix, this send needs to be set to pre-fader, so it can't be affected by the level of your faders. A pre-fader mix means any fader adjustments you make will not be audible in the auxiliary mix because that signal is sent out "pre" or "prior to" the fader adjustments. To choose the pre or post status of the aux sends, click and hold on the bus, and a menu will show up. Select pre for each individual track you are sending to the headphones. Notice the send indicator turns green for all pre-fader sends. This will come in handy when you start dealing with multiple sends for various reasons. Lastly, when you first assigned a send, Logic automatically created a corresponding aux track; rename that track "Headphone Mix" in the Mixer window. After renaming the track it will appear in parentheses next to the associated bus, which is also helpful in tracking down what is being sent where (see **Fig. 5.10**).

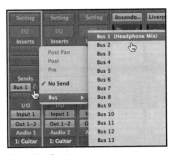

Fig. 5.10: Bus 1 as a Headphone Mix "send."

RECORDING AN INSTRUMENT TRACK

Recording an instrument track is very easy, but here are a few more tips that will help make the recording process a bit smoother. Of course, you can always try to start recording right away without any of this knowledge, but it really helps to know a few important things before you dive in.

Remember, when you create a new session, Logic assumes you are playing in the key of C Major at 120 bpm. While the key is relative and can be changed, it is just as important to figure out your tempo, as your click track and grid will conform to this value.

If you haven't already created an instrument track, go ahead and create one using the keyboard shortcut Command + Option + N. After creating an instrument track, be sure the "Open Library" box is checked. You'll notice that Logic created a track named "Inst 1," armed the track, and opened the Library under the Media bin. We're going to start by recording a simple four-bar drum loop. So as you might imagine we are going to want to load something with drums and percussion. For this example, we are going to be using Logic's Ultrabeat for our drum loops. You can always assign one of Logic's 40 instruments by clicking on the input tab of an instrument and selecting the instrument of your choice, but in this example we will navigate to the Library, select Drums & Percussion > Acoustic Drum Kits > Studio Tight Kit. You'll notice the input to the channel is now Ultrabeat, and the Library setting also loaded a nice compression and EQ for us. We'll go in and tweak those dynamic settings in the mixing stage, but for now it gives us a nice fat drum sound. Double-click the name in the Arrange window and name this track "Drums."

Because we know we are going to be recording a four-bar loop, set your locators to a four-bar length. By default, you will notice that Logic has the locators set at a four-bar length, and they are grayed out from bars 1–4. Click on the set locators or the gray area to make it active. Then drag that selection to bar 2. This way our four-bar loop will start at bar 2 and go through bar 5 (see **Fig. 5.11**). We are moving it to bar 2 in case we are early on the beat when we start recording; MIDI is easier to recover and work with if we start on bar 2.

Fig. 5.11: Cycle range indicating a 4-bar loop.

It is generally a good habit to start recording after bar 1. It allows you more breathing room for editing and creating intros later on in the production process.

With the selection made, pressing Play will prompt the playhead to start from the first locator. When we start recording, the metronome will turn on, and the playhead will give us a one-bar count-in. Once the recording reaches the end locator, the playhead will snap back to the first locator, and recording continues. When working with MIDI we have a few tools we can use to help build our parts. The default Logic setting is what we will use for now. So what will happen? When we start recording, Logic will record all of the MIDI data coming in. When it reaches the end of the cycle to loop back, it will continue to record; however, on the second pass Logic will automatically merge new MIDI data with existing MIDI data, allowing you to build a drum beat one instrument at a time.

This way, instead of trying to play all of the parts of the drum kit at once, you can play them one at a time for each pass, and each time the new part will be added to the existing part. For example, you can record the kick and snare patterns on the first cycle of 4 bars, and then add the hi-hat parts on the second cycle, and maybe cymbal hits or fills on the third cycle.

Overlapping Recording Options

These are various modes of recording MIDI, all of which have unique advantages, but make sure you become familiar with all of them. Awareness of all the functions Logic has to offer is essential to making sure you are the best Logic operator you can be. To set these options, go to the Settings menu, select Recording, then click on the Overlapping Recordings options, and choose the option you desire (see **Fig 5.12**).

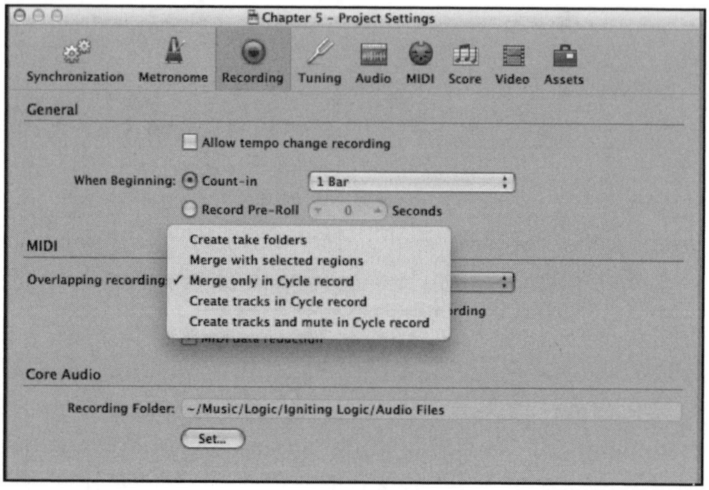

Fig. 5.12: MIDI options menu for overlapping recording settings.

CREATE TAKE FOLDERS

This will create a different take folder with each new pass, and is how audio recording works by default. Some people find this a comfortable way to work, so if you are the type that likes to record the whole pass and then maybe "comp" the takes later, then this will work well for you. Also, added in Logic Pro 9 is the ability to use Replace mode. This allows you to punch in and out of a section from a take folder without creating a new take lane. To use Replace mode, make sure it is turned on in the Transport bar, next to the Autopunch button.

MERGE WITH SELECTED REGIONS

This means each time Logic records MIDI and encounters pre-existing MIDI it will always merge the data. The default is set to only merge when in Cycle record.

MERGE ONLY IN CYCLE RECORD

This is the default and what we will use to build our drum parts. It gives us the luxury of playing each instrument one at a time over each pass, but still allows us to overwrite existing MIDI if we are not in Cycle record.

CREATE TRACKS IN CYCLE RECORD

This is similar to what we are accomplishing with our merge. However, Logic will create a new track with each pass. This still allows you to build your part over each pass, and gives you the flexibility of having each part on a separate track. This might be helpful later if you find yourself wanting to add effects or EQ/compression to an individual instrument like the kick drum. You will still have the ability to separate your parts later if you choose not to use this mode.

CREATE TRACKS AND MUTE IN CYCLE RECORD

This does the same thing as the previous setting; however, after each pass the previously created track will be muted. If you are coming up with different ideas over each pass, this might work for you.

If you have trouble playing your parts "in time," you can use the Quantize feature in the MIDI Thru window in the Inspector. We'll go over quantization in more detail later, and you can always decide to quantize your performance after you record. However, if you select a quantize value in the MIDI Thru Inspector, then your performance will be quantized on input. The best part about Logic's quantize feature is that it is nondestructive. You can always revert to your original performance by turning off Quantize; similarly, you can change to a separate quantize value.

RECORDING AN AUDIO TRACK

Recording audio tracks is very similar to recording MIDI tracks, and many of the same principles will apply to both. Audio tracks are recorded by using your interface in conjunction with Logic. The number of simultaneous inputs you have is limited by your interface. Since I am using the Apogee Duet, I have two inputs at my disposal, and a variety of ways to utilize them. The Duet has two XLR inputs for microphones and two line inputs for direct signals such as guitar, bass, or keyboard. Despite having four ways to get signal into the Duet, the interface can only handle two inputs at a time. The preamp is controlled onscreen using Apogee's Maestro software, which is also used with the Ensemble and the Symphony systems. There are many other interfaces available, and each of them is set up differently. Be sure you have a solid grasp of your recording interface and how to set the input gain properly. Likewise, be sure to check the phantom power settings on your interface. If you are using a condenser microphone, your interface or preamp will need to supply the microphone with phantom power. Most interfaces will generally let you select between various input settings, such as:

- Direct Input

- Instrument/Line Level

- Microphone

Each of these has a different input gain structure, and it is important to select the proper one for your instrument. Plug your instrument into the correct input, be sure your audio track in Logic matches the input on your interface, start to sing into the mic or play the source instrument, and slowly bring up the preamp until you see a nice level on the desired channel strip in Logic. To set good recording levels, turn on the Input button next to the Record-enable button and press Play. This allows you to have the artist play along with the track without recording them, and doing so lets you have them play how they will be playing during the recording and therefore you can set better recording levels. It's a good time saver.

DIRECT RECORDING VS. MICROPHONE RECORDING

Guitar players generally have their sound dialed in with their amplifiers, but you may not have the luxury of being able to track your amp at a nice, loud volume, which usually provides the most desirable tones on many amplifiers. For this reason, Logic allows you to record directly into the program and re-amp your instrument through an amp modeler. Guitar Amp Pro was Logic's flagship guitar amp simulator, and it certainly gets the job done, but most guitar players consider its sound quality to be like that of a toy, possibly only good for "scratch tracks" just to get the idea laid down. However, with the new Amp Designer and Pedalboard plug-ins, all guitar players are going to be pleasantly surprised.

The new Amp Designer plug-in emulates the sound of over 20 world-famous guitar amps and the speaker cabinets that came with them. From full stacks and half stacks to small vintage combo amps and everything in between, Amp Designer does it all. It offers five different EQ types: British Bright, Vintage, U.S. Classic, Modern, and Boutique, each representing the different EQ characteristics found on various amps over the years. It also includes the ability to choose from 10 different reverb types as well as tremolo features that allow you to synchronize to the host application's tempo. Overall, Amp Designer is an incredible-sounding emulator that gives you any combination of vintage to modern tones for recording guitar (see **Fig. 5.13a**).

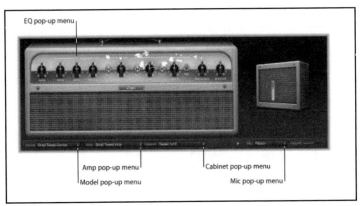

Fig. 5.13a: Amp Designer quick-start "roadmap."

Not only can you choose any combination of amp and speaker setup, but you can also choose between three different virtual microphones. As with all components of the tone chain, different microphone types and their placement will yield very different results. You can also change where the microphone is placed on the speaker. Many engineers call this "voicing the speaker cabinet." Even though placement is restricted to "near-field" range, it still lets you move the microphone around the speaker until you find what you consider to be "the sweet spot" (see **Fig. 5.13b**).

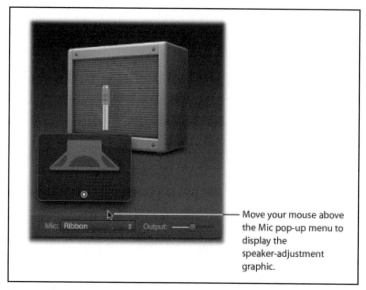

Move your mouse above the Mic pop-up menu to display the speaker-adjustment graphic.

Fig. 5.13b: Microphone placement simulation view.

As if Amp Designer isn't enough to shape your sound, Pedalboard is another new feature that comes with Logic Pro 9. This plug-in simulates some of the most famous and well-liked "stompbox" pedal effects on the planet. You can add or remove pedals as well as change the configuration of their signal routing to give you the ultimate in flexibility. Macro controls can be used to assign up to eight MIDI controllers to control any stompbox parameter in real time. There are also Distortion Pedals, Modulation Pedals, Delay Pedals, Filter Pedals, Dynamic Pedals, and Utility Pedals to choose from, so be sure to set aside a day to enjoy some of this stuff, because there are tons of cool options (see **Fig. 5.13c**).

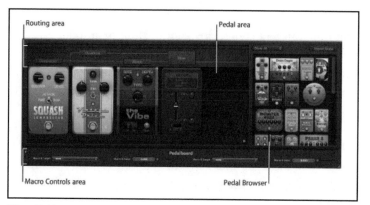

Fig. 5.13c: Pedalboard quick-start "roadmap."

I realize that recording guitar or bass with an amp emulator may not seem ideal at first, but once you start to play around with the beautiful new features and sounds in Logic Pro 9, you will discover the endless tools that are available to help you achieve quality results. Remember, even if you are recording a guitar player who insists on tracking their actual rig (which is quite common), you can connect the output of the guitar into the DI box. The DI box will split the signal, allowing you to send one signal to the player's setup or "rig" to be recorded by a microphone, and simultaneously send another unaltered guitar signal from the DI box to the interface and multitrack, to add modeling to later if you choose. It is always wise to have a few options. Oftentimes I like to blend the two sounds together for "guitar enhancement."

Making the Connection

To record direct, plug an instrument cable out of your guitar into a direct input (DI) on your interface. As previously mentioned, you may not have a separate input for DI signals, so be sure to switch the input to accept a DI. Record-enable the track and make sure you are getting a good signal level by boosting the input as needed. You will notice the sound is very dry and clean. More than likely, that is *not* what you are looking for. So let's go "old-school" Logic and run it through Guitar Amp Pro to shape our sound for this example. You'll see and hear demonstrations of Amp Designer and Pedalboard in the QuickTime tutorials. For now, simply load a channel strip setting from the Library that will add the Guitar Amp Pro plug-in and a few other inserts for you to use as a nice starting point.

Click on the first available insert send, and a menu will appear with the various inserts available to you (see **Fig. 5.14a**). We are going to select Amps and Pedals > Guitar Amp Pro Mono. A floating window appears, showing you all of the available parameters you can tweak in this plug-in (see **Fig. 5.14b**). The interface should remind you of a guitar amplifier, and as you cycle through the various amps, speakers, and EQs, you will notice the parameters adjust accordingly. Separate from the Library settings, most plug-ins have their own settings that can be loaded within the plug-in. Channel strip settings can

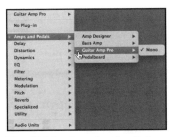

Fig. 5.14a: Inserting the Guitar Amp Pro plug-in.

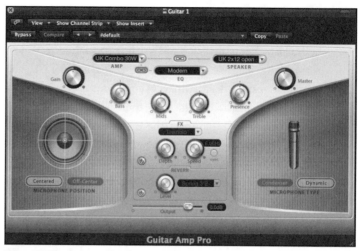

Fig. 5.14b: Guitar Amp Pro interface.

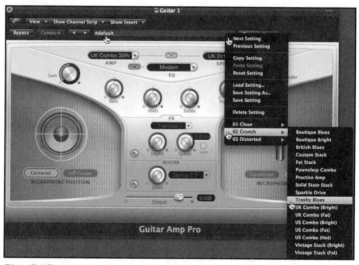

Fig. 5.15: Logic 9 offers a wide variety of tone settings and amp combinations.

be loaded from the Library, and will generally populate your inserts with a few plug-ins and settings. Within a plug-in you can access various presets by clicking on the pull-down menu that is labeled "#default" (see **Fig. 5.15**). From here you can load a ton of various guitar amp settings.

Remember, you can also use the Library to browse plug-in settings. Click the plug-in from the channel strip in the Inspector and be sure your Library window is open. The window updates to show you the various settings/patches you can load based on what is selected. It is a good habit to use the Library to load your settings, as it will help unify your workflow.

Also, keep in mind that when you are recording guitar through the direct input, none of the audio being recorded is from the Guitar Amp Pro plug-in. The audio being recorded is the dry signal we heard before we loaded the plug-in. This is great because it gives us MIDI-like flexibility to change presets on the amplifier or effects without having to commit to them. Of course, if you need to free up your CPU or decide you really like what you have, you can always print your settings. Printing your settings will re-record your audio as a new audio track with the applied settings. As long as you save an original copy of the clean direct signal, you will always be able to go back and make changes later. We'll go over printing plug-ins and freeing up your CPU later in this book.

Checkpoint

So far, we've covered setting up headphone mixes, recording instrument tracks, recording with microphones, and recording direct. If you are following along with this book, you should be recording various instruments in your session. Remember, we started by laying down a four-bar drum loop, then added instrument tracks and direct sources or those recorded with a microphone. At this point, you should start to hear your production come together. If you have been using channel strip settings from the Library, your mix probably already sounds decent without even getting into the mixing process.

INSERTS AND DYNAMIC PROCESSING

Up to this point we have only really used inserts when we loaded channel strip settings and set up our DI recording for guitar. Inserts are most commonly used for dynamic processing. Dynamic processing is anything that changes the amplitude of a sound. Everything from compression and limiting, gating and expansion, to equalization is a form of dynamic processing. We'll learn more about these topics in the mixing chapter, but for now let's get comfortable simply applying inserts (plug-ins) to a channel strip.

To insert a dynamic processor, click the first available insert on a channel; these are identical for both audio and instrument tracks. Notice a floating window appears with a list of categories from which to choose. You will see there are a few categories of plug-ins that do not fall under the category of "Dynamic Processing." This would be effects such as delays, reverbs, phasers, flangers, and other time-based effects. These can be inserted into the channel strip, and are often inserted when loading a channel strip setting from Logic's preset library; however, we will go over best practices with those effects later on. For now, we are going to load an EQ. The equalization plug-in that ships with Logic is the Channel EQ. By default, this is available on every channel strip above the inserts where it says "EQ." Double-clicking the gray EQ space will autoload Logic's Channel EQ onto the first available insert send (see **Fig. 5.16**). If you have already loaded previous inserts, the send will be inserted where it is first available. You may select other EQs, but they will not have the graphic representation that the Channel EQ has on the channel strip. Let's go ahead and load the Channel EQ and check out some of the settings.

Fig. 5.16: Automatic Channel Insert EQ on and off status.

Notice we have eight bands available to us (see **Fig. 5.17**). By default, only the inner six are turned on. Notice both high and low filters are turned off. Remember, using only the bands you need will save some CPU power. Tiny bits of CPU conservation here and there start to add up as sessions grow. You can click-and-drag around the graphical view to get a sense for how your EQ translates. You can also dial in EQ settings by typing in various values along the bottom. Load a preset and take a look at the curve created by Logic. As you hover over various bands, you will notice them highlight in their selected color; as bands overlap, you will see a graphical representation (see **Fig. 5.18**). Play around with a few presets; they are always good places to start.

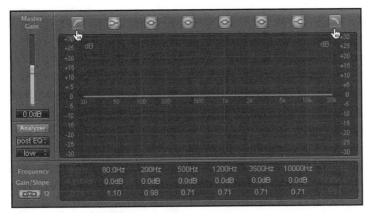

Fig. 5.17: High- and low-pass filters are bypassed by default.

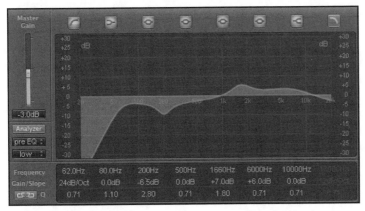

Fig. 5.18: Channel EQ example with high-pass filters engaged.

To get a better idea of how equalization affects your sound, loop a pre-recorded part that has no additional inserts. Open the Channel EQ and start changing the settings. There are no magical EQ presets to make your recording sound great. However, knowing what parameters are available to us and how they work will give us a better shot at achieving the sounds we hear in our head. I would like to also mention that having a good idea of what tonal qualities you are trying to achieve before you start tweaking the option will play a big role in getting a good sound. A good set of ears never hurts, either. Keep in mind that this will take countless hours of trial and error, but the result is usually well worth the effort. To change the EQ parameters, you can click-and-drag within the graphical window, hover over the numbers on the bottom and click-and-drag up and down, or double-click on the parameter you would like to change and type in the numbers to change the values.

TIME-BASED EFFECTS

You might recall earlier in chapter 3 that I mentioned time-based effects. While time-based effects don't rely on dynamics, some effects combine elements of both time-based and dynamic processing. The most common time-based effect is reverb. Reverb is the "special sauce" that can help an artist sing and/or play with more inspiration. When a singer has an independent headphone mix, it is important for them to hear the other instruments, but they also should not sound like they are singing in a bedroom closet. Adding some reverb to the vocal track creates depth and ambience, which will generally give the performer a little more inspiration and confidence. Be careful not to go overboard, though. A singer needs to feel comfortable, but if they get too comfortable hiding behind effects, they can easily lose track of their pitch. Along the same lines, if a guitar player is smothered in reverb and delay, they may feel confident in what they are playing, but typically, it is at the expense of a good performance.

Wet/Dry

So how do you determine the right amount of reverb to put on a track, and how do you control what is sent to a headphone mix versus what you hear in the control room? This is where best practices for applying time-based effects come into play. As previously mentioned, you can indeed add a reverb to an insert send on a track, but you will only have control over the amount of effect from the plug-in window of the reverb. If you open the window of a generic reverb plug-in you will notice a wet/dry knob or slider. This allows you to control how much of the dry, or unprocessed, signal is mixed with the wet, or processed signal.

What we really want is to have more control, free up CPU power, and get a better blend of the wet and dry sound overall. To do this we are going to create an auxiliary send. Click on the first available aux send and select the first unused bus. Logic will create an aux return for that bus. What we want to do is load our reverb and any other time-based effects onto this aux channel strip. If we insert a reverb on this channel strip we can set it to 100 percent wet. Now the amount of dry signal being sent is controlled by the aux send on the original source's channel strip. This also allows you to bus other instruments to the same reverb, as opposed to creating a separate reverb for each individual track. This is what frees up your CPU and gives you more control over your mix.

We are going to create two aux sends: one for reverb and another for delay. Click on and assign the first available aux sends and buses. Make sure to name the auxes in the Mixer window "Reverb" and "Delay." Now, from the aux channel strip you can insert a reverb on the reverb channel, and a delay on the delay channel. Logic comes with an assortment of amazing reverbs, most notably Space Designer, a convolution reverb (see **Fig. 5.19**). Convolution reverb effectively places your sound in locations where impulse responses were recorded. These

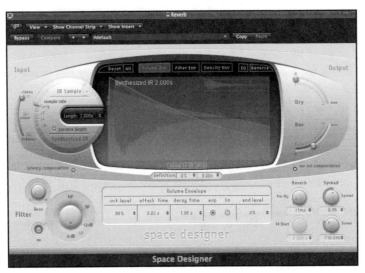

Fig. 5.19: Space Designer interface.

convolution reverbs are captured by sending out a sound, which acts as the impulse. This impulse "excites" the room as the sound bounces off the various surfaces. The sound is then recorded as the response and is compared to the original impulse, and then the reverb is sampled. Logic ships with a full assortment of sound-sampled spaces. Imagine having over 900 acoustic spaces to place your instruments in—anywhere from a "tiny wine cellar to a massive cathedral." The newly added Warped Effects in Logic Pro 9's Space Designer lets you add movement, texture, ghost rhythms, and a few other new parameters that bring this reverb plug-in to another level. There is even a utility bundled with Logic Studio that allows you to record your own impulse responses for spaces you might want to sample. We'll go over how to do that in the last chapter.

For now, load a few different presets and familiarize yourself with the Space Designer plug-in. Notice how the parameters change drastically when switching from a large hall to a small room or a plate reverb. When using this plug-in on an aux track, be sure to keep the wet/dry mix set to 100 percent wet and to use the aux send volume from the source track to determine how much effect you want on each instrument you send to the aux track. Luckily, Logic uses a bit of logic in its design, meaning that even though it's not the best practice to add a reverb or delay directly to your channel, if you do, the plug-in recognizes this, and sets the wet/dry amount to a manageable setting, with a decent and fairly common wet/dry ratio. This allows you to add reverbs and delays to your tracks using the channel strip settings and still have them work properly, and not overwhelm your source with too much of the effect. Also, note that when you add a reverb to an aux channel, Logic recognizes this too, and the plug-in is automatically set to a wet/dry mix of 100 percent wet. To quickly change to the next available preset within a plug-in, press the bracket keys [and] to move backward and forward. Using the brackets to cycle through presets works on any plug-in. You can also cycle through channel strips by using Shift + [and Shift +].

Now we're going to load a delay onto our other aux track. Complementing Space Designer, we have Delay Designer (see

Fig. 5.20). Delay Designer lets you experiment with multi-tap delays in stereo or surround. The intuitive view conforms to your tempo grid, allowing you to graphically change the volume and timing of your delay based on various grid values. Load a few presets to play around with the Delay Designer interface, and compare some of the extreme "Warped" delays to the simpler quarter-note basic pan. Delay Designer gives you full control over the placement of your delay in the stereo or surround field, as well as volume, cutoff, resonance, and pitch transposition. Notice that the wet/dry settings also apply here. Loading this plug-in on an aux send will automatically set the wet/dry mix to 100 percent wet. You can also load channel strip settings for aux channels. Auxiliary channels look exactly like audio and instrument channels, so you might not have noticed, but you can indeed load an assortment of channel strip settings specially designed for time-based effects (see **Fig. 5.21**). You can also load these from the Library.

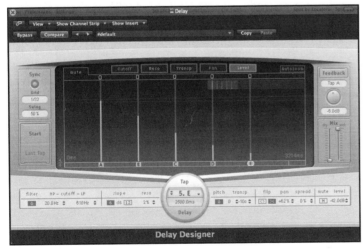

Fig. 5.20: Delay Designer interface.

Now that we have set up our reverb and delay tracks, go ahead and bring up some of the aux sends on the various channels you set up earlier, and send them to your effects tracks until you are happy with the blend between the dry sound and the effect. Once this is done, you should have everything in order to start recording.

Fig. 5.21: Aux and channel-strip template settings.

Start by hovering your pointer over the upper-right-hand edge of your drum loop. The cursor will turn into a looped arrow. Click-and-drag to the right: this will tell Logic to loop this region. Drag it to bar 26 to give yourself some room to play. You can also select the track, and in the Inspector check the Loop button; this will have the four bars loop to the end-of-song marker. Record a few different tracks, and experiment with tracking MIDI instruments as well as microphones and DI instruments. Once you have recorded some parts, we are going to do some rough editing, trimming all of our parts so they are the same length.

To trim your regions using the Pointer tool: hover over the bottom right area of a region until the Pointer turns into a bracket with arrows. You can then click-and-drag to trim the region in either direction, assuming you have room. Trim your regions to four bars to match our original drum loop. Your best performance might not have been in the first four bars, so you can use the Scissors tool as your secondary tool to cut your regions up. We'll go over these editing tools (see **Fig. 5.22**) more in-depth when we get to editing, but for now this is a good way to roughly arrange your tracks. With your regions cleaned up to equal lengths, you can quickly rearrange them with the Pointer tool. Remember that you can have two tools available. Holding down Command will give you access to your second tool. To change tools quickly, press the Escape key once and the Tool menu will pop up. To switch back to the Pointer quickly, press Escape twice.

Fig. 5.22: The tools list.

A BASIC MIX

While working your way through this chapter, you may have made various adjustments to your fader and panning positions. This is quite common, and creating basic rough mixes through the various stages of production helps you gain perspective on how you would like your final mix to sound. When working with channel strip settings and presets, Logic makes it easy for you to achieve a decent-quality, "neutral" mix with very little effort. This means no one instrument overpowers any other. If an instrument is being buried and you have its fader maxed out, try turning down the other instruments instead of trying to boost that fader more. If it is an audio track you are having this problem with, while you are recording, make sure you are tracking at a decent input level. You may need to adjust your preamp's input level to get a better level to the multitrack.

As you start making some changes to your mix and you aren't sure you want to commit to them, you can always execute a "Save As." This allows you to continue with new changes without worrying about losing your previous project settings. Meaning, you will be able to revert to a previously saved mix if necessary, and move forward again. It is a good idea to do a "Save As" each time you create a new mix. Performing a "Save As" takes up very little disk space and is also good for documenting the progression of your project's mix and arrangement.

For example, let's do a quick, rough mix for the project we have been working on. First, set your locators to the four-bar loop and press the Play button. Go to the Mixer window, listen to your mix, and look at your meters. It is important to pay attention to the meters in your mix as well as listen to it. If your master fader is in the red quite a bit, you may need to bring everything down. If your mix sounds crowded and small, try panning some instruments. Placing instruments in different locations in the stereo field opens up your mix and makes it sound bigger, or "fuller." This does not mean you should "hard pan" all of your stereo tracks left and right. It means what it says. Place each instrument in a different location throughout the stereo field. Also, take inventory of all of the parts. Try to make sure the levels and panning positions of the various instruments complement each other.

We will go over a few more mixing tips later in the book, but for the time being, while it may seem limiting, get used to achieving a good mix with just your fader and pan settings, as they are a huge part of a good mix. Everything else is icing on the cake, so apply these fundamentals to your mixing projects.

DUPLICATE TRACK SETTINGS

Now that we have a basic mix going, you might get excited and be inspired to add more parts. If you want to add another part using one of the same instruments that already exists in your project, you can simply duplicate that particular track. In this case, since we already have a decent guitar setting, let's duplicate it so we can have the identical sound playing a different part. When you duplicate the track, the inserts, auxes, fader, pan, and input and output settings will be identical; therefore you will not have to try and match or try to remember what you did to get that sound to begin with. To duplicate a track, select it from the Arrange window and use the keyboard shortcut Command + D. You can also click on the Track menu and select New Track with Duplicate Setting button. Be aware that after the duplicate track is created, any changes made to the track will only apply to that track, not to the previously selected one. After duplicating a track, don't forget to label it before recording so it has its own unique name rather than the duplicate name it was given by default.

FINAL THOUGHTS

Once again, there was a lot of material covered in this chapter. Do not hesitate to re-read any material you aren't clear on. Drill yourself on shortcuts when creating tracks and changing tools by saying them aloud or silently to yourself before you choose them from a menu. Then take note of the keyboard shortcut in the menu when you select it to see if you were correct. While some of the information covered in this chapter has to do with fundamental recording techniques and applies to most DAWs in general, most of the information is specific to Logic, so be sure to familiarize yourself with what we have covered so far. Also, be sure to check out the QuickTime tutorials that come with this book. Seeing a few of these techniques being used in a practical situation will help you to better understand how they are used. Also, take a few minutes to answer the end of chapter Tune-Up questions and review the Power Tips and Keyboard Shortcut summaries.

POWER TIPS FOR CHAPTER 5

1. When recording with pre-roll or a count-in, the audio is recorded as soon as you hit Record; therefore, you can trim back to recover a few pickup notes if your "in point" was a little late.

2. Using the Record Repeat mode and using the Discard Recording shortcut are good ways to keep your regions and hard drive uncluttered. If you know you have several takes that are unusable, there is no need to keep them, and your system will thank you with better performance.

3. You can add members to a group from the Mixer window. Select all of the tracks you wish to include in a group by clicking-and-dragging across the tracks, or by shift-clicking specific tracks. Once the tracks are selected, open the Group menu from one of the selected tracks, and the rest will follow.

4. After setting the Autopunch range, you can quickly set your playback cycle range to the same length as your Autopunch range by clicking-and-dragging the red Autopunch range upward.

5. When customizing the Transport, check the box for "Sample Rate or Punch Locators." You will see a second set of numbers similar to those of the cycle region; these function the same way, except they reflect the punch range instead of the cycle range.

6. If you have trouble playing your parts "in time," you can use the Quantize feature in the MIDI Thru window in the Inspector. Remember that MIDI quantization in Logic is non-destructive.

7. To get a better idea of how equalization affects your sound, loop a pre-recorded part that has no additional inserts. Open the Channel EQ and start changing the settings.

8. When adding a reverb or delay directly to an instrument or audio track, Logic automatically adjusts the wet/dry ratio to a manageable setting; however, it is generally a better idea to properly put time-based effects like reverbs and delays on

an aux channel. This gives you greater control and eases the load on your CPU, because you can share the effect with other instruments in your project.

9. Channel strip settings provide a nice starting point for audio and instrument tracks, but they are also a great way to load presets on an aux channel.

10. Remember that you have two editing tools available at all times. Holding down Command will give you access to your second tool. To change tools quickly, press the Escape key once, and the Tool menu will pop up. To switch back to the Pointer quickly, press Escape twice. Even though Logic Pro 9 offers some very cool new ways to quickly access the different editing tools, get used to choosing your tools this way for the time being. You will not always be on your own recording system, so it is important to be able to work on an older setup without all of the latest and greatest shortcuts.

11. In addition to browsing channel strip settings, the Library window can browse plug-in settings. Click a plug-in from the channel strip in the Inspector and be sure your Library window is open. The window updates to show you the various settings/patches you can load based on what is selected. It is a good habit to use the Library to load your settings.

12. If your recording interface has more than two outputs, be sure to assign your headphone mix to a separate stereo output than your main mix; in most cases this will be outputs 3 and 4.

13. Creating a new track with duplicate settings is a quick way to double a part or add a new part using the same channel strip settings. Click on the "New Track with Duplicate Setting" button in the Arrange window.

14. The Channel EQ offers eight bands of EQ. By default, only the inner six are turned on. You can turn bands on and off to alter your sound; if you are not using a band, you should turn it

15. Use the brackets] and [to quickly cycle through presets of a given plug-in, and Shift + [and Shift +] to scroll through the channel strip settings.

KEYBOARD SHORTCUT SUMMARY

KEYBOARD SHORTCUT	FUNCTION
Command + .	Recording
Escape	Open Tool menu
Escape Escape	Default back to Pointer tool
] and [	Cycle plug-in presets
Shift +] and Shift + [	Cycle channel strip settings
Command + Z	Undo
Shift + Command + Z	Redo

LOGIC 9 TUNE-UP

1. A count-in uses the tempo of the song to count-in a pre-determined number of bars before recording. Pre-roll uses _____ to determine how much time passes before recording begins.

2. In Record/Record Toggle mode, pressing the Record button initiates the recording, pressing it again stops the recording but _____ continues, pressing a third time resumes recording.

3. With the _____ button turned on from the Transport, any existing audio or MIDI in the recorded region is overwritten and deleted.

4. To view all of your takes, click on the triangle on the track for an expanded view; your takes will expand onto "tracks" called _____.

5. The Autopunch range works similarly to the Cycle range. The Autopunch cycle is _____ in color while the Cycle range is _____.

6. You should use headphones to monitor playback while recording with microphones to prevent _____.

7. An independent headphone mix lets the artist hear a separate mix from the main stereo outputs. The independent mixes are sent from _____ _____.

8. Independent headphone mixes sent from auxes should be set to ____ -_____ so that the level of the fader on the channel strip doesn't affect the amount being sent to the headphone mix.

9. When recording MIDI using cycle range, the recording will loop back when reaching the end and continue recording; all subsequent passes will _____ new MIDI with existing MIDI.

10. If you are recording with a condenser microphone, your interface will need to supply the mic with _____ _____ _____.

11. Equalization, compression, and gating are examples of _____ _____.

12. Reverb, delay, phasers and flangers are examples of _____-_____ _____.

13. How much processed signal we mix with our unprocessed signal is generally referred to as our ____/_____ mix.

14. When loading a reverb on an aux channel the wet/dry slider is automatically set to _____wet. We control the amount of wet/dry with the aux send knob.

15. The Space Designer plug-in uses sampled reverbs we call _____ reverb.

Producing with Logic

GETTING READY

Up to this point we have covered a lot of ground in Logic. We've ensured that we have made all the right connections to our interfaces, so that MIDI and audio signals flow into and out of your system effortlessly. We've also explored Logic's interface and gotten to know the lay of the land while learning standard techniques for project management. In this chapter, we are going to dig in deeper, making Logic bend to our creative will by using screensets, creating markers and using custom templates. While covering new ground, we will continue to reinforce the best practices for project management, as well as how to get the most out of your system with some other useful Power Tips.

I recommend that you follow along with your own session as you work through this chapter. Also, remember to watch the QuickTime tutorials that accompany this book and review the Logic Tune-Up questions, Power Tip summaries, and keyboard shortcuts at the end of every chapter. This will help ensure that you are learning the most important information covered in this book.

GETTING THE MOST OUT OF YOUR SYSTEM

Load Meters

You may have noticed by now that as you add more elements to your session, your load meters start to light up. The load meters are located in the display section of the Transport (see **Fig. 6.1**). You will see separate meters for the following items.

Fig. 6.1: System Performance meters.

CPU

The load on your CPU comes from running software instruments and plug-ins. Having several instances of plug-ins or instruments open can make this meter peak. Having several instances of complex CPU-intensive plug-ins such as convolution reverbs will also bog your system down. CPU usage meters will vary from system to system. The variance is based on the number of processors, or "cores," you have. My system has two cores. A Mac Pro can have up to eight cores. When a two-core system is almost maxed out, an eight-core Mac Pro may barely be reaching 25 percent of the CPU's capacity.

NODE

We haven't yet touched on nodes or node processing. In a nutshell, nodes allow you to connect multiple computers on a local network to share some of the CPU load. We'll go over how to set up nodes in greater detail in chapter 8. The Node Meter represents the CPU usage of your nodes.

HD

This represents the amount of load put on your hard drive. While software instruments and plug-ins can put a strain on your CPU, your hard drive is also taxed by having to read and write numerous audio tracks. In this chapter you'll learn some easy ways to ease the load on your CPU. It is generally difficult to conserve hard-drive usage, and this is one of the best reasons why having a fast drive dedicated to audio is so important.

The load meters will give you a rough idea of the strain being placed on your system. Keep an eye on these meters; they will fluctuate throughout the session, during both playback and recording. If one of the meters peaks, you will know because Logic will stop what it is doing and notify you. If your system's CPU is peaking, you will see an error like this (see **Fig. 6.2**). If your hard drive is the problem, you will see this error (see **Fig. 6.3**). Let's go over a few ways to prevent these pesky error messages from slowing you down.

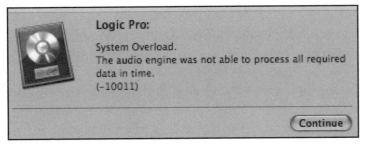

Fig. 6.2: Typical CPU overload error message.

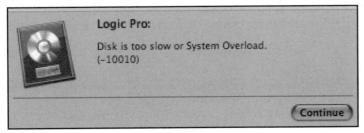

Fig. 6.3: Typical hard drive error.

Freezing

The Freeze function is a very handy tool when dealing with projects that have many software instruments. It is one of the most simple and efficient ways to save CPU power in your session. Freezing tracks will free up nearly 100 percent of the

CPU power required for the software instrument and effects plug-in calculations on the track you are freezing. So how does it work?

When you select tracks to be "frozen," Logic performs an internal offline bounce. All effects and processing directly associated with the selected channel is included in this bounce. This process could also be called "rendering." There are a few new Freeze options that were added in Logic Pro 9, and we'll go over what they are shortly. For now just realize that after a track is frozen, playback will play the rendered track in place of the original track, and the original track and its associated plug-ins are temporarily deactivated and will not use any CPU resources. It's not just cool, it's freezing!

DRAWBACKS

While freezing tracks frees up CPU power and allows you to add more plug-ins and instruments to your session, it has some drawbacks. The rendered track is indeed frozen; you cannot make any changes to the track without unfreezing it. This covers everything from the arrangement in the timeline to individual plug-in parameters. Because the freezing process is so transparent, you can easily forget that a track is frozen, but when you go to make a change Logic will prompt you to unfreeze the track before any changes can be made (see **Fig. 6.4**).

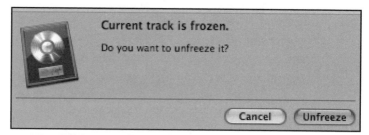

Fig. 6.4: Freeze status selection box.

Even though Logic performs an internal audio bounce for each frozen track, you will never see the printed audio track in the Arrange window, which makes freezing transparent.

HOW TO FREEZE TRACKS

Freezing tracks is very simple; however, by default the button we need to freeze tracks is not shown. Let's start by enabling this button in the Arrange window. To do this, we need to configure the track headers. Currently the track header displays the Record-enable, Solo, and Mute buttons, but we can configure it to show more options. To do this, go to the View menu in the Arrange window and select Configure Track Header, or use the keyboard shortcut Option + T (see **Fig. 6.5**). You can also right-click on any track to select Configure Track Header as well. You will see a few options to choose from in this window. We want to enable the Freeze button, which looks like a snowflake (see **Fig. 6.6**).

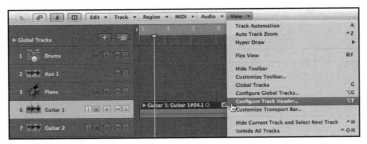

Fig. 6.5: Navigation path to the Configure Track Header option.

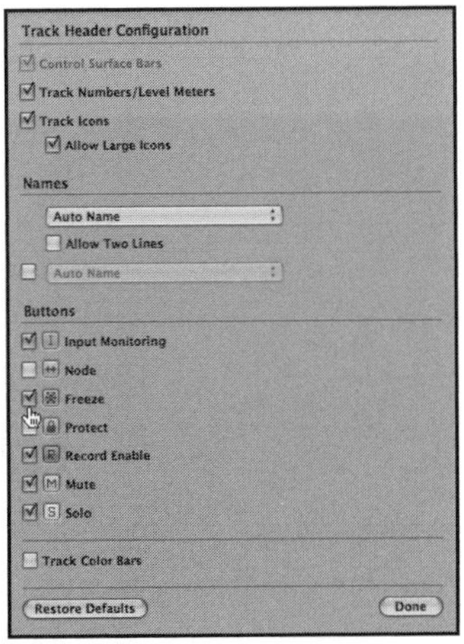

You should now see an extra button to the left of the Record-enable button. When inactive, the button is clear; when active it is green or blue. In Logic Pro 9, freezing a track can now be done as a pre-fader freeze or a source-only freeze. You can make this selection from the Inspector's Track Parameter box. The pre-fader option will freeze the track signal and include all effects plug-ins. The indicator is the standard green color. Source Only freezes the track signal before it hits the first effect plug-in. Choosing this method will turn the Freeze button blue. This is a nice option for CPU-intensive flex modes or software instruments (see **Fig. 6.7a**).

Fig. 6.6: Freeze button selection from the Track Header Configuration menu.

In a real-world situation you would probably wait to freeze a track until you actually needed the extra horsepower, but as an example, let's go ahead and freeze a track. Make sure the track you have selected actually has data in the timeline. Select the Freeze button and notice it turns green. The track is not yet

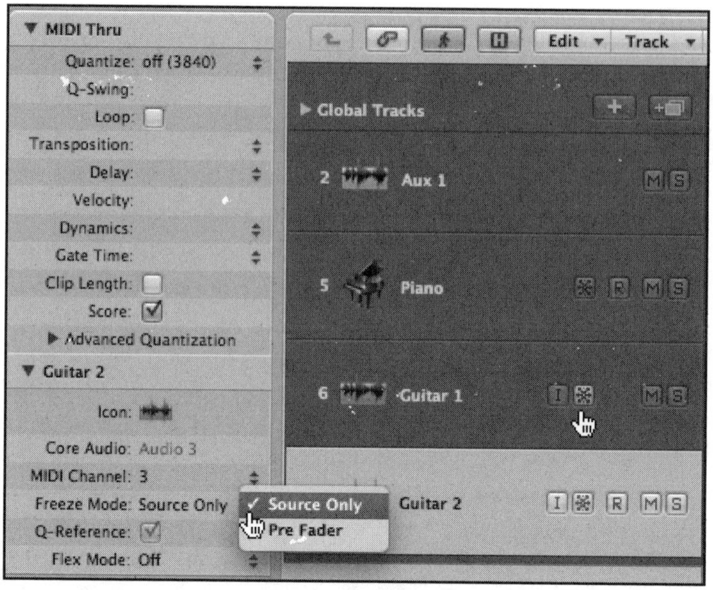

Fig. 6.7a: Freeze Mode selection of Source Only from the Inspector.

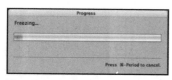

Fig. 6.7b: A "real-time freezing" progress bar with keyboard shortcut to cancel option.

frozen, however. To freeze the track you will have to play it, and you will notice a progress dialog pop up (see **Fig. 6.7b**). You can always cancel a freeze by pressing Command + . You will notice the freeze will go to the end-of-song marker. The regions I need to freeze only go to bar 54, but my end-of-song marker is set to bar 130. Keep this in mind when freezing. If you click and hold down the Freeze button when you enable it, you can move up or down to select multiple tracks to freeze.

If you need to perform an edit, record a function, or alter a parameter, you can always unfreeze the track by deselecting the Freeze button. Take note that you are now using the original amount of CPU power it took to run the selected track. Perform any necessary changes and then re-freeze the track to free up the CPU. Remember, you shouldn't freeze tracks unless your system is straining to play back your session. Freezing can take a while, so constantly freezing and unfreezing tracks can be very time-consuming.

FREEZE FILES

Freeze files are created during the offline internal bounce, and while you don't see the corresponding audio files, they do exist.

These files live at the root level of your project folder in a folder called "Freeze Files." You shouldn't need to access these files, as Logic automatically manages them for you. They will be deleted as soon as the Freeze button is turned off, so there is no need to worry about lots of freeze files eating up your hard drive space.

If you make a global change to your session, such as a tempo change, your freeze files will need to be updated. To do this, go to the Options menu, select Audio, then Refresh All Freeze Files (see **Fig. 6.8**). All of your freezes will be updated.

Fig. 6.8: Navigation path to the Refresh Freeze option (Options > Audio > Refresh All).

Bouncing Tracks or Regions in Place and Manual Internal Bouncing

Freeze files are great, but there are a few instances when you may need more flexibility. Remember that frozen tracks cannot be edited. If you need to free up some CPU but still need full control, the new Bounce in Place function will really come in handy. Essentially this feature allows you to render one or more tracks of audio or software instruments into a new audio file. You have various options that also allow you to include your plug-in and automation settings.

To bounce tracks in place, select the desired software instrument or audio track. Then go to the Track tab and select the Bounce Track in Place option, or use the keyboard shortcut (command + Control + B). Finally, select the relevant parameters from the list of options that appear. All of the options are self-explanatory, so choose as you wish, and enjoy the flexibility of this feature.

Another way of doing the same kind of thing is to use internal routing to perform a manual "bounce." This is a typical way to create "stem mixes," and another alternative for freeing up resources or doing some quick production magic. For example, if you want to create the effect of a reverse piano hit from one of the software instruments, you can bus the output of the selected piano track to a new audio track. Set the input of the audio track to the same bus, arm the audio track, and record. Take a look at the example (see **Fig. 6.9**). Notice the output of the piano is set to bus 1, and the input to the audio track labeled Reverse Piano is set to bus 1. With the track armed, you can see signal getting to the audio track. I am going to record this (see **Fig. 6.10**).

Fig. 6.9: The hands indicate the bus setup (output/input) for an internal bounce.

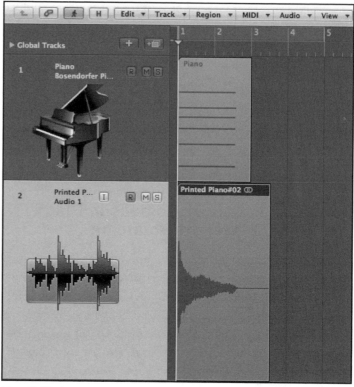

Fig. 6.10: A printed piano track.

Notice how the piano instrument track is transformed into audio from the original MIDI. You can now perform production tricks on the audio track that you could not do with just the original MIDI track. A quick example would be to reverse the bounced piano track for a cool-sounding buildup. Go ahead and record a nice big chord using a piano sound, and then do a quick manual bounce. Once you have the audio file, select it and choose the keyboard command (Shift + Control + R) to reverse the sound. Now move the track to the desired position and enjoy the glorious sounds of a reversed piano chord. This is fairly common and is used on cymbals, snares, reverb tails, and even on vocals.

ORGANIZING YOUR TRACKS

Now that you have some tools available to free up system resources, you will notice that you can add plenty of tracks and other elements to your session. Before you know it, you'll be working with a project with well over 20 tracks. When your session starts to grow by leaps and bounds, it will be easy to get lost if you do not stay organized. Sticking with a consistent naming scheme will help, but another way to quickly navigate your session and know what you are looking at is by using color.

There is no defined way to set up a session; however, certain tools and methods will help you stay organized. You should always arrange your tracks in a way that makes sense. Sometimes this means keeping your software instruments and audio instruments separated; other times it means arranging your tracks based on instrumentation. Some people always like to keep the vocals on top, while others like guitars on top. My session layouts rarely vary from song to song, I like to keep a certain level of consistency and prefer my drum tracks on top, followed by bass, keys, strings, guitars, and then voices. Having a global consistency across multiple sessions will help you navigate your sessions easily. If all of your sessions adhere to a similar setup, then you will be able to work quickly. Naturally, you will also be working with other people's sessions from time to time, so stay sharp on session management and be prepared to navigate anything that comes your way.

Groups

As your session grows, you may find navigating all your tracks a bit difficult to manage. Groups will help you stay organized and allow you to make changes quickly and easily to a group of tracks. For instance, if you have layered a particular guitar part three times, and you would like to bring down the overall volume of all of the guitar tracks at the same time, by grouping them together you can make changes to one member of the group and the other members of the group will follow. There are many parameters a group can control—volume is just one of them. Let's take a look at the group options available to us by creating a group. Start by Shift-clicking on the desired channels you would like to be included in the group from the Mixer window. You can also click-and-drag along the bottom of the channel strip

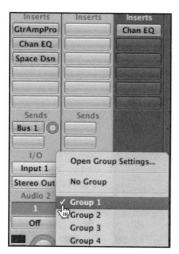

Fig. 6.11: Selecting a group number from the menu.

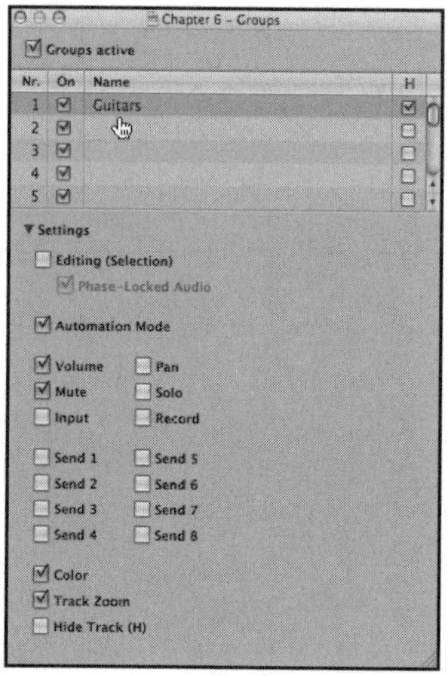

Fig. 6.12: Logic has a wide variety of new group settings.

to quickly select multiple channels. Then, click in the empty gray box below the Output box to bring up the Group Selection Menu (see **Fig. 6.11**).

When you select an inactive group, the Group Settings window will automatically launch. From here you will select the parameters you would like tied to this group. You will also name the group from here. You can always go back and make changes to the group settings. Let's go over the various parameters we can assign from this window.

Defining Group Settings

The default behaviors for Groups are shown in **Fig. 6.12**. These are the most common elements you will find yourself grouping; however, by exploring the other parameters in detail, you will soon see the power that groups can give you.

GROUPS ACTIVE/ON CHECKBOX

This will allow you to turn selected groups on and off. When a group is off, it is inactive, but all its settings are retained. Changes can be made while a group is off, and the channel strips will act individually. Enabling the group again will bind the tracks to the group settings again. Active groups appear in yellow, and disabled groups appear in black (see **Fig. 6.13**).

NAME

Just as important as naming your tracks is naming your groups. Groups are named by number by default; typing in a relevant name for your group helps you stay organized. While your track names may be more specific, your group names will tend to be more generic. For example, if you tracked a guitar with two microphones and a DI, you might label your tracks "GTR 57," "GTR 421," and "GTR DI"; however, when grouping the tracks together, it is common to name the groups "Guitar 1," "Guitar 2," etc.

Fig. 6.13: Enabled and disabled groups, indicated respectively by bold and dark coloring.

EDITING (SELECTION)

This checkbox allows you to link your region selection to your group. Selecting a region on a track that is a member of a group will select the same horizontal range on all members of that group.

TRACK ZOOM

For added convenience when zooming in on any member of a group, the same zoom values will be applied to the group.

HIDE TRACK

This works in conjunction with the Hide feature in the Arrange window. When active, you only have to select one member of the group to hide, and the entire group will be hidden. This is a quick way to show and hide many tracks at once.

RECORD ENABLE

By checking Record Enable you will arm all members of the group at once. Citing our previous example with the guitar with two microphones and a DI, we only have to arm one track to enable all tracks. Not only is this convenient for when you record overdubs, it's a safety precaution. If you accidentally forgot to arm one of the tracks, you would be out of luck, and you might just miss that perfect take. Be aware though that you can only use this feature if the tracks all have unique inputs.

AUTOMATION MODE

We're going to go into automation features in the Mixing chapter, but for now know that there are different automation modes. With this selection on, we can tell the group to follow the automation settings that we choose.

CHANNEL STRIP COLOR

By default, audio tracks are blue and software instruments are green. This allows you to quickly glance at your Arrange window and differentiate between the two. To take it a step further, you would ideally assign colors to groups. Doing so allows you to quickly identify groups in the Mixer and Arrange windows. When you enable this feature, changing the color on one group member will change it on all members. To change the color of a track, click on the Colors button in the upper right-hand side of the Arrange window. Notice a floating color palette appears (see **Fig. 6.14**). Select any of the colors, and your channel strip and regions will change to that color. This can be done outside of grouping, but it is convenient to group selected tracks and then change the color once. You should stick to a consistent color scheme that you can remember. If you always make your Guitars bright blue, then you can quickly see all of your guitar tracks in any of your sessions. If you learn to associate instruments with their color, then you will find it easier to navigate, edit, and arrange your sessions. Colors are very powerful when combined with groups. They help organize your workflow and make your sessions easy on the eye. Applying colors in the Arrange window does not carry over into the Mixer window. Select a track in the Mixer window to apply color; the color will still affect all group members.

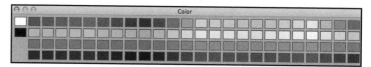

Fig. 6.14: The color palette (double click on a color for more options).

VOLUME

This is certainly one of the most common reasons for grouping tracks. You can set up a blend of different instruments and still want to change the overall volume of the blend. For example, you may have a perfect volume blend between your guitar tracks, but you feel the overall guitar needs to come down in volume. If you change all of the guitar tracks independently, you may lose your exact blend ratio if you aren't really careful. By linking your group to include volume, raising and lowering the volume will maintain the same relationships at all times. One of the subtle, but really nice, new features in Logic Pro 9 is that the fader resolution from +6 dB to –6 dB is set to 0.1 increments. This is a nice addition when trying to fine-tune a mix.

NOTE

Remember that the fader throw is on a logarithmic decibel scale, so as you bring a group down, the volume blend may look like it is scrunching up, but it is still maintaining the same relative relationships. Notice in **Fig. 6.15** and **Fig. 6.16** the same volume ratio at different levels.

MUTE

This will mute all the members of the group when active.

PAN

Similar to volume, this will link the channels in the group to one pan knob; when active, the group members will maintain their initial relationship to each other.

SENDS

The checkboxes for sends 1 through 8 allow you to link auxiliary send levels in the group. As with volume, initial levels are maintained.

Group Clutch

Let's say you want to make a change to your guitar group mix, but the group volume is enabled. This means if you change the level of any one of the faders, all the faders in the group will follow relative to your changes. To make a quick change, we need to temporarily suspend the group. It would be a hassle to go into the Group Settings window to disable the group, make a small change, and then re-enable the group. So Logic offers a simple solution called Group Clutch. Group Clutch works the same way the clutch on a car works. With the clutch engaged, you are free to change gears; when you release the clutch your engine is in the new gear. When Group Clutch is on, you can make changes to any group in Logic; it will temporarily allow you to "change gears," and reorganize anything you want, very quickly.

To enable Group Clutch, go to the Options menu from within the Mixer window and select "Group Clutch" or use the quick

Fig. 6.15: Relative fader level for the guitar group.

Fig. 6.16: Relative fader level for the guitar group after bringing the faders down.

key Command + G. You'll notice the group turn gray. Make whatever changes you please; when done you can release Group Clutch by pressing Command + G again.

This sums up the Group Settings window and grouping functions. You will find that different groups will benefit from different settings. Remember that none of these settings are permanent. You can add and remove settings at any time. You can also add and remove channel strips for a group at any time. Simply click the gray box beneath the output selectors on the channel strip you wish to add or remove from the group, select the group name or number, and the change is made.

ORGANIZING YOUR AUDIO BIN

The Audio Bin is where all the audio related to your project is stored. From the Audio Bin we can see important information regarding each track, such as its sample rate and bit depth, as well as whether the track is mono or stereo. The Audio Bin is where we keep our audio organized. Oftentimes the Audio Bin will be overlooked in this regard because it's not as visually important as the Arrange and Mixer windows; however, keeping your Audio Bin organized will allow you to quickly reference audio tracks and keep your system running smoothly.

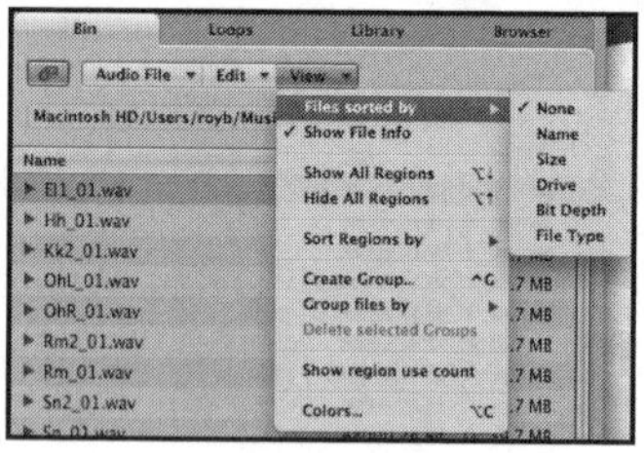

Your Audio Bin can fill up quickly. To find things fast you'll need to know how to properly sort your audio files. There are a few different ways you can sort your bin; these options are available under the Audio Bin's View menu (see **Fig. 6.17**). By default the sort option is set to "None." Let's go over what each of these sorting options will do.

Fig. 6.17: View menu options for Audio Bin content with sorting options and overall content information.

NOTE

The default sorting view actually sorts your audio files by the order they were loaded or recorded: older files on top, newer ones on the bottom.

NAME

Audio files are sorted in alphabetical order.

SIZE

Audio files are sorted according to size; larger files are at the top of the list.

DRIVE

If you have audio files residing on different drives or partitions, this will sort your files by their location. Usually all of your audio files will be on the same drive. But if they aren't, this is a great way to track down where they are.

BIT DEPTH

Audio files are sorted by bit depth in descending order. Again, your audio should be consistent, but this is a quick way to see if you have any audio of a different bit depth.

FILE TYPE

This view sorts the bin by file type. For instance, maybe you are tracking or mixing in the AIFF format but you imported an MP3 file to reference something you did on an earlier pre-production project. To quickly find it, you can sort by file type. You can quickly switch to Sort by Name from any of the other sort options by clicking on the "Name" column header.

Grouping in the Audio Bin

Just like you grouped tracks to organize them, you can also group files in the Audio Bin. This comes in handy for finding specific files you don't know the names of. While Logic provides us with a few great sorting options, the application is not smart enough to sort by what instrument a file is. If we manually group audio files by instrument, we can see at a glance all the audio files for a particular instrument. **Fig. 6.18** gives an example. This Audio Bin has audio files for guitar, bass, drums, and vocals. But the naming scheme is not consistent, so we may have to audition the files to identify them.

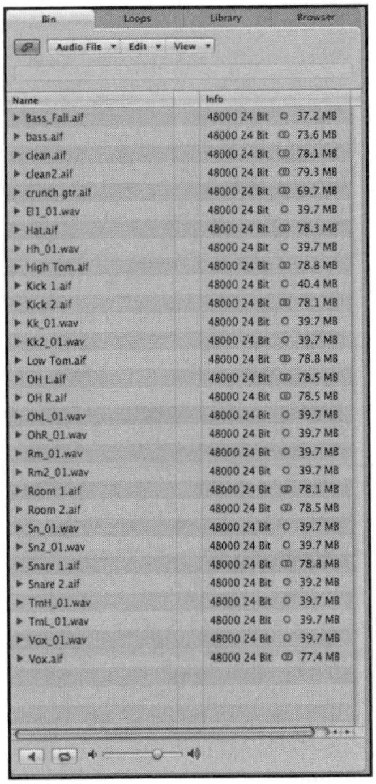

To audition a file from the Audio Bin, select the file you wish to identify and press the Prelisten button on the bottom left of the

Fig. 6.18: Zoomed-out view of the Audio Bin and its contents.

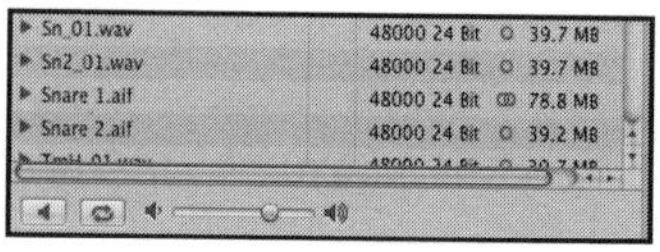

Fig. 6.19: The Prelisten button is directly relative to the Prelisten fader in the Mixer.

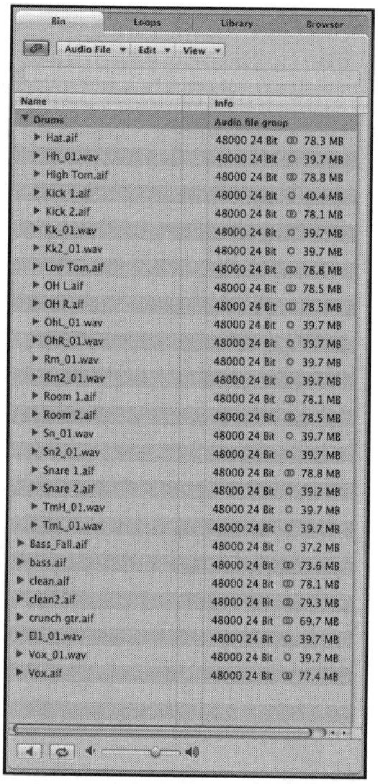

Fig. 6.20: Example of all of the drums in their own folder in the Audio Bin.

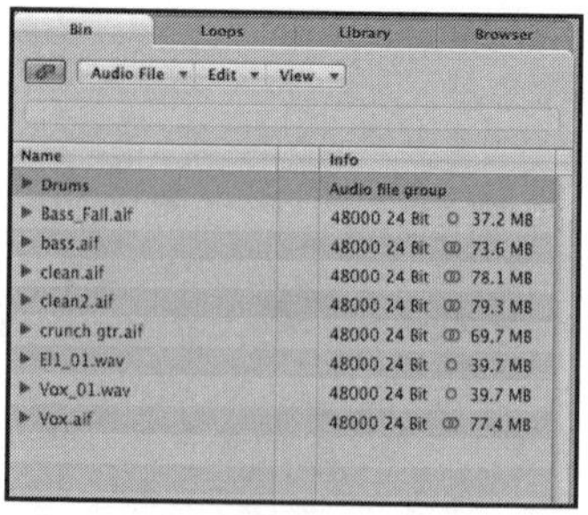

Fig. 6.21: Drums group folder collapsed.

Audio Bin (see **Fig. 6.19**). There is a separate volume control for you to adjust while listening to the selected file. Let's say I want to know what Hh_01.wav is. After auditioning it, I can tell it is a hi-hat track; hence the "Hh." However, not all the drum tracks conform to this naming scheme. For instance, one snare track is named Sn_01.wav, but another snare track is named Snare1.aif. To stay organized, I am going to group all of the drum tracks. You can select all of the drum tracks by clicking on one and then pressing Command to select the other tracks. If the tracks are in relative order already, you can quickly select all of them by selecting the top track, then holding down Shift and selecting the bottommost track; all tracks in between will be selected. You can add or deselect tracks by holding down Command and selecting tracks to add or remove. This can be a time saver when done properly.

Once the tracks are selected, go to the Audio Bin's View menu and select "Create Group" or simply press Control + G. You are prompted to name your group; label it accordingly and press Return. You have now created a group for these audio files. My drums now appear in a group labeled "Drums" (see **Fig. 6.20**). I can now expand and collapse this group (see **Fig. 6.21**). This one organizational tool alone cleans up the look of my Audio Bin considerably. If I am looking for the vocal track, I don't have to sift through the many drum tracks to see it.

You can always delete a group by selecting the group name in the Audio Bin and pressing Delete; a window will prompt you to delete the group. It is important to note that deleting groups does not delete or alter the audio files in any way; it is purely an organizational tool.

Renaming Audio Files

You may want to rename certain audio files to conform to a standard. In the above example I had a few inconsistencies with my naming scheme. To fix this I am going to rename the files to be more consistent. It is important to realize however that renaming an audio file will change the name of the file where it is stored, so it can be dangerous to change the name. For example, if another session uses the same audio file, it will not know to reference the new name. You can also rename audio files by using the Text tool in the region. Double-click Escape to bring up your Tools menu and select the Text tool. Now you can click on a region and rename it. Notice in the Audio Bin, however, that the change affects only the named region. It is therefore a better idea to rename the file from the Audio Bin as it gives you more flexibility and consistency. Chances are you will want to rename all associated audio files. Doing so from the Audio Bin will allow that, whereas renaming a region only changes the region and not any associated files. When working in the Audio Bin you will find yourself expanding and collapsing track components and groups many times. This can make your Audio Bin seem out of order and hard to navigate. To quickly expand or collapse all tracks, Option-click on one of the triangles; all tracks will follow suit.

Moving Audio Files

If you have audio files on various partitions or drives and wish to collect all of them in a single location, you can do that in the Audio Bin with the Move command. You'll probably want to sort by location to start, then select all of the files you wish to move and select Move from the Audio File menu, or press Control + M. A dialog box will ask you to confirm the move (see **Fig. 6.22**), after which you'll be prompted to choose a location to move the files to. This location should be the Audio Files folder of your current project. If the audio tracks already reside on this partition but are in a separate folder, the move will be instantaneous; if they are on a separate drive or partition, you will have to wait while the files are moved to the new location. Be careful, as other projects using the same files can be affected

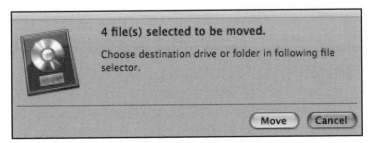

4 file(s) selected to be moved.

Choose destination drive or folder in following file selector.

Move   Cancel

Fig. 6.22: Move File confirmation menu.

by this. Collecting all of your audio in one place will help keep you organized.

Copying vs. Moving

Similar to moving is copying. By copying selected files you are creating a copy of the file in a new location. This takes up twice the disk space but it can be safer. If another project references the original file, that relationship will be maintained. Copying files will also allow you to make destructive edits to the copied file without affecting the original. To copy a file, select the file and select Copy/Convert Files from the Audio File menu, or simply press Control + C. There is also the option to convert while copying. Like moving files, copying files will collect your audio in a single location; however, the copy dialog gives us the option to convert the files as we see fit. This is a good opportunity to

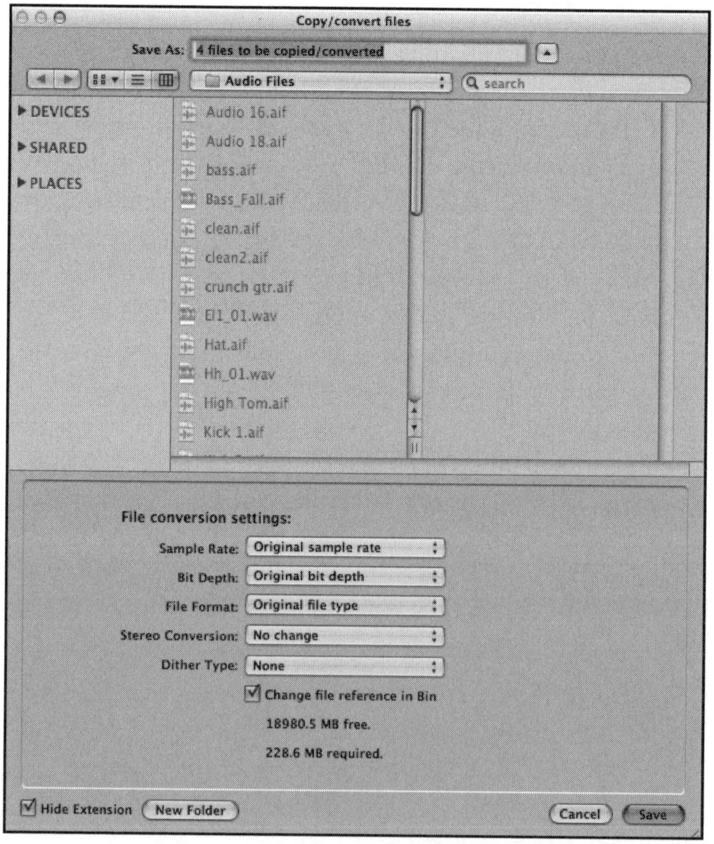

Fig. 6.23: Copy/convert files browser and options menu.

convert your files if needed. You can alter the sampling rate, bit depth, file format, stereo interleave, and dither type (see **Fig. 6.23**). If you have a sample you want to cut up and make changes to, chances are you will want to leave the original intact. Using the Copy/Convert = command will allow you to alter samples and loops as you please. For example, if you wish to edit an Apple Loop, Logic will not let you (see **Fig. 6.24**). After copying an Apple Loop, however, you are free to edit it freely.

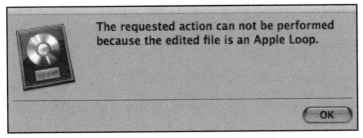

Fig. 6.24: Error message when trying to edit an Apple loop, which cannot be edited.

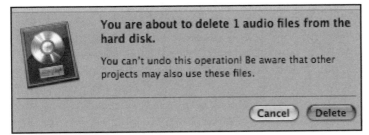

Fig. 6.25: Common delete warning.

Deleting Audio Files

You may want to clean up your Audio Bin and delete some files. Because the session and Audio Bin are referencing files from your hard drive, you can delete them from the Finder, but this is not recommended as the session will not update after the files are deleted. Opening the session after deleting the files will then prompt you to locate them. For this reason you should only delete audio from your session via the Audio Bin. Select the files you wish to delete and choose Delete File(s) from the Audio File menu. A dialog will ask you if you are sure (see **Fig. 6.25**). After deletion, the files are moved to the Trash, where they can be recovered until you empty the Trash.

NOTE

Deleting a file in the Audio Bin removes it from the Bin and the Arrange window; however it does not actually delete the file. You can use this method to keep your Audio Bin looking clean, but know that the files still reside in their original location.

Optimizing Audio Files

Deleting audio files is a great way to clean up your session and stay organized, but an even more effective way to do this is to optimize your audio files. Optimizing files will delete the unused portions of audio files in your Audio Bin, and will free up lots of wasted hard drive space. Select the files you wish to optimize from the Audio Bin. A great way of doing this quickly is to choose "Select Used" from the Audio Bin Edit menu. This will select all the audio used in your session. Then select Optimize Files from the Audio File menu, or simply press Control + O for Logic to delete all the unused portions and retain only what is in use. The optimization dialog will appear and tell you how many samples Logic is about to delete, and that this cannot be undone. There is also a Preservation slider that allows you to adjust the amount of samples to preserve on either end of the file for pre- and post-roll. By default it is set to one second (see **Fig. 6.26a**).

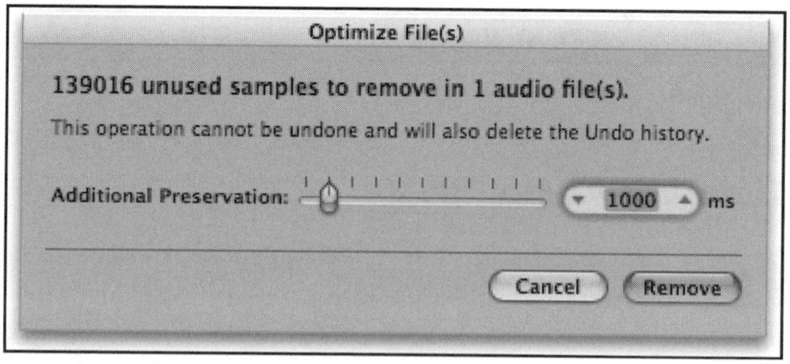

Fig. 6.26a: File optimization parameter settings.

Saving Regions As and Exporting Regions

You might have a region that is part of an audio file that you wish to convert into its own audio file. For example, if you need to make a lot of edits to a particular audio region, you may want to consider turning the region into its own audio file; that way all associated edits will only reference that file, instead of clogging up your Audio Bin. To do this, simply select the region and select Save Region(s) As from the Audio File menu. You'll be prompted to name or rename the file and choose a save location. You may also want to export a region or an entire track as an audio file. Select the tracks or regions you wish to export and choose "Export Region as Audio File" or "Export Track as Audio File" from the Audio File menu. The quick key for track export is Command + E. You'll be prompted to name and choose a location as well as the file type.

PRODUCING WITH LOGIC'S SOFTWARE INSTRUMENTS

Logic Pro 9 features a plethora of amazing instruments to tap into your creative potential. Each of the 40 instruments has a wide array of effects and patches that can be loaded, and if that's not enough, the Library channel strip settings allow you to combine instruments and effects for creating massive soundscapes. The possibilities are endless. You may recall that Logic Studio used to come with a manual dedicated to the instruments and effects used throughout the program. Now you can simply use the Help menu, which quickly references the user's manual, to find the answers to any questions you might have. In the next few pages we're going to go over a few of the best instruments available to us in Logic Pro 9.

Learning Has Never Been Easier

Before we get into using the bundled instruments, let's take a moment to learn how to map certain parameters to your MIDI controller. By mapping knobs, buttons, faders, and more to your MIDI controller, you can quickly and easily tweak instrument parameters. You may want to hold off on assigning parameters to your MIDI controller while you are getting to know a particular plug-in or instrument, as you may not be aware of which parameters you'll be using the most. But when the time comes and you want to stop using that mouse in favor of something more fitting, go ahead and do the following.

Bring up the Controller Assignments window by pressing Command + L, as in "learn." A small yellow text box appears, telling you that Logic is waiting for a MIDI signal, and the Controller Assignments window pops up (see **Fig. 6.26b**). From here you can click on any assignable fader, pan knob, or other available parameter in a plug-in or instrument window. After you click once on the parameter you wish to assign, you can assign it to a MIDI controller simply by manipulating the MIDI controller (button, knob, switch, or slider) to which you would like the parameter assigned. If you wish to assign a knob to your MIDI controller, turn the knob. If you wish to assign a fader, move the fader up and down, etc. Logic will tell you when the parameter has been successfully mapped. To continue mapping, select another parameter and then choose a free MIDI controller to assign it to. When finished, hit Command + L again to exit learning mode, close out the Controller Assignment window, and start turning knobs and moving faders.

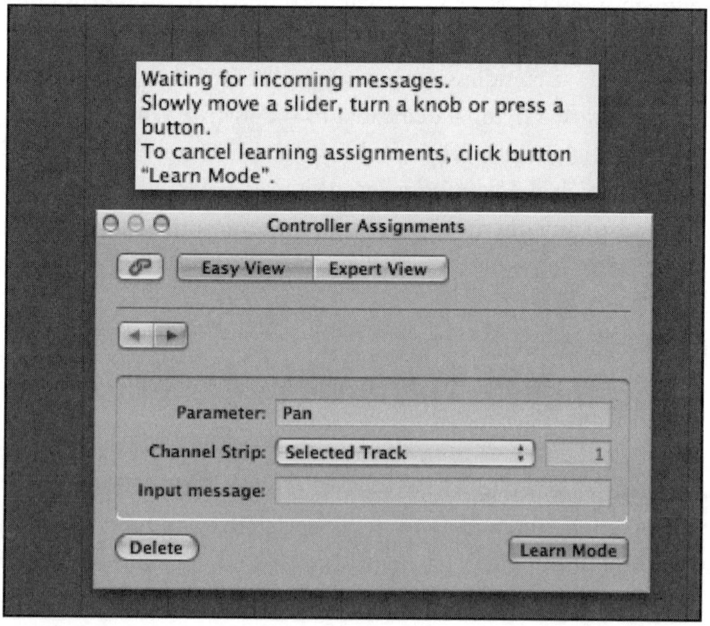

Fig. 6.26b: Controller assignment learning-mode options.

ULTRABEAT

Ultrabeat is Logic's one-stop shop for drum sounds and sequencing. A combination of a synthesizer, sampler, and sequencer, Ultrabeat has 25 synthesizers, or voices, at its disposal for loading sounds. Each is optimized for drums and percussion, with a rich palette of effects built in to allow you to shape your drum sounds. Ultrabeat automatically maps to the first 24 keys of a MIDI keyboard, corresponding to MIDI notes C1–B2. To load Ultrabeat, create a new software instrument track, click on the Input tab of the track, and select Ultrabeat (Drum Synth) Stereo from the menu.

Ultrabeat is broken into three main sections (see **Fig. 6.27**).

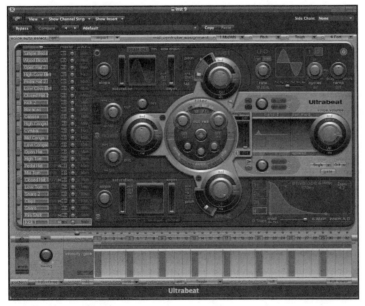

Fig. 6.27: Ultrabeat's main GUI.

Assignment Section

This shows all of the drum voices available to you. You can rename and organize them from here, as well as pan and adjust the volume of each voice.

Synthesizer Section

Each voice has its own synthesizer. Selecting different voices from the Assignment window will load a different instance of the synthesizer. This synthesizer is very powerful and includes tools for shaping your sound to make it your own.

Step Sequencer Section

This is where you create and control various sequences and patterns within Ultrabeat. Sequences reference a single voice, while a pattern references up to all 25 voices.

To load sounds into Ultrabeat, click on the drop-down menu labeled "#default." You will see a few options for loading various drum kits and patches. Remember that loading settings in both instruments and effects is universal; the load menu is always in the same place. Also remember that you can use the Library to browse through settings and patches. Whatever you select will replace "default #." Go ahead and load up "Studio Tight Kit." Loading a patch in Ultrabeat will load all 25 available voices along with each of their unique synthesizer settings, as well as default sequence and pattern presets.

Assigning and Organizing Your Voices

Let's take a closer look at the Assignment section. Notice the names of the voices are shown here. To rename a voice, simply double-click the name and type a new one. To move voices, simply click-and-drag on the number (not the name) and drag up or down. Wherever you release, the moved voice will be swapped with the original voice's location. For example, if you drag Kick 1 up to Low Tom, you will notice that Low Tom is now number 1 and Kick is now number 6 and the mixer settings (volume, pan, mute, solo, output) all follow suit; however, the sequences are not swapped. To swap sounds and sequences, hold down the Command key while swapping. Holding down Option while swapping will actually copy the sound and mixer settings to the new location, but the sequences will not be copied. Holding down Command and Option while swapping will copy the sound, mixer settings, and sequence.

Notice in the Assignment section that voices are labeled in blue. That blue color actually represents the volume of the selected voice. You can click-and-drag left and right to adjust the volume accordingly. Note that this is the maximum volume for the selected voice. If your kick is set to –4.5 dB, the kick voice still has a velocity range of 0–127. In this case hitting the key at maximum velocity would yield an output of –4.5 dB. Next to the blue volume slider are Mute and Solo buttons, which are convenient for isolating and mixing voices from within Ultrabeat. To the right of these is a panning knob, which will place the voice in a stereo field within the plug-in. Last is the output selector. This is set to "Main" by default, which means the output of all voices in Ultrabeat will play through outputs 1 and 2. Should you wish to assign certain voices to different outputs, simply click on Main and select your output. This may come in handy if you choose to process different voices outside of Ultrabeat. If you bus them to a separate output, then you can have a separate channel strip's worth of settings for that one voice.

NOTE

If you select a mono output, the panning knob is disabled. As you play your MIDI controller (C1 represents the lowest voice in Ultrabeat), you will notice an onscreen keyboard to the left of the voice name. The keyboard will light up blue as a key is pressed. You can also audition sounds by mouse-clicking on this keyboard.

Changing It Up

Let's say you love the "Latin Kit," but you want to load a different kick drum. You can do this with the Import function. Just above the Assignment section and slightly to the right, you will see an Import button. Pressing this will prompt you to load another drum kit. Load the "Vintage 08 Kit," and you will notice a transparent blue column appear to the right of the assignment section (see **Fig. 6.28**). Here you see the entire voice mapping of the Vintage 08 Kit. You can audition sounds from this kit by clicking on the voice name. Voices that have sequences are denoted with an "sq" next to their name. To swap out a voice from your current kit simply drag-and-drop to replace it; remember,

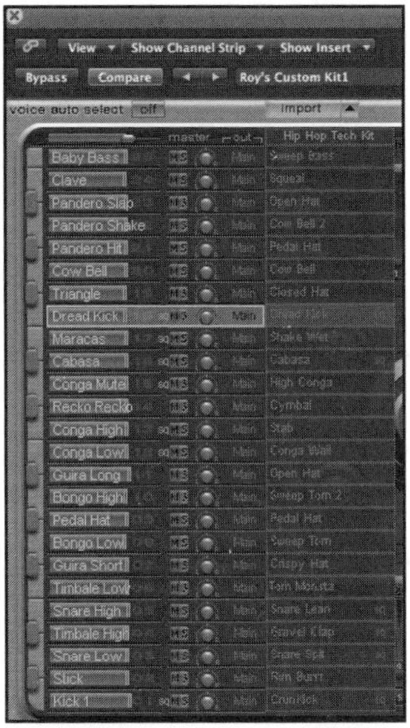

Fig. 6.28: Importing different sounds within a custom Ultrabeat kit.

the same modifiers work here as with copying sequences. Also, you aren't limited to only copying the kick to a kick track; you can click-and-drag from the Import window to any voice you wish to reassign. You can create custom kits as you find sounds you like in the various presets. To save your custom kit, click on the same drop-down menu you used to load the initial patch and choose "Save Setting As." The default save location is in the Ultrabeat folder, which is probably where you want to keep it. Name your custom kit and press Save.

Shaping Voices with the Synthesizer

The synthesizers in Ultrabeat can appear a bit scary at first. There are just so many parameters available for tweaking, it is hard not to get intimidated quickly. For instance, Ultrabeat's synthesizer uses basic subtractive synthesis. You see? Already intimidating, but fear not. This only means that a basic tone is created by an oscillator and noise generator (things that generate sounds or fixed frequencies), then an EQ filter subtracts certain frequencies from the original sound, followed by volume shaping using various envelopes. The filter section in the middle receives its input from Oscillators 1 and 2, the Noise Generator, and the Ring Modulator. In the center section are a few buttons that tell the signal to enter the filter section or bypass it and go straight to the output, as seen in **Fig. 6.29**. Two of the three buttons are red and on, with arrows indicating they are flowing to the filter section. Notice that Oscillator 1 is not going through the filter in this example.

You may also notice red power buttons for each module of the synthesizer. When a module is off, no signal is being created or passed through the module. When on however, you can shape the sound using the parameters. The volume controls for each parameter are the knobs in the middle of each of the circles (see **Fig. 6.30**). To go over every parameter of each plug-in would fill this entire book, but let's take a look at Oscillator 1. We can change the type of synthesis engine by selecting from Phase Oscillator, FM (Frequency Modulation), or Side Chain. Let's take a closer look at the Side Chain input.

Fig. 6.29: Ultrabeat signal-flow buttons.

Fig. 6.30: Ultrabeat volume control.

If you select the Side Chain input, Ultrabeat will use an external source such as another audio track or aux track. This external track will be run through the Ultrabeat plug-in, and Ultrabeat will be triggered based on this input. Select the Side Chain input tab for Oscillator 1. You'll see an arrow showing the signal flow of the sidechain; now we have to select the source of our sidechain input. This is found from the Side Chain menu in the upper right corner of the Ultrabeat plug-in window (see **Fig. 6.31**). I am going to select my audio kick drum track to be the input; now the sound of the kick will run through the various filters and the step sequencer of Ultrabeat.

Fig. 6.31: Sidechain source track selection in Ultrabeat.

I highly recommend checking out Logic's Instruments and Effects manual for more detail on each synth engine. Much of the theory applied to the drum synths will carry over when sculpting sounds with other plug-ins. Loading and creating kits takes seconds to do, but by shaping your sound you will make it your own.

Using the Step Sequencer

The step sequencer built into Ultrabeat allows you to create patterns that use all 25 of the available voices. It's a great visual way to create beats quickly and effectively. The step sequencer can hold 24 voices, and each sequence can contain up to 32 steps. Let's take a closer look at the Step Sequencer window (see **Fig. 6.32**). Notice it is broken up into three parts.

Fig. 6.32: Ultrabeat's basic pattern sequencer.

Global Parameters

These functions apply to patterns in the step sequencer, such as the On/Off button, which enables and disables the sequencer. You can trigger Ultrabeat using MIDI sequencing on a MIDI track in Logic, or you can use the step sequencer. It's generally a matter of preference. Ultrabeat is very powerful, but you do not have to use all aspects of it for it to sound good. However, you should be aware of all its functions. The Edit Switch toggles between Voice and Step mode.

Voice and Step Modes

VOICE MODE (DEFAULT)

Voice mode controls the parameters of the drum sound itself, such as the velocity and gate.

STEP MODE

Step mode allows you to automate parameters, changing from one setting to another. In this mode notice all of the knobs and faders turn yellow; as you grab them you will see the changes reflected in the step sequencer. This is what makes sequencing within Ultrabeat very powerful. Having the ability to automate each module and parameter in a sequence gives you near-infinite flexibility.

The Transport button allows you to start and stop the sequence. When Logic is playing back and the sequencer is on it will automatically play along with Logic; however, should you wish to audition the sequence with Logic stopped, you can do so by pressing Play.

The Swing knob allows you to humanize Ultrabeat enough to "swing" notes. This gives you more of a syncopated, jazzy feel. Play with this knob while listening in Logic to make your drum patterns sound more musical and less like a computer. You can turn on Swing by pressing the blue button next to the word "Swing."

Pattern Parameters

Patterns can contain up to 32 steps, and can use all 25 available voices. Patterns apply to all sounds.

PATTERN MENU

Ultrabeat can use 24 patterns. These can be selected in the lower left-hand corner (see **Fig. 6.33**).

LENGTH

This sets the length of the pattern. The length is measured in steps. While the sequencer is limited to 32 steps, the number of bars this translates to will depend on the meter of your song and the resolution of the grid.

RESOLUTION

This sets what each step in the pattern represents. When set to 1/8, each step is an eighth note in 4/4 time. At 32 steps that

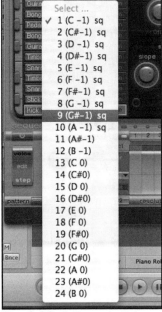

Fig. 6.33: Pattern-selection menu.

means we would have a four-bar drum pattern. Be sure to adjust your resolution and step length based on the meter of your song so that the sequence is an even number of bars.

ACCENT

An accent means the sequencer will emphasize that step more strongly. There is a volume slider for the accent volume. To enable accents, turn on the blue button next to the slider; to accent certain steps, click on the blue light above the step. Accents can be turned on or off for each voice.

SWING

Similar to the accent setting. When enabled the swing value will be determined by the value of the Swing knob.

The Step Grid

In the step grid the pattern is displayed in steps on two rows. The Trigger row indicates a voice being triggered on a specific step. The Velocity/Gate row sets the length and velocity of the triggered voice. The Velocity/Gate row displays information graphically; the taller the bar, the greater the velocity. The wider the bar, the longer the duration of the triggered note. You can trigger the selected voice by selecting the various steps. Each of the 25 voices has its own step grid.

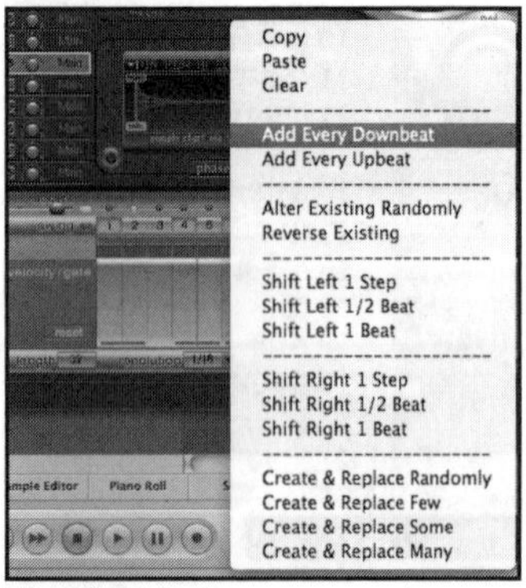

To enable a voice on a step, simply click on one of the step numbers. The step turns blue to indicate it is now active in the pattern. There are a few shortcuts that can help you build beats quickly and effectively. Right-click on any of the steps and a contextual menu will appear (see **Fig. 6.34**).

Copy, Paste, and Clear are all pretty straightforward. Copy and Paste allow you to copy patterns from one voice and paste them into another; Clear allows you to start with a clean slate. Notice when you paste that you don't have to remember the step you copied from or where you are going to put it; Paste will know exactly where the pattern is supposed to go.

Fig. 6.34: Step-sequencing shortcuts menu.

The remaining tools will help you construct a beat with fewer clicks, or change an existing beat with little work. You will find it convenient to Add Every Downbeat or Upbeat; these settings give you a good place to start while building your beats. Some more creative options include the following.

Alter Existing Randomly tells Ultrabeat to randomly create a pattern from the existing steps; only the amount of selected steps will be used, though. Reverse Existing does exactly what it says and is great for coming up with unique ideas if you find your beats are getting stale. The Shift Beats option allows you to shift the entire pattern by a certain amount; this is great for auditioning how a beat will sound with an instrument offset by half a beat or so. If this isn't enough, you can always use the Create and Replace Randomly option, which will give you a new random pattern each time. You'll be hearing new ideas in no time and creating unique beats with these great tools.

To change the velocity and gate of the triggered step, simply click-and-drag in the Velocity/Gate Row. A blue graphical bar will adjust according to how you click-and-drag. Remember that taller bars have a greater velocity and wider bars have a longer length. Similar to the tools we discussed for creating random patterns, you can also randomize the velocity and gates by right-clicking and selecting one of the options. Alter Gate and Alter Velocity will randomize their respective parameters while retaining the Trigger row. Randomize Gate and Randomize Velocity will also retain the Trigger row but will create a more pronounced change in velocities and gates.

Step Up to Full Grid View

Now that you have a grasp of how to create sequences using various drum voices, wouldn't it be nice to see them all at once? You can by opening up Full Grid View (see **Fig. 6.35**). The synthesizer view is now hidden, replaced by a full view of all 25 voices and their associated sequences; all of the sequences combined create a pattern. When you play the sequencer you can see graphically how the step sequencer is working as it goes through up to 32 steps of 25 voices. It's a very simple idea: as

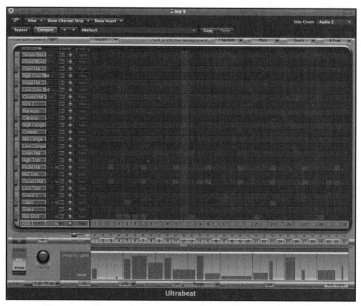

Fig. 6.35: Full-grid view for step sequencing.

the sequence playhead moves through the sequence, voices will trigger if they are enabled on the step. You still retain control over velocity and gate settings. By selecting a voice, the active voice will show the velocity and gate row along the bottom. You can add or delete triggers simply by clicking them in this grid window. Using Full Grid View in combination with randomizing sequences, velocities, and gates is a great way to see your beat come together. As the pattern plays, feel free to experiment with adding and removing various triggers.

Pattern to Arrange Window

Remember that you can create up to 24 different patterns, so experiment with creating patterns with Logic playing and with it stopped; you'll come up with unique ideas each time. To copy a pattern to your Arrange window, simply drag it from the Pattern Selector menu onto the Arrange window. Once it is in the Arrange window you have the flexibility of editing the region using all of the tools available in Logic. You can create multiple patterns, then drag them in as separate regions to create different drum beats in the Arrange window. You can create a four-bar loop for a verse, another for a chorus; drag them both into the Arrange window; copy and paste accordingly; and you'll have drums for your whole song in no time.

Pattern Mode

An alternative to dragging your patterns to the Arrange window is to play them on your MIDI controller by assigning the patterns. To do this we need to turn on the Pattern Mode button found along the bottom of the Ultrabeat window. You'll notice the Transport head turn blue. The 24 patterns are mapped chromatically from C1 through B0. In Pattern Mode you have a few options for triggering various patterns. These can be set via the menu next to the Pattern Mode button.

ONE-SHOT TRIGGER

This means you trigger the pattern to play from your MIDI controller and the pattern plays until it ends; when it ends nothing else happens. You can interrupt the one-shot by pressing another note or the same note, and playback of the first pattern will stop and the new pattern will start immediately.

SUSTAIN

The note triggers the pattern to start, and for as long as the note is depressed or sustained, the pattern will loop; as soon as the note is released the pattern will stop.

TOGGLE

This is the default when in Pattern Mode, and makes the most sense for live performance. A note triggers a pattern, and the pattern plays indefinitely until another note is received. If the next note is the same note, the pattern will stop immediately; if it is a new note, a new pattern will begin playing at bar 1 of the old pattern. This is ideal, as it will allow you to trigger the next pattern without worrying about triggering it in time, as you would have to do with the One-Shot option.

VOICE MUTE MODE

This unique mode allows you to mute various elements of your pattern. Muting MIDI note C1 will mute the voice corresponding to C1. This mode is great for live performance and allows you to reprogram the pattern without deleting anything in the sequence.

That's a good look at Ultrabeat for Logic. Keep in mind that we only scratched the surface of what Ultrabeat is capable of. With more than 50 new drum kits in this version, along with 400 new patterns and over 1,000 new sounds, you will find yourself building massive beats with little effort.

EXS24 MKII

The EXS24 is an extraordinary sampler that ships with Logic Pro 9. While synthesizers uses a tone generator to create sounds, a software sampler uses prerecorded audio for playback; these prerecorded bits are called *samples*. Collections of samples that are organized and tuned accordingly are called Sampler Instruments. These sampler instruments are what we load into the EXS24. An extensive library of sampler instruments is included with the EXS24 mkII, but because EXS is a known standard, you can also use sampler instruments from many third-party developers. The EXS24 can also support sample formats for Akai S1000 and S3000, SampleCell, GigaSampler, DLS, and SoundFont2. Having this flexibility in a software sampler allows Logic to use just about anything you throw at it, all with amazing flexibility and ease of use.

Logic's EXS24 mkII is broken down into two main windows. When you launch an instance of the EXS24 mkII you will see the Parameters window, which is shown in **Fig 6.36**. From this window you can alter the sound of the samples you have loaded using basic synthesis and transposition tools. The other window is the Instrument Editor, which is used to edit existing sampler instruments as well as create new ones. Both of these windows can seem very complex, but learning how to use the EXS24 mkII is very similar to learning Ultrabeat. It's very simple to learn, but it will take a long time to master shaping your sound using the available parameters. Let's go over the basics of using the EXS24 mkII in Logic.

Fig. 6.36: The EXS24 GUI.

Go ahead and launch an instance of the EXS24 mkII on a software instrument. Remember, a software instrument is loaded via the input tab of a channel strip. Be sure to select EXS24 (Sampler) Stereo. To load a sampler instrument, click on the arched black empty field just underneath the Copy function. A drop-down menu will appear, allowing you to select from a list of various instrument types (see **Fig. 6.37**). Under Acoustic Pianos, select Classical Piano. Logic will bring up a loading dialog box; what's going on here is that Logic is loading up the individual samples. Depending on the size and complexity of the instrument, this can take a while. Some of the most complex sampled instruments are composed of hundreds of samples. In order to properly recreate the actual instrument, it was sampled at various velocities to pick up the different subtleties in timbre. While it is possible to transpose pitches within reason so you don't have to sample each note of an instrument, instruments that take multiple samples of each note are the most accurate. They also take up a lot more space on your hard drive. If you want to know where these samples reside on your hard drive, they are located here: Library/Application Support/Logic/EXS Factory Samples.

Let's take a look at the Classical Piano sampler instrument we have loaded. Click on the Edit button next to the Load menu. The Instrument Editor launches in a separate window (see **Fig. 6.38**). You'll notice a long list of the audio files that make up this

No Instrument
Next Instrument
Previous Instrument
Clear Find
Find...
Refresh Menu
01 Acoustic Pianos ▶
02 Bass ▶
03 Drums & Percussion ▶
04 Keyboards ▶
05 Synthesizers ▶
06 Pop Strings ▶
07 Pop Horns ▶
08 Guitars ▶
09 Orchestral ▶
10 World ▶
11 Textures ▶
12 Legacy Instruments ▶
GarageBand ▶

Fig. 6.37: EXS24's list of instruments.

particular instrument. If you look under the Pitch column you will see the original note the audio file was sampled at. There are 88 keys on a standard piano; if you were to sample each key at soft, medium, and hard velocities, you would end up with 264 samples. Because of the advances in modern samplers with pitch- and time-stretching, we can get away with sampling every few notes and adjusting the pitch to fill in the missing notes. The more you stretch the pitch of a given note, however, the less accurate it becomes. So with the exception of the lowest note, each sampled note is stretched over no more than a whole step. If you look at the key range column, you can see that each sample is theoretically capable of being stretched over the entire keyboard. This may be an interesting effect for sound design, or for creating some crazy-sounding instruments, but doing this will not recreate what the actual instrument sounds like. Along the bottom of the window above the keyboard you will see sets of boxes. These boxes represent the individual audio files. If you select one from the list, the corresponding box (above the keys) will highlight. There are three sets of boxes because this instrument was sampled three times to capture the various velocities.

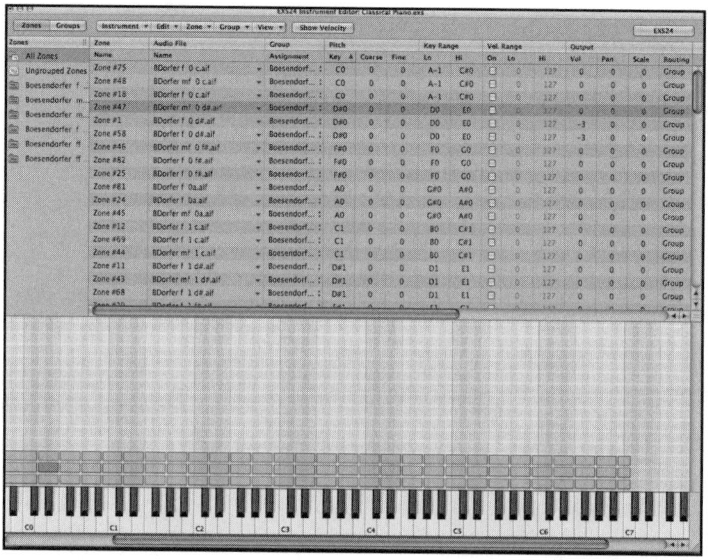

Fig. 6.38: Detailed audio file list for an EXS24 Classical Piano sample.

When you load a sampler instrument, all of the associated audio files are loaded into your computer's RAM. The files live on your hard drive, but hard drives aren't fast enough to keep up with live performance, so the EXS24 loads them into a faster cache where it can access them quickly. The amount of RAM your system has greatly affects the amount of instances of the EXS24 you can load. Each instance that is open makes a call on your RAM to allocate enough space to hold the entire instrument. Each instrument can have hundreds of audio files, and while these files are generally small, hundreds of them can quickly add up. Seeing as your computer also relies on RAM to run other processes inside and outside of Logic, it is imperative that you have a decent amount of RAM when working with sampler instruments to allow for ample real-time access. Remember that you can always freeze tracks after recording them to free up CPU and RAM, but be aware that you will need that free power initially. If you are taxing your system, be sure to close unnecessary applications and set your buffer accordingly.

Now that you have an idea of what makes up a sampler instrument, let's take a closer look at the interface of the EXS24 mkII. To quickly switch to the next available sampler instrument, hit the + button to advance forward, and the – button to roll back (see **Fig. 6.39**). Just like all other settings, when this window is active you can always load settings and instruments from the Library window. Logic comes with quite a few sampler instruments, but you can also add third-party instruments. You may find it hard to keep track of all of them, so the ESX24 allows you to conduct searches using filters. If you click on the Load menu and select Find, you can type in a filter that will only show instruments containing your search item. Notice if you type in "vibraphone," the list of EXS24 instruments is much smaller (see **Fig. 6.40**). Only the EXS24 instruments that have "vibraphone" in their title appear, with the exception of your currently loaded patch. In this case the Grand Piano still shows up because it is our currently loaded sampler instrument.

Back in the interface window, we can see that we have a few different parameters at our disposal. These are broken down into the following categories.

Fig. 6.39: How to scroll through various instruments in the EXS24.

Fig. 6.40: Example of finding an instrument (vibraphone).

General Parameters

This lets you configure various sampler preferences. The Legato/ Mono/Poly buttons allow you to determine the polyphony of the sampler instrument, which is basically the number of voices that can play at one time. Mono and Legato both only use one voice at a time, the difference being that Legato mode does not trigger the envelope when switching notes, creating a tied legato effect. Poly is short for *polyphonic*, meaning "many voices." The amount of voices can be set next to the Poly button: 64 is the maximum. Keep in mind that while you only have 10 fingers, you can still max out your polyphony by sustaining notes and triggering multiple voices. When you max out your polyphony, some voices will suddenly cut off. Keep an eye on the meter next to the voices, which shows you how many voices are currently in use. Remember that even after you let go of a key, the release time will determine the length of time the voice will play for.

The Options menu gives us a few ways to load presets for the selected instrument. Recalling the default EXS24 settings will reset the EXS24 mkII to the default settings. Go ahead and play the piano patch after recalling these default settings. Hear when you release a note how it is instantaneously cut off; this helps us to realize exactly what the ESX24 is helping us do. Go ahead and load the "Recall Settings From Instrument" option and notice that the piano sounds much more realistic. You can tweak the various parameters as you please, but should you wish to Revert, you can always use that option. You can also save any changes you make to an instrument, though it is recommended that you perform a "Save As" so that you don't overwrite the default settings of the original instrument. Under the Options menu you will notice an option for Virtual Memory (see **Fig. 6.41**). Virtual Memory helps you load instruments and samples that are far too large for your RAM buffer. Essentially this feature tricks your computer into using a portion of your hard drive as RAM. While the hard drive isn't as fast as RAM, you can still use this feature because only the attacks are loaded into the RAM buffer, meaning that you can still play in real time without worrying about latency issues. The remainder of the sample or samples is pulled from this virtual memory on your hard drive. You can configure this based on a few settings; first you need to know the

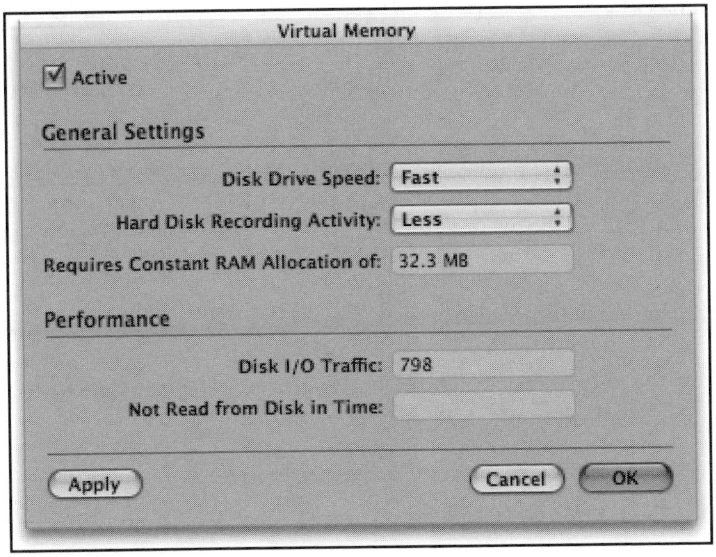

Fig. 6.41: Virtual memory preferences and options menu. .

speed of your hard drive. A fast drive is 7,200 rpm or more; a medium-speed drive is around 5,400 rpm. You shouldn't need to select the slow option on any modern Macintosh. You also need to know roughly the amount of recording activity you are doing. If you are tracking a full band you'll want to set this to Extensive. If you are working primarily with software instruments, go ahead and set this to Less. Notice as you change these settings that the amount of constant RAM allocation will change. You can also monitor the disk input and output traffic.

Velocity Offset allows you to adjust the incoming velocity of your MIDI signal. This can be offset by +/−127, allowing you to maximize your dynamic range. If you find your MIDI controller hits the maximum velocity of 127 too easily, setting this offset to a lower number will give you more flexibility with your dynamics.

The Hold Via parameter is something you probably won't change; this allows you to tell the EXS24 which MIDI controller you wish to hold, or sustain, the note; by default it is set to CC 64, which is the standard for the sustain pedal. If you want to get experimental, you can always reassign this to a free MIDI parameter such as a knob or fader.

The Xfade, or crossfade parameter, allows you to adjust the amount of fade-in and fade-out between voices in adjacent velocity range settings. Basically the ESX24 triggers individual audio files and crossfades between samples to help the instrument sound more natural. You can adjust the amount of crossfade as well as adjust the type. You can choose from a linear curve, a decibel linear curve, or an equal power curve; experiment with these settings to find what works best for you. Again, remember that the default settings loaded with each instrument are designed to work best with that particular instrument. The above settings are more for creating your own instruments or experimenting with sound design.

Pitch Parameters

The pitch of the loaded sampler instrument can be altered using the pitch parameters. We can also alter the tuning and transposition of the selected instrument.

The Tune knob allows you to change the pitch in semitones by +/–24 semitones, or two octaves; when set to 0 nothing is altered.

The Transposition window acts similarly to Tune in the sense that we are transposing the pitch by semitones; however, the associated zones are also moved with the Transposition tool, making it sound more natural. Take a piano, for example. If you play a middle C and tune it up an octave using the Tune knob, you are essentially telling that middle C to double in frequency. When you take the same middle C and transpose it up an octave, you are only telling the EXS24 to play that note an octave higher. Both can be used differently to suit your tastes. Try the example with the piano and listen to the difference in timbre.

The Random knob tells the pitch to waver within a specified amount, simulating a modulating string on a violin, for example. The values are measured in cents; 50 cents is equal to one semitone.

The Fine tuning knob allows you to adjust the pitch in finer increments using cents. You may need to do this to play in tune with an instrument that cannot be tuned, such as a recording that did not use A 440 as the reference pitch, or a sampled instrument was sampled out of tune. Using this knob can fix all three of these things. You can also intentionally make your instrument slightly out of tune with this knob to create a chorusing effect.

Note: A 440 wasn't always 440 Hz. Handel's *Messiah* used a tuning fork set to A 423; almost a half step away from what we know today. Some purist orchestras will tune to this reference pitch; having the ability to fine-tune within the ESX24 allows us to do the same.

The amount of pitch bend up and down can be set to different settings. By default the range that you bend up or down is a whole step. Generally this is the typical bend on a guitar, so synthesizers with pitch wheels or joysticks are usually set to move a whole step up and down, or two semitones. You can set the pitch-bend up value to an octave, or 12 semitones. By default the pitch-bend down setting is linked with the up setting so they match. But you can have a different setting on the pitch-bend down if you choose; for example you can set this to jump down 36 semitones, or three octaves. This can be cool because it allows you to bend your pitch up normally to emulate a guitar bend, but also allows you to go down three octaves, creating the effect of a whammy dive.

The Glide and Pitcher sliders work in conjunction with each other to create portamento effects. Portamento is the amount of time it takes to glide from one pitch to another. The Glide slider is the amount of time it takes to go between the two pitches, measured in milliseconds. When the Pitcher slider is set to the middle we have true portamento. Playing a note and then playing another note will tell the EXS24 to glide between the two notes based on the amount of time set on the Glider. When the Pitcher is set higher, the note will start the set amount of semitones higher and glide down to the selected pitch; conversely, if the Pitcher is set below 0, then the note will glide up to the selected pitch.

Filter Parameters

These filters allow you to tweak the resonance, drive, slope, and envelope of the selected sampler instrument. This section is where you will tweak the ADSR of your samples. ADSR stands for Attack, Decay, Sustain, and Release. Remember in our example when we set the EXS24 to default settings for the piano how computerized it sounded? To make it sound more natural, these filters are applied to the samples in various ways to emulate the actual instrument. The principles of basic synthesis and ADSR all apply here. By default any patch you load will be set up to sound great with no tweaking, but having these parameters at your fingertips allows you to have complete control when shaping existing instruments as well as creating your own. If you want to go deeper, be sure to reference the Logic manual Instruments and Effects.

VOLUME AND PAN

A local Volume and Pan control allows you control the overall volume and panning placement of the instrument in a stereo field from within the EXS24 mkII.

LFO PARAMETERS

LFOs, or Low Frequency Oscillators, allow you to modulate the signal passing through the instrument.

MODULATION MATRIX

This is a complex routing matrix that allows you to route various parameters using other parameters as a source. This matrix can route and reroute various modulation sources to different modulation destinations. For instance you can set the destination to "Pan" and the source to Pitch Wheel, and you'll notice as you raise the pitch that the sound will pan to the right channel. This is just one example of how you can experiment with routing various modulation effects from within the EXS24 mkII. Load some channel strip settings for software instruments that use the EXS24 as their input, and take a look at the main interface window to get a better idea of how to tweak these settings for your own use.

CONVERT AUDIO REGION
TO SAMPLER INSTRUMENT

This is a new feature added to Logic Pro 9, and it can be a very powerful creative tool. This option enables you to take audio tracks or regions and turn them into sampler instruments, allowing you to create different arrangements with your new "sampled instrument." To do this, simply start by selecting a specific audio selection from the Sample Editor. Try to make it a perfect loop to keep things simple and concise. Next, choose the Convert Regions to New Sampler Track option from the Audio tab or use the keyboard shortcut Control + E (see **Fig. 6.42**). From here you need to make a few decisions. First, select Transient Markers option, then name the instrument and set the Trigger Note Range, then click OK (see **Fig. 6.43**).

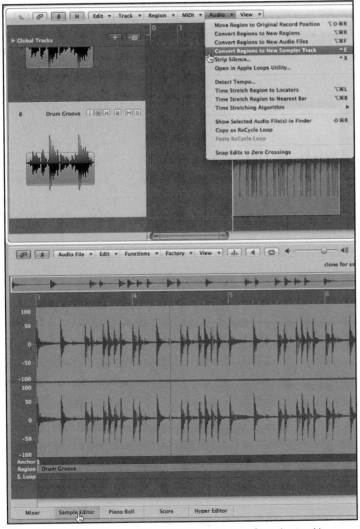

Fig. 6.42: Audio Menu > Convert Region (to new Sampler track).

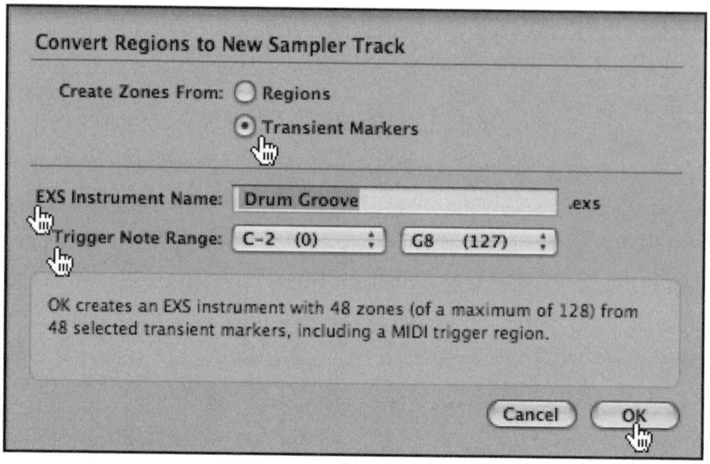

Convert Regions to New Sampler Track
Create Zones From:
Regions
Transient Markers
EXS Instrument Name:
Drum Groove
.exs
Trigger Note Range:
C-2 (0)
G8 (127)
OK creates an EXS instrument with 48 zones (of a maximum of 128) from 48 selected transient markers, including a MIDI trigger region.
Cancel
OK

Fig. 6.43: Convert Regions to Sampler Track, step 2. Pointers indicate important settings.

Logic will automatically create a new instrument track just below the audio track. It slices all of the transients and maps them across the keyboard (see **Fig 6.44**). This allows you to trigger each section, sound, or beat that was in your original audio. If you use the Inspector, you can change region parameters to create new musical variations. Remember, since this is now a new sampler instrument, you can change any of the instrument parameters you just read about, making new sounds, or noises with your new create tools. You can even use the use the exs editor to modify the individual slices, or "zones" and add effects is you wish. Last but not least, Logic 9 has given the EXS24 a 5.1 Surround output option from the channels output selector.

Edit
Track
Region
MIDI
Audio
View
Global Tracks
Drum Groove
Drum Groove
EXS

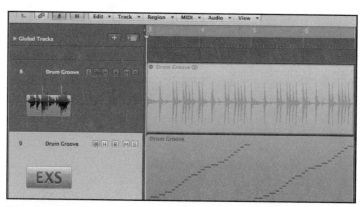

Fig. 6.44: Converted region track view.

OTHER INSTRUMENTS

We have learned about Ultrabeat and the EXS24 mkII. The remaining Logic instrument bundle cater more to individual sounds. A wide array of "vintage" instruments are included in the Logic Studio bundle. Let's go over some of the basics. Remember, if you want to learn about these instruments in detail, be sure to check out the Logic guide from the Help menu.

Sculpture

Sculpture is Logic's powerful component modeling synthesizer (see **Fig. 6.45**). The core of Sculpture's synthesis is based on the vibration of a string or bar. That sounds very abstract, and believe me, it is. Sculpture takes advantage of additive and subtractive synthesis. On top of the basic synthesis functions there are many parameters unique to Sculpture, such as the String element. The central sound generator relies on the user to tell Sculpture what material the string is made out of and how it is being struck or played, as opposed to an oscillator that just generates a simple waveform. Sculpture's base waveform is always changing, whereas an oscillator will never change, even if the signal is interrupted.

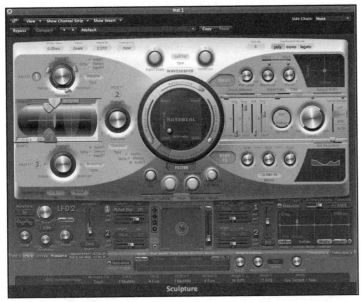

Fig. 6.45: Sculpture's GUI.

The virtual string also oscillates; however, when a new signal is fed into the generator, it will react with the existing string's vibration, which is far closer to the real-world physics of acoustic instruments. Oddly enough Sculpture isn't designed to sound like a real-world instrument, but it can create out-of-this-world-sounding synths by emulating the physics and principles of real-world acoustic instruments. Sculpture is very fun to play around with; try creating new sounds and even loading existing presets to learn the ins and outs of the synth. What really sets Sculpture apart, aside from being "string"-based, is its ability to output in 5.1 surround. Assuming your interface and studio is set up for 5.1 monitoring, you can instantaneously create soundscapes that fill a room with a few clicks and twists. Be aware that Sculpture is very CPU intensive. You may find it interesting to record a part, or take a prerecorded MIDI part, and put it on a Sculpture track; loop your selection and start playback. You will find that changing parameters in Sculpture is very much a performance unto itself.

EVB3 Tonewheel Organ

Modeled after a Hammond B3, the EVB3 (see **Fig. 6.46**) gives you full control of a drawbar organ with two manuals and a pedalboard. Each manual can have its own drawbar setting, just

Fig. 6.46: EVB3 organ GUI.

like the real thing. Also included in this amazing instrument is the ability to choose a Leslie effect, or the rotating speaker cabinet that gives the B3 its signature sound. The lowest octave on your keyboard will recall different drawbar presets to allow you to change them seamlessly during performance. The changes are crossfaded into each other. If you have a MIDI controller with faders, it's a good idea to map them to the individual drawbars so you have even more flexibility in your performance.

EVP88 Electric Piano

Here is another great vintage keyboard emulator. The EVP88 (see **Fig. 6.47**) simulates that classic Fender Rhodes sound, as well as other classic electric pianos such as the mighty Wurlitzer and the Hohner Electra. The synthesis engine at the core of the EVP88 is designed to emulate the vintage hardware down to the reeds, tines, bars, and pickups of the original. You'll hear the percussive, bell-like attack as well as hammer and damper noises. The EVP88 is a very authentic representation of these classic keyboards. Be sure to hit the Open button (see **Fig. 6.48**) for access to more parameters in this instrument; adding some chorus, tremolo, and drive can really fatten up the tone.

Fig. 6.47: EVP88 closed-lid example.

Fig. 6.48: EVP88 open-lid example.

EVD6 Clav

The EVD6 (see **Fig. 6.49**) is a faithful emulation of the classic Hohner Clavinet D6. The Clavinet is a keyboard instrument known for its percussive, funky attack. Much like the EVP88, the EVD6's main synthesis engine is designed to recreate the inner workings of this classic keyboard down to the plucking

Fig. 6.49: EVD6 clavinet GUI.

of the strings and the sticking hammer pads. No detail was left out in creating this emulation. You will notice that you have quick and easy access to change the position of the pickup on the strings to shape your tone; you can only imagine the amount of work this would have taken on the original model.

Some might say nothing beats the original vintage keyboards, but having them all in your computer means you don't have to carry them around—they also don't break as often!

Rounding out Logic's collection of instruments are the basic synthesizers: the EVOC 20, EFM1, ES E, ES M, ES P, ES 1, and ES 2 all have their own unique flavors. The EFM1 synthesizer is a basic frequency-modulation synth that gives us rich digital sounds synonymous with the '80s. The ES synths are more simple, with low CPU overhead. These are good for doubling up a bass part to cut through your mix, and come in monophonic and polyphonic varieties. The ES 1 and ES 2 give you classic analog sounds with full control at your fingertips. I can't go into how amazing each of these synths are, but I would like to go into the EVOC 20 in a little more detail.

EVOC 20 PolySynth

The EVOC 20 PolySynth (see **Fig. 6.50**) combines a simple polyphonic synthesizer with a vocoder. *Vocoder* is short for *vo*ice en*coder*. Basically a vocoder receives its input from an audio signal. The signal is analyzed and passed through to the input of a

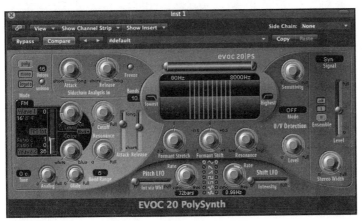

Fig. 6.50: The EVOC 20 PolySynth Vocoder GUI.

synthesizer; the synthesizer is triggered by the audio input, and the two signals are mixed together, creating a synth vocal effect you have probably heard many times in electronic music. Let's go over how to set up a vocoder to receive input from a vocal track.

First we need to have a vocal track. It doesn't have to be prerecorded, but for the sake of example, let's take an existing vocal track. Notice in **Fig. 6.51** that we have set the sidechain input to be our vocal track. After selecting your sidechain input be sure to change the signal input to "Voc." I have also loaded the preset Clear Voice Vocoder and set a cycle range for the audio. Now if I play back the cycle, I can play notes on my MIDI controller and will only hear the synth when the vocal is present. The synth is mixed with the vocals, creating a very computerized-sounding harmony. Be sure to mute the original audio track at first to get an idea of what the vocoder is actually doing.

Fig. 6.51: EVOC 20 Vocoder setup.

FINAL THOUGHTS

We covered a lot of territory in this chapter. Logic comes with many instruments, providing us with a near-infinite palette of sounds; be sure to play around and get comfortable with the software instruments. The more you use them the more comfortable you will become with signal flow, as well as how emulation and synthesis work. Also, as you become more familiar with these instruments, consider mapping their various parameters to your MIDI controller and remember them so you don't find yourself reaching for your mouse during a performance. Feel free to go back through this chapter to brush up; also be sure to check out the QuickTime tutorials that come with this book, go over the Power Tips, and answer the Tune-Up questions before moving on; we still have a lot more ground to cover.

POWER TIPS FOR CHAPTER 6

1. If you click and hold down the Freeze button on a given track you can drag up or down to select multiple tracks to freeze.

2. Sticking to a consistent color scheme between projects will help speed up your workflow and will be easier on the eye.

3. Sorting your Audio Bin is essential, to sort by name click on the "Name" column header.

4. You can quickly select multiple files from your Audio Bin by pressing Shift when selecting files. To select multiple files that aren't adjacent, use the Command key.

5. When working in the Audio Bin you will find yourself expanding and collapsing track components and groups many times. This can make your Audio Bin seem out of order and hard to navigate. To quickly expand or collapse all tracks, Option-click on one of the triangles; all tracks will follow suit.

6. In Ultrabeat when you drag and drop voices in the Assignment section, the two sounds switch places, and the mixer settings (volume, pan, mute, solo, output) all follow suit; however, the sequences are not swapped. To swap sounds and sequences, hold down the Command key while swapping. Holding down Option while swapping will actually copy the sound and mixer settings to the new location, but the sequences will not be copied. Holding down Command and Option while swapping will copy the sound, mixer settings, and sequence.

7. The samples in Logic are installed by default in this location: /Library/Application Support/Logic/EXS Factory Samples.

8. Remember that you can always freeze tracks after recording them to free up CPU and RAM, but be aware that you will need that free power initially. If you are taxing your system, be sure to close unnecessary applications and set your buffer accordingly.

9. Load some channel strip settings for software instruments that use the EXS24 as their input, and take a look at the main interface window to get a better idea of how to tweak these settings for your own use.

10. To better understand how instruments like Sculpture work, pre-record a MIDI part and loop it while you tweak the various parameters within the instrument.

11. If you have a MIDI controller with faders, it's a good idea to map them to the individual drawbars of the EVB3 so you have even more real-time flexibility in your performance.

KEYBOARD SHORTCUT SUMMARY

COMMAND	FUNCTION
Command + .	Cancel freeze
Command + G	Group Clutch
Command + E	Export Track as Audio File
Command + L	Controller assignments/Learning Mode
Control + C	Optimize Audio Files (Audio Bin)
Control + G	Copy/Convert Files (Audio Bin)
Control + M	Move Files (Audio Bin)
Control + E	Bounce in Place
Option + T	Configure Track Header

LOGIC 9 TUNE-UP

1. Freezing tracks is an effective way to free up _____ _____.

2. Freezing tracks doesn't affect _____ _____, _____, or _____ -_____.

3. You can make changes to several tracks by assigning them to a _____.

4. To make changes to individual tracks in a group you must enable the _____ _____.

5. To clean up your Audio Bin you'll want to get rid of unused portions of audio; you can do this by _____ your files.

6. Logic Pro 9 features _____ amazing software instruments.

7. Logic 9's primary instrument for percussion and drum sequencing and sampling is called _____.

8. Each of the 25 voices in Ultrabeat has its own _____ that helps you shape each sound within the instrument.

9. The _____ _____ _____ command tells Ultrabeat to randomly create a pattern from existing steps in the sequencer.

10. The software sampler that ships with Logic Pro 9 is known as the _____.

11. Software instruments such as the EXS24 mkII require CPU power from your host computer, but more important they require large amounts of _____ so that the samples may be stored for real-time access.

12. The _____ knob allows you to change the pitch of an EXS24 instrument by semitones, whereas the _____ _____ knob allows you to adjust in cents.

13. ADSR stands for _____, _____, _____, _____.

14. Sculpture is Logic's powerful component modeling synthesizer. It can output sound in _____ if your recording interface has enough available outputs and your studio is configured accordingly.

15. To use a voice as an input signal in the EVOC 20 PolySynth you must enable it as a _____ _____ _____.

The Logical Approach

7

CUSTOMIZING AND EDITING YOUR PROJECT

Of all of the creative tools made available to us by Logic, the program's customizable features and new editing functions will ultimately become some of your most valuable assets as a power user. On the surface, creating custom templates or editing your audio and MIDI may not seem to be as fun or creative as shaping your sound with Sculpture, programming beats with Ultrabeat, or using any of the other cool instrument plug-ins Logic has to offer. However, you will soon learn that editing is an art form unto itself. Possessing current, professional editing skills allows you not only to arrange projects, fix mistakes and polish up a slightly flawed performance, but also to create unique performances by giving you more creative control than ever before. If you are currently an aspiring audio engineer in today's competitive market, keeping up with constantly evolving digital audio editing techniques may be what sets you apart from competitors and keeps your clients coming back.

Logic Pro 9 features some major advances in the editing department. While it's not possible to cover every one of them here, we'll cover the most important and practical features in this book and the accompanying QuickTime tutorials. These new features bring Logic even closer to being a "must-have" application for professional DAW operators and producers as well as self-produced musician-engineers.

It wasn't too long ago that the only way for professional audio engineers to edit multitrack recordings was to edit the analog tape that was used to record albums in the past. This type of editing was employed by engineers to help create the timeless music that has inspired the majority of bands and artists you know and love today. As little as 20 years ago, in order for producers and engineers to change an arrangement of a song or simply fix bad punch-ins on a multitrack recording, they had to physically cut and splice the tape the music was recorded on. This form of audio editing took years of experience using a simple razor blade to create seamless edits.

Needless to say this was a destructive way of editing, but when there is no alternative, professional audio engineers do whatever is necessary to get the job done. Imagine having to actually cut and splice a piece of tape just to make a simple edit. Once someone was committed to making a cut, there was no turning back. The only insurance or safety net available was to go back to the copy of the reel they made as a backup before they started cutting the tape. Understanding part of what audio editing used to be like should help you truly appreciate how far technology has come in the audio engineering industry.

Luckily for the modern engineer and most of today's musicians, DAWs have made editing audio and MIDI hundreds of times easier and far more efficient than it ever was in the past. It has taken major technological advances in computers and a dramatic increase in the overall sound quality of digital audio for professional audio engineers to take DAW editing and mixing seriously. The ease of use and affordability of DAWs have not only made creating and recording music for the modern musician a breeze, but editing audio is now just as simple as editing text with a basic word processor.

This technology didn't happen overnight. Musicians had to wait a long time for computers to come this close to catching up with the creativity of artists. In the early days of computer-assisted music making, computer technology was paired with MIDI instruments. Soon after, MIDI composition and editing took off, and we've never really looked back. However, I feel it is important to know about past technology, so that you can respect today's technology and get genuinely excited about tomorrow's. Keep in mind, MIDI sequencing is what the first versions of Logic were designed to do. In subsequent releases of Logic, audio recording was added, planting the seed for the powerful application we know today.

In the final chapters of this book, we will also learn how to use some of Logic's handy session management features. Having the ability to create custom templates and screenshots to streamline your workflow will come in handy on your journey to becoming an efficient and well-organized Logic Pro 9 user.

ADVANCED SESSION PREPARATION

By now, you should be comfortable creating tracks for your various needs. Now we are ready to dive into more advanced techniques for setting up sessions. We'll go over more ways to improve your project's workflow, and we'll also go over setting up professional sessions prior to recording. When you are recording yourself at home you might not think twice about creating a project prior to actually working on it; you'll probably create it as you go. However, when working in a studio or with a client, it helps to map out your session ahead of time. If you or your client is recording a band that consists of drums, guitar, bass, keys, and vocals, you should build a project template long before you even set foot in the studio. Arriving at the studio with a pre-made session template is not only professional, but also will save you time and money.

Template Overview

By now you should be somewhat familiar with the built-in templates that are bundled with Logic. When you are first getting to know Logic, you'll probably find yourself loading the "Explore" templates, or you may find yourself creating projects with a blank canvas. In this chapter, we're going to take an in-depth look at the "Rock" template under the "Compose" category (see **Fig. 7.1**).

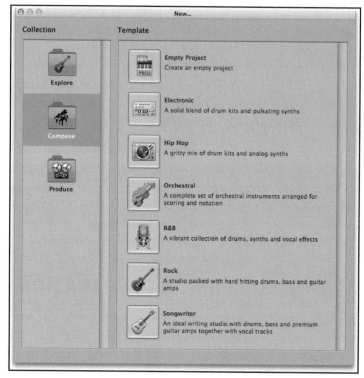

Fig. 7.1: Template browser with Compose File selected.

Notice that there are 15 tracks in this template. Since the band we're planning on tracking is a rock band, let's have a look and see if this template will work for us. At first glance, we see tracks for guitar, bass, drums, and vocals (see **Fig. 7.2**). The only things missing from this template for our "mock" project are keyboard tracks. Not a problem; we can add these tracks ourselves if we need to. Next, let's have a look at the Mixer window to learn more about this particular template. Use the keyboard shortcut Command + 2 (numeric keypad) to launch the floating Mixer window (see **Fig. 7.3**).

Here, we can see that very little detail has been left out of this template. Each channel strip has preloaded settings for various instruments, dynamic processing, and even time-based effects. Also, take note of the bus assignments. The first insert is green, indicating it is a pre-fader send on bus 20, used for a headphone mix. We can verify this by seeing the aux channel labeled Headphone Mix. Notice that its input is set to bus 20. Below the first send are two other sends: one for reverb and another for

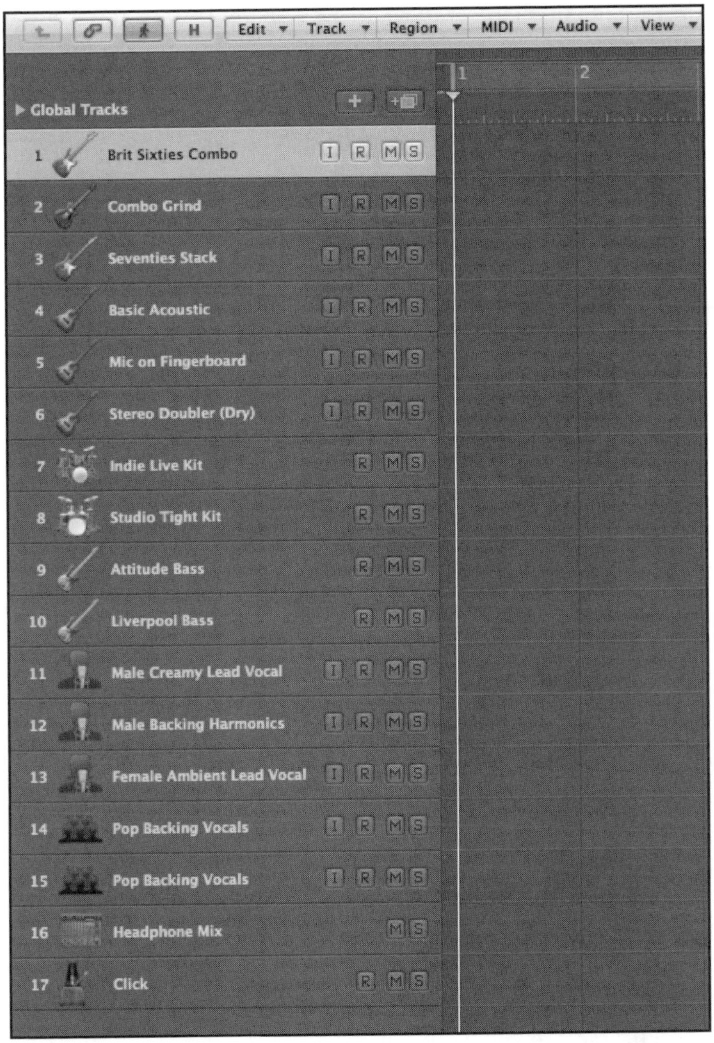

| ⬐ | ⬗ | ✦ | H | Edit ▼ | Track ▼ | Region ▼ | MIDI ▼ | Audio ▼ | View ▼ |

▶ Global Tracks   [+] [+▦]

1	Brit Sixties Combo	[I] [R] [M][S]
2	Combo Grind	[I] [R] [M][S]
3	Seventies Stack	[I] [R] [M][S]
4	Basic Acoustic	[I] [R] [M][S]
5	Mic on Fingerboard	[I] [R] [M][S]
6	Stereo Doubler (Dry)	[I] [R] [M][S]
7	Indie Live Kit	[R] [M][S]
8	Studio Tight Kit	[R] [M][S]
9	Attitude Bass	[R] [M][S]
10	Liverpool Bass	[R] [M][S]
11	Male Creamy Lead Vocal	[I] [R] [M][S]
12	Male Backing Harmonics	[I] [R] [M][S]
13	Female Ambient Lead Vocal	[I] [R] [M][S]
14	Pop Backing Vocals	[I] [R] [M][S]
15	Pop Backing Vocals	[I] [R] [M][S]
16	Headphone Mix	[M][S]
17	Click	[R] [M][S]

Fig. 7.2: The Rock template's global tracks list view in the Arrange window.

Fig. 7.3: Rock template Mixer view with convenient channel presets for a typical rock band recording session.

delay. The auxiliary channel strips associated with those buses already have their reverb and delay settings preloaded. We can also see that there are aux tracks dedicated to submixes. This template appears to be pretty convenient!

Although this is a well-thought-out template, unfortunately it's not exactly what would work best for our recording project. But by looking at Logic's built-in templates, we often can get some good ideas for how we may want to create our own custom template. In the next section, we will learn how to make a custom template that is geared toward a band we are about to record.

CUSTOM TEMPLATE BUILDING

Close out any open session and bring up a new Empty Project. Let's say we are tracking a band that consists of a drummer, bass player, guitar player, keyboardist, and vocalist. Let's break down what we would need to accommodate all of the parts for this type of project.

1. Kick Drum

2. Snare Top

3. Snare Bottom

4. Rack Tom

5. Floor Tom

6. Hi-Hat

7. Overhead L

8. Overhead R

9. Bass Amp

10. Bass: DI

11. Guitar Mic 1

12. Guitar Mic 2

13. Guitar: DI

14. Keyboard: Stereo

15. Keyboard: MIDI (**Note:** will not pass audio)

16. Vocals

Obviously for this type of project you will need to have an interface with more than two inputs in order to multitrack the drums. If you have an interface with at least eight inputs, you should have no problem making this type of session come to life.

A portable interface such as an Apogee Duet or an Mbox 2 is likely to have only two analog inputs. A mid-level interface like an Apogee Ensemble or a Digi 003 generally has eight analog inputs and outputs. If you need more than eight inputs at a time, you'll need to look into high-end professional studio interfaces. These are generally scalable so more I/O can be added as needed.

In the above example, the total track count is 16, 15 of which require analog inputs (remember, one is a MIDI input). If you have a Symphony system, you are good to go, but if you have an Ensemble system, here are your options. The drums will use up all eight inputs, so the drummer will have to record alone, preferably to a click track, or a pre-recorded guide track that was recorded to a click track.

Once the drums are recorded, you'll have the option of either recording everyone else at the same time or overdubbing the tracks one part at a time. Let's start building our session and see how it looks.

1. Start by closing any open Logic Session.

2. Create a New Empty Project.

3. When prompted to create tracks, type in 8 mono audio tracks (see **Fig. 7.5**). To save time while setting up your tracks, select the checkbox for Ascending Input. Channel 1 will have Input 1, Channel 2 will have Input 2, and so on; this is limited to the number of inputs available on your interface.

4. We know we are going to create more tracks eventually, but let's do this methodically, one instrument at a time. Let's label our drum tracks according to the previous list we

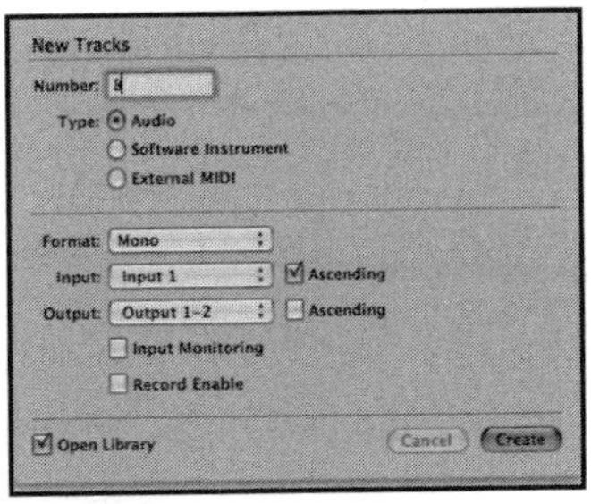

Fig. 7.4: New Tracks menu with eight mono audio tracks and ascending numbers for inputs selected.

made. Double-click the first track to rename it. After typing in the new name, simply press Tab to advance to the next track. This will save having to reach for your mouse. When you finish labeling them, they should look something like **Fig. 7.5.**

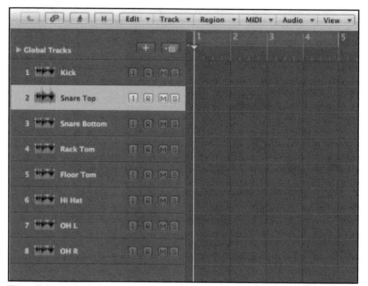

Fig. 7.5: Arrange window view with all drum tracks named.

5. Save your session. You wouldn't want to lose all of the work you have done up until this point. Now create six more mono audio channels, also with ascending inputs. These will represent the bass, guitar, and vocal tracks. Label these six tracks accordingly.

6. We haven't forgotten about our keyboardist. Bring up the New Track dialog and create one audio track, but be sure to change the selection from mono to stereo. Label the track and bring up the New Track dialog again, this time to create a software instrument track. Your session should look something like **Fig. 7.6**.

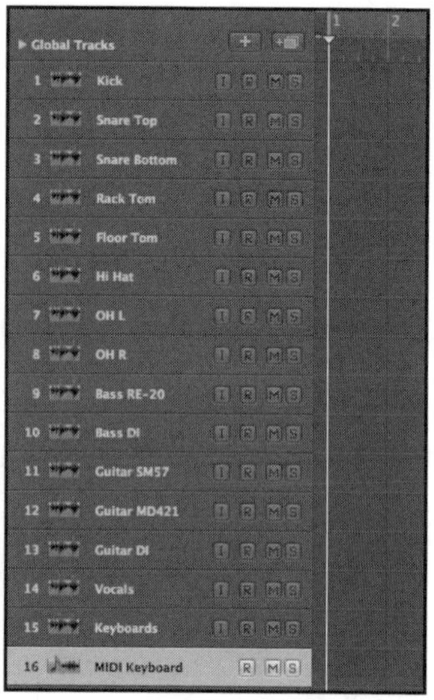

7. Remember to periodically save your progress in case of an unforeseen computer crash, which still manages to sneak up on us on occasion. Okay, so our project is starting to look like the pre-made Logic template we had a look at earlier. Now let's add some of the nifty things the previous template had.

Fig. 7.6: Arrange window view, with a custom "rock session," every track named.

Let's begin with our headphone mix. On the first track, click the first blank bus assignment tab and assign it to Bus 1. This is going to be our headphone mix, so after selecting it as Bus 1, be sure to click and hold to bring up the bus dialog again and select "pre" to designate it as a pre-fader send. When we first initialized Bus 1, Logic created a corresponding aux track labeled Bus 1. Let's rename that "Headphone Mix." Now underneath Bus 1, enable Bus 2, and label the aux track Reverb. Underneath that, enable Bus 3, and label the aux track Delay. We now have a pre-fader headphone mix and dedicated buses for sending reverb and delay. Add all three buses to each of the tracks (see **Fig. 7.7**). It can be very time-consuming if you assign the buses to each track, and then make each of the first buses a pre-fader send one at a time. However, if you quickly make a group for all of your tracks before you start the busing assignments and include the aux buses with the group settings parameters, then you can assign all of your bus settings at once. When you are finished, you can simply turn the group off. Remember to work smarter, not harder, whenever possible.

Fig. 7.7: Bus setup including a reverb, delay, and headphone mix.

8. We're almost finished now. To keep our tracks organized and easily identifiable, we are going to add icons to them. By default, audio tracks have a blue box with a waveform and MIDI tracks have a green box with an eighth note. We can customize these in the Inspector. Select the first track, and in the Inspector make sure that the triangle next to the track name is expanded. Click on the icon button to bring up a visual list of the available icons (see **Fig. 7.8**). Assign icons

to the appropriate instruments as you see fit; you should end up with something that looks like **Fig. 7.9**. You should recall how to create custom colors from the previous chapter. Using custom colors in conjunction with icons is a sure-fire way to visually know where you are at all times. We are going to make all our drum tracks red, bass tracks orange, guitar tracks yellow, keyboards green, and vocals blue.

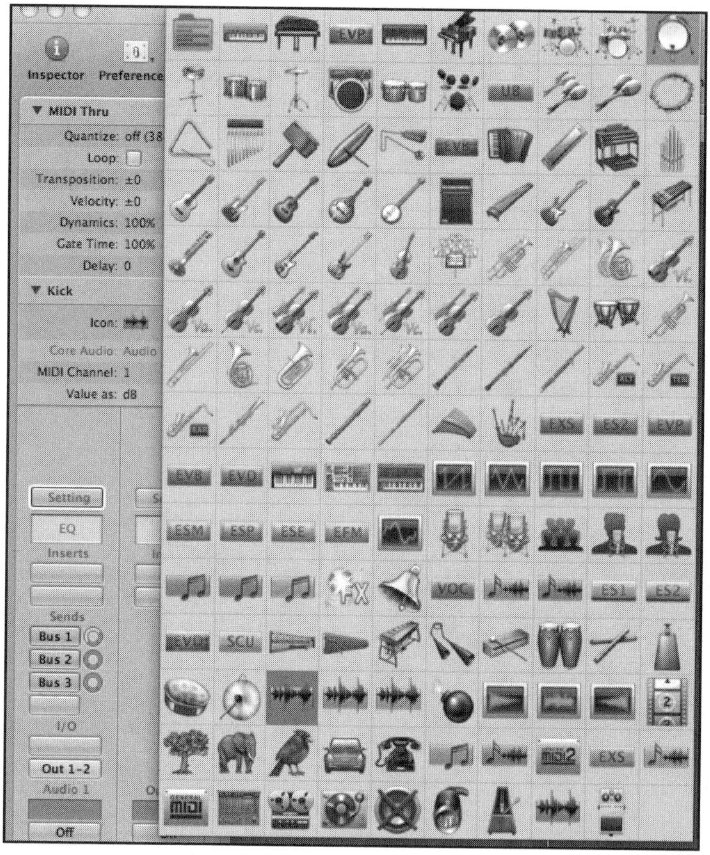

Fig. 7.8: Semi-custom icons to use on your tracks for quick visual reference.

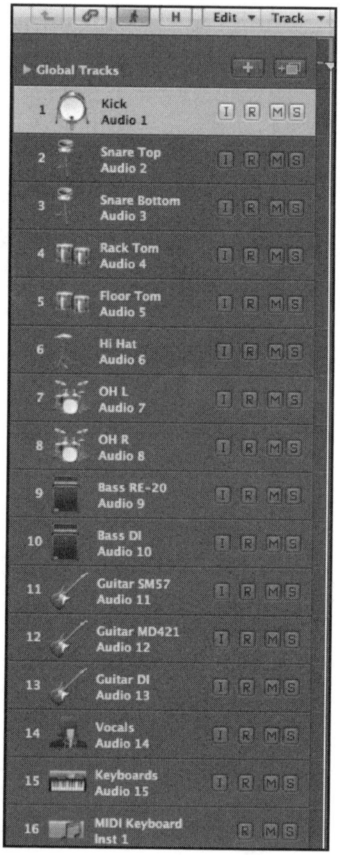

Fig. 7.9: Icon setup on our custom project.

This should just about do it for this template. You may have noticed that we didn't assign any channel strip settings, or insert any plug-ins or instruments, for that matter. That's because we want to hear what the incoming signal will sound like before we process any audio. Remember, the fewer plug-ins you have enabled, the more smoothly your system will run when recording. However, in this case it wouldn't hurt to load a channel strip setting for the reverb and delay aux channels in order to add a little bit of effect on the musician's instrument or voice. Also, notice that we didn't set the tempo or key for the song since this session is only serving as a template, but hopefully not all of your songs will be in the same key or played at the same tempo.

Now that this template is finished, we can save and recall it for each new song we track with this band. To save this session as a template that is readily available to you when you create a new session, go to the File menu and select Save As Template. By default, this template will be saved in the Project Templates folder at: User/Library/Application Support/Logic/Project Templates (see **Fig. 7.10**).

Fig. 7.10: Save As Template selected from the File menu.

Congratulations! You have set up a custom template that better suits your particular project's needs. For the same reason the pre-built Logic template didn't meet your every need, this example template won't either, so get used to creating a few custom templates based on your needs and daily routines. A couple of well-built templates for recording, editing, mixing, or even mastering will save you time in the long run and help you run an organized session. Remember, the next time you go to create a new session you will now see a new folder labeled My Templates. This is where you will find all of your custom templates (see **Fig. 7.11**).

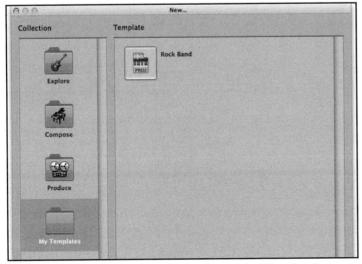

Fig. 7.11: My Templates folder added to the standard Template Browser.

Go ahead and create a new session from this template, and have a look around. Everything should be just as you saved it (see **Fig. 7.12**).

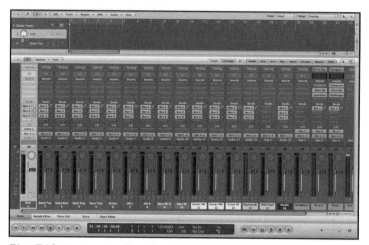

Fig. 7.12: Final custom template, fully set up and ready to use.

GETTING TO KNOW YOUR SCREENSETS

By now you probably realize the unified Logic Pro 9 interface can handle just about anything you require from within one window. Previous versions of Logic relied on multiple floating windows. While many people found these floating windows confusing, power users swore by them. Logic Pro 9 represents the best of both worlds. While the unified interface will get you by most of the time, there will be situations where you might want a little more screen real estate, so you may find yourself opening the Mixer in its own window instead of in the Arrange window. Logic Pro 9 allows you to use floating windows from previous versions of Logic in all of their glory.

What Are Screensets?

Prior to the one-window interface Logic has now, sessions would often have several floating windows positioned across one or more screens. Logic allows you to save and recall these positions using screensets. A screenset is geared toward a particular activity.

You might set up one screenset for score editing, and another for audio editing. It wouldn't make much sense to have the Score Editor taking up precious screen real estate when you are trying to edit audio, so if you find yourself switching between editing, mixing, and arranging, creating custom screensets will come in very handy. With the press of a button, Logic will recall the window layout associated with the saved screenset. This also includes display size, position, and zoom level. Screensets are as powerful as you choose to make them.

You can have from 1 to 99 screensets, but it is important to note that none of the screensets uses the number 0, as 0 is designated as a Stop command in Logic. Editing and creating screensets is as easy as typing in a single keyboard shortcut. Let's quickly go over which floating windows we'll potentially be working with here.

Arrange	Command + 1
Mixer	Command + 2
Event List	Command + 0
Score	Command + 3
Transform	Command + 4
Hyper Editor	Command + 5
Piano Roll	Command + 6
Transport	Command + 7
Environment	Command + 8
Audio Bin	Command + 9
Loop Browser	not preset
File Browser	not preset
Sample Editor	not preset

NOTE

The last three windows do not have keyboard shortcuts associated with them; however, you can assign them from the Key Commands window. Be sure to choose key commands that don't conflict with other Logic commands or system-wide key commands.

If you haven't touched your screensets yet, you are in Screenset 1. You can always tell which screenset is active by looking at the Menu bar. In between Window and Help is your Screenset indicator. Go ahead and open a floating Mixer window and size it so all tracks are visible. Position the window at the top of your screen. Press the number 2 and see what happens. The Mixer window disappears. It did not hide itself underneath another window; it closed. Take a look and you'll notice you are now in Screenset 2. Press the number 1 and you'll be taken back to Screenset 1, and your Mixer will return to the same place it was in before.

Whatever screenset you are currently in, you are always editing. Logic will remember wherever you place your windows. Pressing a number not yet assigned to a screenset will automatically create one for that number. The Arrange window will appear by default. To select screensets 1–9, press numbers 1–9; however, to select two-digit screensets hold down Control when pressing the first digit. For example, to get to screenset 45, you would press Control, then 4, and then 5.

Screensets are also stored in templates, so, just as we browsed the premade Logic templates for ideas, let's open a Logic template to get a sense for how screensets can be customized for various workflows. Close any open session, and from the template browser select Explore > Instruments. You probably used this template to explore the various channel strip settings and software instruments Logic has to offer.

Once you have this template open, have a look at the Screenset menu and notice that this template has custom screensets. They even have names (see **Fig. 7.13**).

Screenset 1: Pick Instruments & Record Tracks. This shows the Arrange window with the Media area open to the Library tab (see **Fig. 7.14**). This is a very common layout for selecting instruments and recording tracks.

Screenset 2: Edit Regions. This screenset is split in half, the top half being the Arrange window, and the bottom half being the Piano Roll MIDI editor (see **Fig. 7.15**). You will probably find yourself editing most of your MIDI regions in the Piano Roll Editor. Having the Arrange window on the top half allows you to select the regions you wish to edit.

Screenset 1	Help	
✓ 1 Pick Instruments & Record Tracks	1
2 Edit Regions	2
3 Add Loops	3
4 Edit Arrangement	4
5 Edit MIDI Region	5
6 Set Track Volumes	6
7 Produce Final Mix	7
Duplicate...	
Rename...	
Delete	
Lock	⇧L
Revert to Saved	

Fig. 7.13: Logic 9 screenset templates.

Fig. 7.14: Screenset 1: Pick Instruments & Record Tracks.

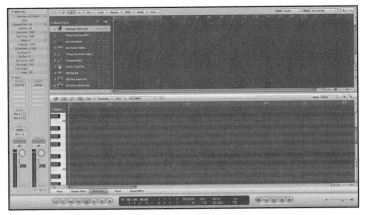

Fig. 7.15: Screenset 2: Edit Regions.

Screenset 3: Add Loops. Similar to Screenset 1, this one shows the Arrange window. This time, however, the Media area is open to the Loops Browser (see **Fig. 7.16**). This is convenient for auditioning loops, while allowing you to set a cycled selection in the Arrange window.

Screenset 4: Edit Arrangement. This simple screenset (see **Fig. 7.17**) hides all open tabs and windows from view. Only the Arrange window is shown, maximizing your available screen real estate for building and arranging your tracks and regions.

Screenset 5: Edit MIDI Region. This is another simple screenset (see **Fig. 7.18**), optimized by closing all windows and maximizing the floating Piano Roll Editor.

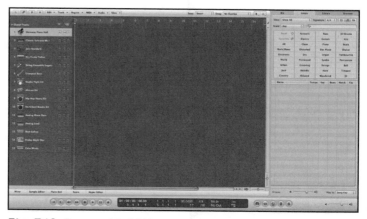

Fig. 7.16: Screenset 3: Add Loops.

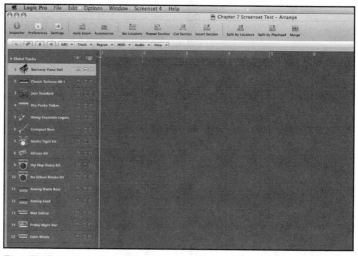

Fig. 7.17: Screenset 4: Edit Arrangement.

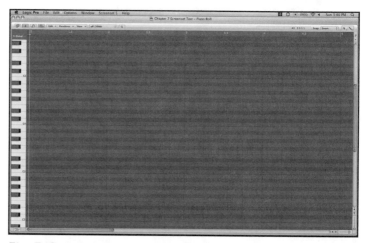

Fig. 7.18: Screenset 5: Edit MIDI Region.

Screenset 6: Set Track Volumes. This is an interesting screenset (see **Fig. 7.19**). The top three-fourths of the screen is taken up by the Arrange window, and along the bottom is the Mixer. However, the Mixer has been resized to take up less height. Notice on the right you can see that the scroll bar is set somewhere in the middle. This allows you to set the fader level and see the input and output of the channels.

Fig. 7.19: Screenset 6: Set Track Volumes.

Screenset 7: Produce Final Mix. This template (see **Fig. 7.20**) primarily focuses on the Mixer window, which takes up the bottom three-quarters of the screen. Here we can see the entire channel strip for each track.

Fig. 7.20: Screenset 7: Produce Final Mix.

The above screensets are from the Instruments template. If you explore other Logic templates, you will find other screenset examples. Experiment with changing between screensets and doing the various tasks associated with each one. When you finish, go ahead and open your custom template again; we're going to build a custom screenset. By default there is only one screenset listed in the Screenset menu, but as you press new key numbers, new screensets will be created. Press 3 to create Screenset 3. You have a blank canvas; basically you only see the Arrange window. Open a floating Mixer, and close the Arrange window. Resize the Mixer so only the eight drum tracks and two bass tracks are visible. Position the Mixer in the upper left-hand corner of the screen. Now open the Loop browser, position it to the right of the Mixer, open the File browser, and position it to the right of the Loop browser. Along the bottom, open up the Sample Editor. You will be prompted to open or create a new audio file (see **Fig. 7.21**).

Fig. 7.21: Custom screenset as described above.

We might use a layout like this if we wanted to audition loops over our drum tracks while mixing to get a good blend. We may also have the File browser open to find an external audio file. We would then load that file into the Sample Editor. This is just one example of how screensets allow you to customize your workflow. We've taken a lot of care to create this workflow. It would be a shame to have to reopen, resize, and reposition these windows every time we wanted to run this workflow. We can always switch back to it by recalling the screenset number—3 in this case. However, if we accidentally close a window or resize it, the screenset is updated in real time, so if we navigate to another screenset and back again, the changes we made will remain. To prevent accidents like this from happening to your precious screensets, you can lock them.

To lock a screenset, select Lock Screenset from the Screenset menu on the menu bar, or use the keyboard shortcut Shift + Command + L. Locked screensets are designated by a dot before the number of the screenset. Now that our screenset is locked, we can close windows, resize them, change screensets, then change back again, and our default locked screenset will appear. While the Revert to Saved command in the Screenset menu allows you to revert to your screenset's state before any changes were made, it is a better idea to lock the screensets you wish to protect.

Some other valuable screenset tools include the ability to name, copy, and delete screensets. To name your screenset, make sure you are in the screenset you wish to name, and from the Screenset menu select Rename. Type in a name that best describes what your screenset is for. To create an exact copy of an existing screenset, select the screenset you wish to duplicate, and from the Screenset menu choose Duplicate. You will be prompted to name the copy and select the screenset number. Remember, the screenset number you choose cannot end with a 0. Duplicating a screenset can come in handy when you want to make some changes yet still keep your existing screenset. With the vast number of options and screensets available, there is no harm in creating dozens of screensets to find what works best for you. After you have created several screensets, you may want to clean them up and delete the ones you are no longer using. Select the screenset you wish to delete and from the Screenset menu choose Delete. To rename, duplicate, or delete screensets, you have to use the Screenset menu; there are no keyboard shortcuts assigned to these functions.

Screensets are session specific, so each project can have its own set of custom screensets. This gives you great flexibility; however, it would be very frustrating to have to recreate all of your custom screensets with each new session. Screenset data is saved when you create a template, so if you begin a new project from a custom template with pre-made custom screensets, you are all set. But let's say you started a new project from scratch because none of your templates met your needs. We already know that building a project from scratch isn't difficult, and you can build it as you go; however, it would still be convenient to have your custom screensets available to you. Luckily, we can import screensets from other projects. To import screenset data, go to the File menu, and under Project Settings select Import Settings, or use the keyboard shortcut Option + Command + I. You will be prompted to browse for a project that has the settings you wish to import. Navigate to the project file that has your custom screensets and load it. If you want to start your own session from a blank template, but would like to use the premade Logic screensets from one of the templates, you can load it by navigating to Library/Application Support/Logic/ Project Templates and then select Open at the lower right (see **Fig. 7.22a**). After selecting Open, you will be prompted with an Import Settings dialog. In Logic 9, there are three sections to make multiple choices as import options. Some of the newer settings to choose from are Sync, Metronome, Record, Tuning, Audio, MIDI, Video, and Asset. Let's choose the Screenset settings from the Rock template to import into our Rock Band template (see **Figs. 7.22b** and **7.23**).

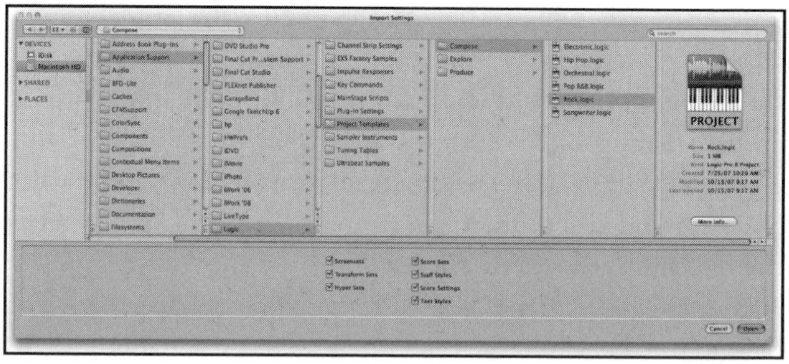

Fig. 7.22a: Import Settings view used to look like this, and you would choose specifics from this menu.

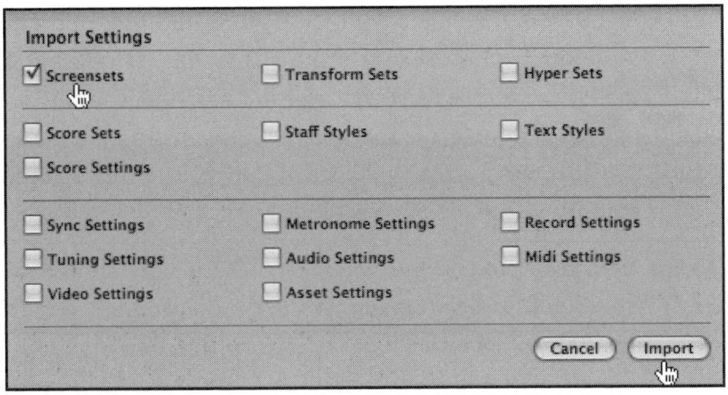

Fig. 7.22b: Import Settings view in Logic Pro 9 shows this menu with a few more options.

Fig. 7.23: Post import, showing the custom screensets we just imported from the other project.

EDITING YOUR ARRANGEMENT

Now that we have gone over the fundamentals of how to create and customize your projects, it is now time to learn about the editing tools at your disposal. Because you have already learned proper naming conventions, project organization, and how to create streamlined workflows with screensets, using these tools will come much easier to you. There are two ways to look at editing: the big picture and the small picture. Big picture editing is editing the arrangement of your song. This is done in the Arrange window. Most of the time, you are probably zoomed out enough to see the majority of your tracks and the length of your song. From here, you can see your entire song. On the other hand, small picture editing, such as editing individual audio and MIDI regions, is done while zoomed in on the instrument being edited. For this reason, you will want to be in either the Sample Editor for audio or the Piano Roll Editor for MIDI.

To get used to the edit tools, we are going to start with basic editing functions at the arrangement level. The simplest way to edit your arrangement is to drag regions to different locations. When working with music, chances are you want your regions to move in a musical way, meaning you want to move your regions by bars and beats as opposed to moving them by samples. This lets you stay relatively zoomed out while still making accurate region moves that will stay in time with your arrangement. We can set how our regions will snap from the Snap menu of the Arrange window (see **Fig. 7.24**).

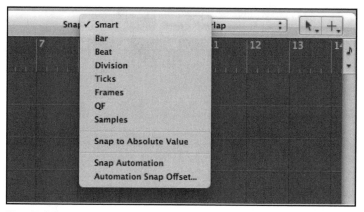

Fig. 7.24: Snap options menu.

There are a variety of ways we can have our Regions snap; by default this is set to Smart. Let's explore what each of these snap options does for us.

Smart. Snapping regions using Smart will snap them to the nearest bar, beat, or subdivision. The smart snap is dynamic and changes based on your zoom level. For instance, if you are zoomed out pretty far and you drag a region, chances are the region will snap to the nearest bar, whereas if you are zoomed in, your regions will snap to beats. Smart is the default snap setting because since it is dynamic it may easily meet all of your needs. However, if you want more control over how your regions snap, you can use one of the other snap options.

Bar. When dragging regions and releasing them, the region will snap to the nearest bar. If your region starts on beat 2, and the snap value is set to Bar, then dragging this region to a new location will still maintain its position within the bar on beat 2.

Beat. Moving regions with your snap set to Beat will snap them to the nearest whole beat. Naturally, this will depend on your time signature. In 4/4 time a quarter note gets one beat, and there are four beats in one bar, so the region will snap to one of these four beats. In 6/8 time the eighth note is worth one beat and there are six of them; therefore the region will snap to one of the six eighth notes.

Division. On the Transport beneath the time signature is the division (see **Fig. 7.25**), which represents the resolution of the grid. When set to /16 in 4/4 time, each quarter note has four 16th notes; there are a total of 16 divisions in this situation. With snap set to Division, you can drag your region to snap to the subdivision of the beat. This will change based on your current division setting.

Fig. 7.25: The Division settings box.

The last four snap settings are not "musically" based. Snapping regions to Ticks, Frames, Quarter Frames (QF), and Samples are all ways to accurately snap your regions for super-fine editing. If your regions are recorded properly and in time, then you will very rarely use any of these tools. However, if your region starts ever so slightly out of time, you may find yourself nudging the region by small values. In such a case you can be sample-accurate by setting your snap value to Sample. Be sure you are zoomed in close enough; otherwise your edit operations will not be sample-accurate. When working with SMPTE and film-related projects, you will find it convenient to be able to snap your regions based on frames and time code settings.

The snap values are all relative. We touched on this briefly when describing the Bar snap setting, but the same applies to all snap values. When you move a region, it will retain its relative position. To override this, you can tell Logic to snap to an absolute value. If you have a region that falls in between beats and you set your snap value to Bar, when the Snap to Absolute Value setting is enabled, the region will land on the downbeat of the nearest bar. Absolute and relative snap values both have their place.

To temporarily override the snap value, you can press Control when moving regions. This will override the snap and allow you to move regions based on the division setting. Holding down Shift-Control while moving a region overrides the snap and allows you to move regions based on ticks. Remember that this is only accurate based on your zoom level. We are still learning about arrangement, but it's important to realize that the snap value pertains to any edit operation, not just moving regions. We'll learn more about edit operations as we proceed through this chapter, but be aware that the snap settings will apply to all of our edit operations. Now that we know how our regions will snap as we move them, let's take a look at how regions will work with each other when placed on the same track. Audio and MIDI regions will perform slightly differently, as you will see. Directly next to the Snap menu is the Drag menu (see **Fig. 7.26**). The Drag menu shows the five different modes available to us (see **Fig. 7.27**).

Fig. 7.26: The Drag menu.

Overlap. This is the default Drag mode. This will allow you to drag one region on top of another; the region borders are still preserved, though. Take a look at the two audio regions shown in **Fig. 7.28**. It would be highly unlikely for you to combine

Fig. 7.27: The various Drag modes.

Fig. 7.28: Two random audio regions.

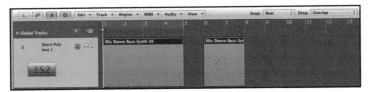

Fig. 7.29: Two random audio regions "overlapped."

a drum beat with a synth on the same track, but for the sake of example, let's drag the synth track so it overlaps our drum beat (see **Fig. 7.29**). If we play from the beginning, we hear the drums until bar 3, when the synth takes over. MIDI regions behave slightly differently. When MIDI regions are overlapped, the regions are summed; i.e., the notes in both regions are played simultaneously. **Fig. 7.30** shows two MIDI regions, which are overlapped in **Fig. 7.31**. When you press Play you will hear both regions play back simultaneously.

Fig. 7.30: Two MIDI regions.

Fig. 7.31: Two MIDI regions overlapped.

Fig. 7.32: Two MIDI regions, before selecting no-overlap.

Fig. 7.33: MIDI Drag set to no overlap.

Fig. 7.34: Region after no-overlap settings.

No Overlap. On the surface No Overlap appears to act the same as Overlap. When moving one region on top of another (see **Fig. 7.32**), the first region is edited. You can see this by dragging a region onto a pre-existing region (see **Fig. 7.33**), then moving it back (see **Fig. 7.34**). This is still nondestructive; however, you can always trim back the edited region. We'll go over trimming a little later. With MIDI regions the two regions are not summed, as they are in Overlap mode, and react more like audio regions did, with one taking over when the other one stops.

X-Fade. This mode automatically crossfades two audio regions when they overlap. This does not work with MIDI regions or Apple Loops.

Shuffle. This automatically aligns regions (to the left or right, respectively) when you move, resize, or delete them.

When you use Shuffle R (or Shuffle L), moving a region to the right (or left) aligns the region end point with the start point of the following region, ensuring that there is no space between the two regions. Regions that are dragged over each other will swap positions. When deleting regions, the remaining regions (those to the left or right of the deleted region) are moved to the left or to the right by the length of the deleted region. If a region is stretched or shortened when either Shuffle option is active, the other regions on the track will be moved to accommodate the new length. In Shuffle L mode, the right side of the region will be stretched or shortened, and the regions to the right of the edited region will be moved. In Shuffle R mode, the left side of the region will be stretched or shortened, and the regions to the left of the edited region will be moved. The regions that precede the edited region can only be moved as far as the project start point. If the stretching of a region results in preceding regions being forced to the project start point and exceeding the space available, the edited region will overlap the existing content.

Now we know how our regions react to the various modes, how they snap, and how they act when they come in contact with one another. We are now going to start editing with some new tools. Before we start actually cutting up our regions, though, remember that our zoom level greatly affects how accurate our edits will be. In Logic 9 you can make sample-accurate edits in the Arrange window. You can even nudge by 1 or 10 ms, assuming you are zoomed in enough to make these micro edits.

EDITING IN THE ARRANGE WINDOW

Now that we have covered how to move your regions around in the session, there will come a time when you will want to make an edit on a single take, move a piece of a region to a new position in the timeline, or anything else you need to do to the region to meet your needs. Each edit window in Logic allows us to assign tools for use in that specific window. In the Arrange window, we can assign two tools for quick access. By default, these two tools are set to the Pointer tool (as the primary) and the Marquee tool (as the secondary). You should recall from earlier chapters how to change these tools. To quickly change a tool, press Escape to bring the menu up without having to mouse all the way over to the menu. However, you can also assign a third tool for easy access. To do this, go to the Preferences menu, select General, then click the Editing tab, and the first option will be Right Mouse Button. Click on this and make your selection. Notice that Logic 9 now offers four options; the newest option is to open the Tool and Shortcut Menu (see **Fig. 7.35**). If you select the right-click to be an assignable tool, the new tool selection will appear next to your first and second tool selections at the top of the Arrange window.

Fig. 7.35: Assignable Third Tool is set under Preferences > General. Select the Editing tab and set the Right Mouse Button to "is Assignable to a Tool."

Fig. 7.36: The Tools menu.

We're going to be using many of these tools to edit, so let's go over what each tool does for us (see **Fig. 7.36**).

Pointer Tool. The Pointer tool is the most commonly used tool in Logic. It is used to select regions or events and to move and copy regions. You can adjust the length of your region with the Pointer tool by clicking-and-dragging on the bottom left or right corner. When you do this, the Pointer tool changes from a typical cursor to a bracket with two arrows on either side, indicating that you can click-and-drag to change the length. You can also use the Pointer tool to loop a region. This is similar to resizing a region: click-and-drag in the upper left-hand corner and dragout to the right for the desired length of your loop. If you go to theGeneral option from the Preferences pane, and select the Editingtab, you will see that you can set the options for the Pointer tool to show the Fade tool or the Marquee tool in the click zones.This kind of turns the Pointer into a "super tool." Nice!

Pencil Tool. The Pencil tool is used to add new regions or events. By default when creating a new region with the Pencil tool, it will be one bar in length. This can be changed by adjusting the length. The Pencil tool is similar to the Pointer tool because it can adjust length, toggle looping on and off, and move the selected regions.

Eraser Tool. True to its name, the Eraser tool erases selected regions. You can also delete unselected regions simply by clicking on them. The Backspace button accomplishes the same task. This can generally be undone, unless Logic tells you otherwise.

Text Tool. The Text tool very simply lets you name regions, or add text to a musical score.

Scissors Tool. This very useful and powerful tool lets you cut a region into multiple regions. This is very convenient as it allows you to quickly move regions around to rearrange a part. It also lets you copy or delete regions once they have been cut from an existing region. If you have a continuous take, you may find yourself using the Scissors tool to separate your region into various sections (verse, chorus, etc.).

Glue Tool. Complementing the Scissors tool is the Glue tool, which as you may have guessed will glue separated regions into a single region. If you piece together a part from multiple regions and wish to consolidate the regions into a single region, use the Glue tool.

Solo Tool. The Solo tool is great for quickly soloing a region during playback. While this tool is active, you can click and hold on a region during playback, and while your mouse is depressed you will only hear the selected region. Click and hold on different regions to solo other parts. You can move the playhead simply by moving to a different area in the Arrange window during playback. In Logic 9 you can scrub the audio with the Solo tool by clicking-and-dragging over a region. If you press the Option key and click on a region, it will play from the beginning of that region.

NOTE

The Solo tool works for audio and MIDI tracks; however, frozen software instruments will not play back.

Mute Tool. Similar to the Solo tool, the Mute tool will let you mute a selected region during playback. If you want to hear your mix without a specific region, simply click on the region using the Mute tool. If multiple regions are selected, the mute will apply to all of them. If a track is frozen, the Mute tool will not work without unfreezing it first.

Zoom Tool. The Zoom tool lets you rubber-band a selection; your selection will then fill the screen. To return to the normal zoom, simply click anywhere in the window. You can also access the Zoom tool without making it one of your two or three default tools or bringing up the Tools menu. Simply press Control + Option to temporarily use the Zoom tool.

Crossfade Tool/Fade Tool. The Crossfade tool is also referred to as the Fade tool, as it can create normal fades in addition to crossfades. To create a fade, select this tool and click-and-drag from the beginning or end of the region. However far you drag away from the beginning of the region will determine the length of the fade (see **Fig. 7.37**). When using this tool you can drag in either direction as long as you end past the beginning or end of the selected region. Clicking-and-dragging within a region with the Crossfade tool will do nothing. You can always adjust the length of your fade by clicking-and-dragging to a new length. Set your fade, audition it, and then adjust it by dragging to select a new length. To create a crossfade, simply apply the same technique to two regions that are close to each other or overlapping. Notice in **Fig. 7.38** and **Fig. 7.39** how crossfading works. To delete a fade, make sure the Crossfade tool is selected, hold down Option, and click on the fade you wish to delete.

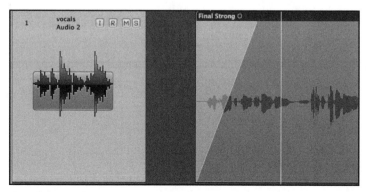

Fig. 7.37: A close-up view of an audio fade-in.

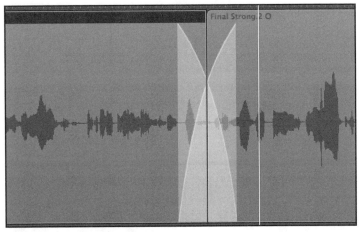

Fig. 7.38: A close-up view of a typical crossfade.

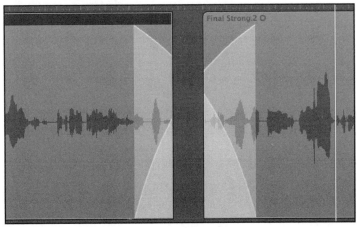

Fig. 7.39: A close-up view of a crossfade that is not connected.

To adjust the curve of your fades, press Shift + Control while clicking-and-dragging on the curve. **Fig. 7.40** shows you the various curves you can use. Fine-tuning your fades will help make your edits seamless.

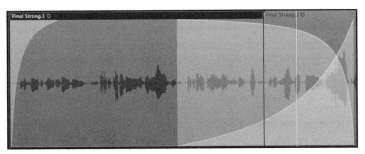

Fig. 7.40: A close up of a typical fade curve.

If you desire, you can get really precise and manipulate your fades mathematically by adjusting them in the Inspector's Region Parameter box. Here you can adjust the length in samples, as well as the curve (see **Fig. 7.41**). Also keep in mind that if you have your Pointer tool set up properly, you can access these functions while you have the Pointer tool selected. This may take a little getting used to, but it will certainly speed up your workflow.

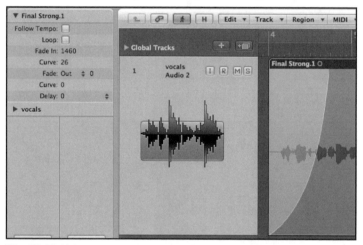

Fig. 7.41: You can customize a curve from the Inspector's fade curves area.

Marquee Tool. The Marquee tool is also very powerful and useful. Between the Pointer, Marquee, and Fade tools, you can accomplish most of the everyday editing tasks you will be faced with in Logic. One of the more common things you can do with the Marquee tool is to use it to rubberband or highlight, a particular selection. Notice after the region is selected with the Marquee tool that it is highlighted by a shaded rectangle. You can make Marquee selections in a single region or multiple regions across multiple tracks. To add a track to the Marquee selection or exclude a track, simply Shift-click. The Marquee tool doesn't seem powerful by itself, but when used with other tools it gives you ultimate flexibility when making selections. If you use the Pointer tool as your primary tool and the Marquee tool as your secondary tool, you can make a selection using the Marquee tool by holding down the Command key. When you release, you are back to your Pointer tool. You can now click-

and-drag your selection out to a new region. You can also create a selection with the Marquee tool and then use the Eraser tool to remove the selection. If you would like to make your Marquee selection as accurate as possible, hold down Shift + Control while making your selection. This will make your selection accurate to the sample or tick. This only works if the Marquee tool is the secondary tool. Also, you can set your locators to your Marquee selection. To do this, go to the Region menu in the Arrange window and select Set Locators by Regions, or use the keyboard shortcut Control + =.

A few more Marquee tool features have been added to Logic Pro 9 that should be mentioned. For instance, you can make a Marquee selection that does not include part of the region, and the empty space that was included in your selection will be included in your cut, copy, and paste. This makes regions that don't start on the beat incredibly easy to edit. You can also double-click with your Marquee tool to cut regions, events, and folders without having to use the Scissors or Pointer tools. Also, you can paste content from the clipboard at the Marquee selection. If there is no Marquee selection, the clipboard content will be placed at the playhead's position on the selected track. Another nice addition is that you can hold down the Option + Command keys while clicking on a region to make a Marquee selection based on the region's borders. Another cool enhancement is to hold down Shift + Option + Command to add to your Marquee selection.

MULTIPLE TAKES

When recording it is almost impossible to capture a perfect performance in one take. For this reason we record multiple takes. Takes are usually created in Cycle mode when recording, but are also created when recording over an existing audio region. When you record over the previous region, you aren't deleting any prerecorded audio; you are just creating a new take. Takes are stored in the same audio track. You can change which take will play back by clicking on the disclosure triangle in the upper right-hand corner of the audio region. From here, you can select any take (see **Fig. 7.42**).

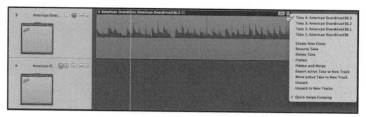

Fig. 7.42: The Takes options menu.

Even when you have multiple takes, it is still nearly impossible
to have one solid take that is perfect. More often than not you
will find yourself wanting a piece from Take 1, another piece
from Take 3, and so on. To do this we create what is known as
a "comp." A comp is essentially a super-take, a compilation of
multiple takes that will make up your finalized part.

Take folders are created by default, unless Replace mode is active.
Remember, in Replace mode each new take replaces the previous
one, saving disk space.

To view all of your takes at once, click on the triangle in the
upper left-hand side of the audio region. This will expand all
your takes for viewing (see **Fig. 7.43**). Notice that these takes are
expanded into lanes. These lanes are not individual tracks. The
take that is selected is represented on the top track, and will be
heard during playback. To audition other takes, click the take's

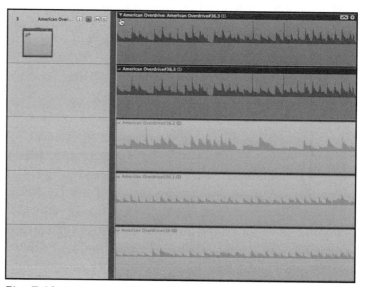

Fig. 7.43: The expanded view of the multiple takes.

header to select it and make it active. Audition your takes to get an idea of what you like and dislike about each one. When "comping" a vocal track, pay close attention to the inflection and emphasis placed on certain words. It might help to open a blank text file to type out your notes, or if you're old-fashioned, write them down on paper. These notes will help you stay organized when referencing your various takes.

Now that you have an idea of what you like and dislike in your takes, we're going to create a comp and assemble one good take out of our various takes. Comping is an industry-standard editing technique that has existed since the beginning of multitrack recording. Logic 9's Quick Swipe Comping is probably one of the best ways of creating a single seamless performance from multiple takes. Other programs have similar features these days, but Logic's Quick Swipe Comping feature truly sets the new standard for creating one "great" take out of many "good" takes.

QUICK SWIPE COMPING

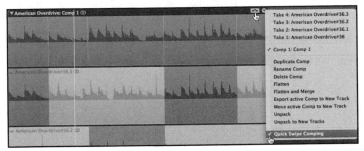

Fig. 7.44: Two ways of turning the Quick Swipe Comping feature on and off.

To use Quick Swipe Comping, first expand your takes so they fill in the lanes, and then either select Quick Swipe Comping from the Takes menu or click on the new Quick Swipe Comping icon just to the left of the Takes menu selector (see **Fig. 7.44**). Remember how the selected or highlighted take is the active take? Well, with Quick Swipe Comping, when you select a portion of another take you like by clicking-and-dragging with the Pointer tool to make a new selection, the newest selection is the active take (see **Fig. 7.45**).

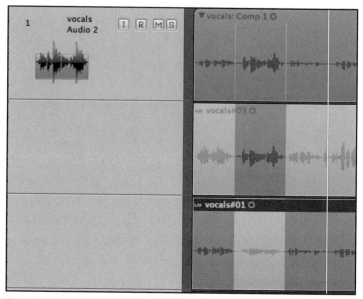

Fig. 7.45: Example view of Quick Swipe Comping.

Notice in **Fig. 7.45** how the first phrase is coming from the second take, and the second phrase is now coming from the first take. The comp is realized on the actual track (top track), and will update as you select various parts from the different takes. You will see a checkerboard-like appearance based on your selections, but the topmost lane (which is the actual track) will always show the waveform of your comp.

Using your notes, you can quickly audition various options to create a perfect comp. Even if you didn't take notes, you can quickly and effectively audition various comps by swiping over different takes. For maximum efficiency, set a play range cycle that is the length of your comp. As playback loops, you can audition your changes in real time without worrying about parts overlapping. As you drag a selection into another selection's phrase, only what you recently selected will be highlighted and selected for playback. Only one track can play back at a time. If you create a comp you like but wish to make another one without losing the changes you made to your first comp, you can easily create another comp. Click on the upper right disclosure triangle to bring up a floating menu. We used this menu previously to select takes and turn Quick Swipe Comping on and off; we can use it now to create and select new comps (see **Fig. 7.46**). Remember to stay organized and name your comp something recognizable to distinguish it from your other comps. You may quickly end up with multiple comps because of how easy it is to create them. As you swipe over various areas of the takes, you will notice that nothing can overlap.

Logic Pro 9 now allows you to perform expanded take folder editing. Simply turn off Quick Swipe Comping by de-selecting it in the upper right side of the audio file. While your take folder is expanded and comping features are off, you can perform edits such as separating and dragging a selection to a new section, or you can experiment with the new Flex tool and get creative with the phrasing. Flex Time editing is a powerful new feature that we will dive into in the final chapter. For now, just get familiar with the new expanded take folder editing option.

The main goal for now is to combine multiple takes that are okay, and "have their moments," and turn them into one glorious take that sounds like it was performed naturally and in real time. For example, in **Fig. 7.47** we have created a great comp. This uses pieces from all four takes to create our final master take. The track's waveform represents our comp. Notice the white vertical lines through the comp. These lines serve as a reference to show us how our comp is divided into the various takes. We can collapse the view and hide the lanes, and our comp will still be in place. Use these lines as a visual guide; you may wish to go back and select a different take for a particular phrase.

Fig. 7.46: Create a New Comp from the drop-down menu.

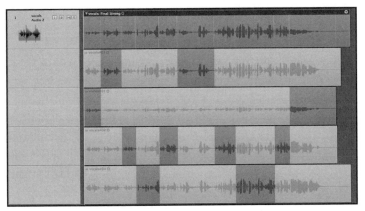

Fig. 7.47: An overview of the final comp.

Try Quick Swipe Comping with various instruments to get a feel for how comping works on various instruments and parts. Please keep in mind that a lot goes into making Quick Swipe work that you don't see. For instance, Logic automatically adds crossfades to all of your swipes to make your edits flow seamlessly. If an edit occurs in mid-waveform, normally you would have an annoyingly audible click or pop. But luckily Logic has some very user-friendly, intuitive tools that help us easily create a great comp. If you wish to adjust the default length of the crossfade time used in each edit, you can do so by going to the Audio Preferences pane; you can adjust the length under General. The default is 20 ms (see **Fig. 7.48**).

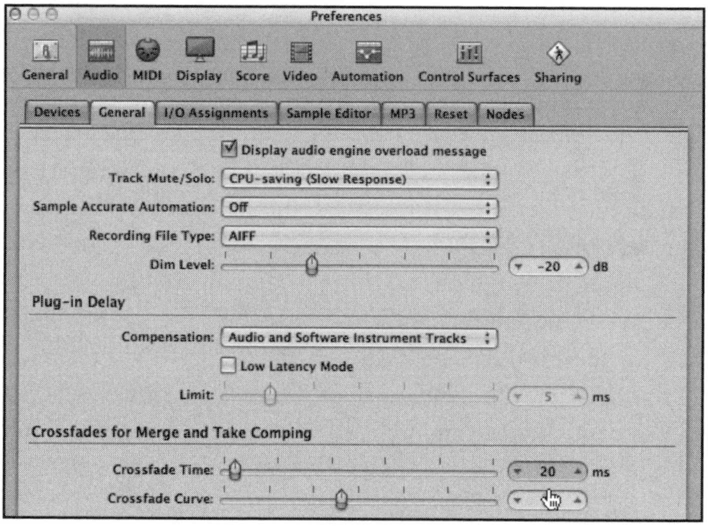

Fig. 7.48: Set the crossfades for Merge and Take Comping (bottom) in the Audio > General section of Preferences.

Your comp references multiple takes, which are stored across various sectors of your hard drive. Playing back a comp while playing back many other audio tracks places an unnecessary strain on your system. Once you have decided on a final comp, you can save some CPU and lighten the load on your hard drive by flattening your comp. *Flattening* is similar to bouncing, as it prints your final comp onto a single audio track. You'll notice you have the option to Flatten as well as the option to Flatten and Merge. Let's discuss what makes these two options different.

Flatten. This will take all the referenced portions of your audio regions and place them into one track to represent your comp. You will notice that each highlighted portion is an individual region, and the regions are marked with crossfades. This means you can manipulate the various regions in the Arrange window. You'll also notice you can see the crossfades for the first time (see **Fig. 7.49**).

Flatten and Merge. This function also takes all the referenced portions of your audio regions and places them into a single track; however, the final track is represented as a single region. Both of these functions will replace your take folder. You can always undo these moves to return to your take folder; or if this presents an issue, you can always select the Export to New Track option. This is essentially the Flatten command; however, the flattened comp will appear as a new track, leaving your take folder intact.

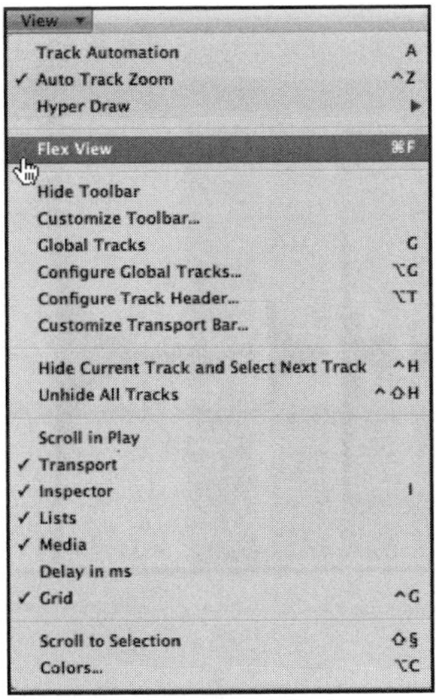

Fig. 7.49: Choose the Flatten option to create a comp with crossfades and various takes included in one complete take.

FLEX-ABILITY

Logic Pro 9 has really stepped up to the plate with its new editing features. These new additions make this incredibly musical software more like the other pro DAWs that have dominated the market for so many years. The program's multiple track editing capability, complex transient detection, and different types of time compression and expansion, all with specific algorithms for different types of audio, are key new features. Having the ability to phase-lock tracks is the way to go for editing drums or anything recorded with multiple microphones. The list goes on and on regarding what a big step Logic has taken in the audio editing area. Longtime Logic bashers will have to "man up" and admit that Logic Pro 9 is starting to set the pace, or has at least caught up with the main frontrunners in professional audio engineering.

Flex Time Editing

"Flex Time Editing" is pretty much the same thing that other programs call "elastic audio." It's a nondestructive way of editing audio to fix the timing on single or multiple tracks. You can even use it to quantize audio as if it were MIDI information. My best advice for using Flex Time Editing is to experiment with it a lot and learn what you can about the modes and how to use them.

Flex Time Editing revolves around a set of markers called transient markers that identify specific points, or transients, in an audio file. The type of audio you are manipulating will play a big role in which "mode" of Flex Time you use. When you choose a mode for a track, you are choosing the way your computer analyzes the audio on that particular track. There are six modes to choose from.

SLICING FLEX MODE

This mode is unique compared to the other Flex modes, because it does not apply time compression and expansion to the original audio while you are applying Flex Editing. It slices the audio at all transients. This makes it the best mode for drum tracks, percussion tracks, or any other type of track in which you would like to preserve the attack, release, and length of the original audio. Be aware of the Fill Gaps, Decay, and Slice Length settings that are found in the Inspector.

RHYTHMIC FLEX MODE

This is the best mode for rhythmic guitars, keyboard parts, and even Apple Loops. Its main parameters of interest are Loop Length, Decay, and the Loop Offset function, all found in the Inspector.

MONOPHONIC FLEX MODE

This mode time-stretches material in real time, with very good sonic quality. Solo instruments, vocals, and bass lines are best suited for this mode. If there is a lot of reverb and "junk" on the track this may not work for you, but if the track is dry, you will get the best results using this mode. The parameter of interest is the Percussive option. Turning this on from the Inspector is better for plucked string instruments and tonal percussion. It helps preserve the area around the transient markers, providing better "timing" results. Leaving it off is better for bowed or wind instruments.

POLYPHONIC FLEX MODE

This mode uses time-stretching based on phase vocoding. It is the most CPU-intensive of all the Flex modes, but it is awesome for complex polyphonic material. Use it on guitar tracks, piano, or choir tracks, and even complex mixes, and you'll be amazed at how well it works.

TEMPOPHONE FLEX MODE

This mode emulates the effect of a historical tape-based time-stretching instrument known as a tempophone. It has a machine-like sound that contains many artifacts. It is used more for creative processing and special effects. You can choose the Grain size and Crossfade length from 0, which produces hard artifacts, to the full grain length of 1, which tends to sound softer.

SPEED FLEX MODE

This mode time-stretches audio by playing the source material faster or slower, with the pitch changing accordingly. This is more of a fun mode, but can sometimes be used to fix percussion tracks.

MAKE A CHOICE

Now that you have an idea of which modes to use when experimenting with Flex Time, it is probably a good idea to learn how to turn it on and use it. First go to the View tab and turn on the Flex View selection, or use the keyboard shortcut Command + F (see **Fig. 7.50a**). Once on, you will notice a new Flex mode drop-down menu in the Global Tracks area of the Arrange window (see **Fig. 7.50b**). From there you can select the Flex mode options from the Inspector and use the Flex tool to manipulate the audio. Experiment as much as possible, and take a look at the QuickTime videos that come with this book. They will cover some of the more practical uses for Flex Time audio, including drum editing, quantizing audio, manipulating timing, and creative production techniques. Also, do yourself a favor and use the included drum tracks to do some drum comping and editing on multitracked drums using the new grouping features, as well as phase-locking and quantizing techniques.

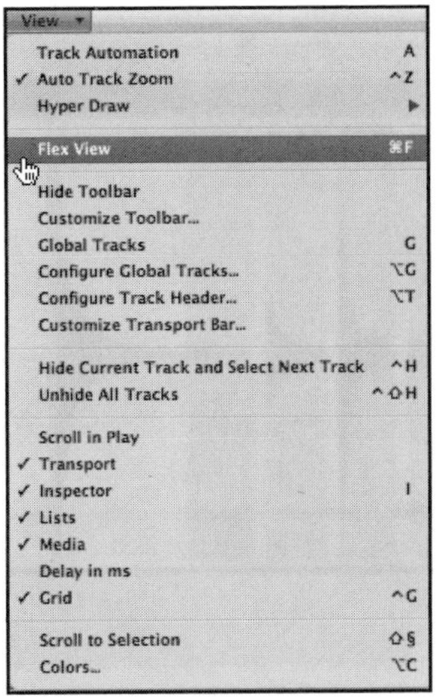

Fig. 7.50a: The Flex View on or off selector from the View menu.

Fig. 7.50b: The various Flex Modes drop-down menu.

THE SAMPLE EDITOR

The Arrange window is capable of sample-accurate editing. So why would Logic still include a dedicated Sample Editor? There are a few reasons why you might want to edit your audio with the Sample Editor instead of in the Arrange window. The ability to edit in the Arrange window is convenient, but for your serious audio editing needs the Sample Editor provides a few more functions, collectively known as the Digital Factory. This feature set gives you the ability to stretch time and pitch, as well as adjust levels and employ some creative techniques like reversing waveforms.

Let's have a look at the interface of the Sample Editor to get used to how to navigate it (see **Fig. 7.51a**). Along the top of the window are five menus that are specific to the Sample Editor. When we need to make edits and perform operations on our files, we'll visit these menus. Next these familiar menus is the on/off selector for a cool, brand-new feature of Logic Pro 9. This button turns on the Transient Editing mode. When you turn this mode on, two more buttons appear (see Fig. **7.51b**). These are the "transient confidence" buttons that allow you to add or subtract how many transient markers are detected. Next to the Transient Editing mode button is the Play button, which looks like a tiny speaker. Clicking it allows you to play your current selection in the Sample Editor. Next is the Loop button, which will loop your selection. Next to these buttons is a volume slider. Similar to the Loop browser, the Sample Editor has a dedicated volume that is conveniently connected to the Prelisten fader. Below and to the right of that is the info display, which shows us pertinent information about our selection—in particular, the length. Next to that you'll recognize the familiar tool selectors. Similar to the Arrange window, you have two tools—a primary and a secondary tool made available by holding down the Command key. You will notice that the selection of tools varies slightly. You have access to the Pointer, Eraser, Hand, Zoom, Solo, and Pencil tools. The Eraser and Hand tools are new. The Pointer tool lets you make a selection and, using the Hand tool as your secondary tool, easily move it. This is a "handy" complement to the Pointer tool in the Sample Editor. Spanning the length of the Sample

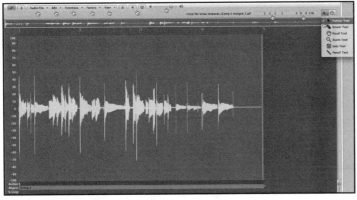

Fig. 7.51a: A close-up view of the Sample Editor.

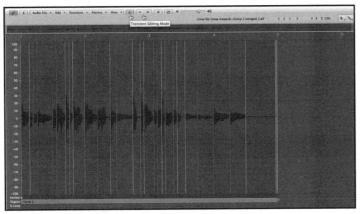

Fig. 7.51b: The new Transient Editing Mode on and off selection.

Editor is the Waveform overview, which represents the entire waveform, regardless of your zoom setting. You'll notice a shaded rectangle around your selection to let you know what part of the waveform you are viewing and editing. Similar to the Arrange window, you'll see the Ruler, which serves as a basic frame of reference for your waveform. Underneath that is the Waveform display, which shows us our current selection in detail.

Everything in this window is handled independently from the rest of Logic. Playback occurs independently of the playhead's position in the Arrange window. If you wish to hear your selection in context with your arrangement, simply use the Transport controls. To play back your selection, press the Play button in the Sample Editor window, or press the spacebar. Just be sure the Sample Editor is the active window. You can also make the Sample Editor start playback by double-clicking on any position on the Ruler. Also, if you would like to use the scrub audio function, click and hold on the Ruler and move the mouse over the selection. Playback will follow the speed and direction of the mouse. This is handy when you're trying to find a specific part quickly.

Another very nice feature is while you are looping playback, you can change your selection and the loop will update in real time. If you are trying to extrapolate a drum loop from an audio file, you can set the loop and keep changing your selection until it loops perfectly in time. Once you have made your selection, you can create a region from the selected area by going to the Sample Editor's Edit menu and under Selection choosing Region Function.

Zooming and scrolling in the Sample Editor functions the same as in the Arrange window. Be sure to adjust your scroll and zoom settings to match your needs. For even more accurate and focused editing, open the Sample Editor in a floating window and stretch the window to maximize your screen real estate. This will make your zoom and scroll settings seem less extreme. You should create a custom screenset to incorporate this feature.

Get used to using the following keyboard shortcuts for easy navigation in the Sample Editor. To go to the start of a selection, press the Left Arrow key. To go to the end of a selection, press the Right Arrow key. To go to the region's anchor, press the Down Arrow key. The region anchor is a reference point for the file. It is a small orange marker that is found in the Sample Editor on the lower left beneath the waveform. By default, the anchor is placed at the beginning of the region. This anchor is how the region is tied to the Ruler in the Arrange window. If you have an audio file that starts with silence, you may have to adjust the anchor to the peak of the first transient to keep the region in time. Click-and-drag the anchor to reposition it.

Here are a few more useful navigation tools we can explore. To find the loudest point in your audio file, under the Functions menu, select Search Peak; the playhead will jump to this peak. To do this quicker, use the keyboard shortcut Shift + P. To navigate to silent passages in your audio file, under the Functions menu select Search Silence, or press the keyboard shortcut Shift + S. This will place the playhead at the first point of silence.

To make a selection, simply click-and-drag with the Pointer tool. To select the entire audio file, under the Edit menu choose Select All, or press Command + A. Shift-click to resize your selection. The selection will change based on the proximity of your click. If you Shift-click closer to the in point, the selection will update by moving the in point to the new location. If your selection is closer to the out point, then the out point will update to your new selection. Also, by pressing Option-Shift when changing your selection, you are able to force your selection to the farther boundary.

Before we go any further with the Sample Editor, it is important to realize that all edits and processing done in this window are destructive. Any edit you make alters the original audio file. You can undo commands in the Sample Editor, but realize that the undo for the Sample Editor is separate from the rest of Logic's undo. To be safe, you should copy your audio files and edit the copies.

After you have made your selection, you can use the basic edit tools such as Copy, Paste, Delete, and Cut. These are all accessible in the Sample Editor's Edit menu. Cut and Copy both copy the selection to the clipboard so it may be pasted elsewhere. The difference between them is that when a selection is "cut," the original is removed. Paste will insert the contents of your clipboard at the position selected by the Pointer tool. Be careful, however: if you paste over existing audio, that data will be deleted and replaced. The Delete command is pretty simple, as it simply erases the selection and will shuffle the audio to the right of the deletion point to fill the gap.

One of the more advanced tools available to us in the Sample Editor is the Pencil tool. You can use this tool to manually correct pops and clicks. These annoying pops and clicks are generally located at the peak of a waveform. To find them, go to the Functions menu and select Search Peak. Scrub around the peak until you hear the anomaly. Be sure you are zoomed in enough to make an accurate edit. With the Pencil tool you can manually redraw the waveform; this will replace the spike and get rid of the pop. Remember that this type of editing is destructive and sometimes can do permanent damage to the files, so please be sure to editing duplicate audio tracks and not the originals.

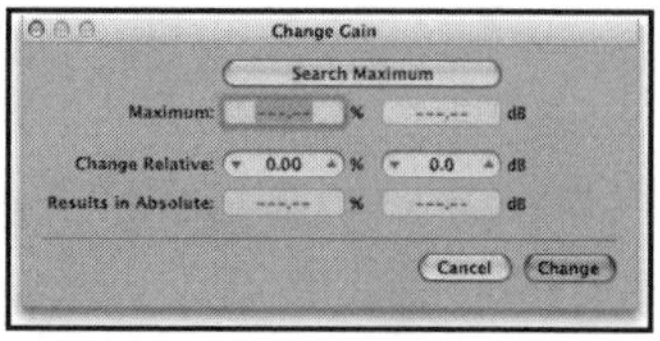

Fig. 7.52: Close-up view of the Change Gain function.

Another advanced tool available to us is the ability to change the level of an audio file. This feature is found in the Function menu under Change Gain (see **Fig. 7.52**). You can manually enter the amount in decibels you wish to change. If you click on Search Maximum, Logic will search for the maximum peak and use that as a reference for changing the gain of the audio file.

To perform a destructive fade, make a selection in your audio file and, from the Functions menu, choose Fade In or Fade Out, or press Control + I for a fade-in and Control + O for a fade-out. While you may not want to use fades in the Sample Editor the same way you do in the Arrange window, they are still very important. Using a fade-in will ensure that your region starts at zero volume, minimizing the risk for clicks and pops later on. The fades you perform in the Sample Editor are likely to be very short.

Remember that when you delete a portion from the Sample Editor, the selection gets shuffled so there's no gap. If you wish to overwrite audio with silence, you can tell the Sample Editor to stripe an amplitude value of zero over the selected area. This is great for removing background noise. To add silence to your selection, go to the Function menu and select Silence, or simply use the keyboard shortcut Control + Backspace.

The Reverse command is generally applied to the entire audio file, but can be used to reverse a selected portion of your audio file. To reverse your selection, select Reverse from the Functions menu, or use the keyboard shortcut Shift + Control + R. The Reverse command is an excellent creative tool. Try creating your own reverse cymbal or piano hit at the beginning of a song or as a "break" in the song to grab the listener's attention. Another cool trick is to reverse the reverb tail and place it at the beginning of your file. I suggest you take the time to play around with some of these ideas just for the sake of adventure and curiosity. It is important to make copies of your audio files before trying any of these ideas, however, as this type of editing is destructive.

Similar to changing the gain of an audio file is normalizing. When we normalize an audio file, we are essentially setting the maximum output of the file to a specified amount. This process will maximize the volume without distorting. Make a selection and choose Normalize from the Functions menu, or press Control + N.

NOTE

Because normalizing works by finding the highest volume peak, make sure you don't have any rough peaks that don't belong. If you have a low signal and you accidentally hit the microphone, you'll notice a spike—you do not want this as your reference for normalizing. Be sure to tame these peaks before normalizing your tracks. By default, the settings for normalizing an audio track are set to peak at 100 percent, or 0 dB. This will give you maximum volume, but leaves you no headroom if you want to apply EQ or other dynamic processors. You should try and leave approximately 3 dB of headroom when normalizing if you plan on applying any further processing to the track. To bring the peak value down, go to Settings under the Functions menu and bring it down at your discretion (see **Fig. 7.53**).

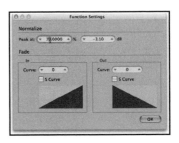

Fig. 7.53: Close-up view of the Normalize window.

THE DIGITAL FACTORY

Beyond the tools for basic editing and volume changes are powerful tools for pitch shifting and audio quantization. These Digital Factory tools can also be used to extract pitch and rhythm data from audio files. The Digital Factory features are all available from the Factory menu. We'll also go over the keyboard shortcuts for these tools.

It is important to note that Digital Factory processes will overwrite existing audio information. Be sure to work on copies of your audio files or leave yourself enough room to undo your changes. For this reason Logic has included a prelisten function so you can hear roughly how the processed file will turn out.

This way you don't have to wait for the process to finish before deciding it's not what you were going for.

One of the most amazing Digital Factory Tools is the Time and Pitch Machine (see **Fig. 7.54**). The Time and Pitch Machine allows you to tweak time and pitch simultaneously or separately, based on your preference. You may need to change the tempo of a track, but want to keep the pitch intact. Or you may want to change the pitch of a file without changing the time, or you may find it necessary to change both. This is a useful tool for shaping audio, and is great for creative applications. To open up the Time and Pitch Machine, press Control + P. Be sure to select the Time and Pitch Machine tab.

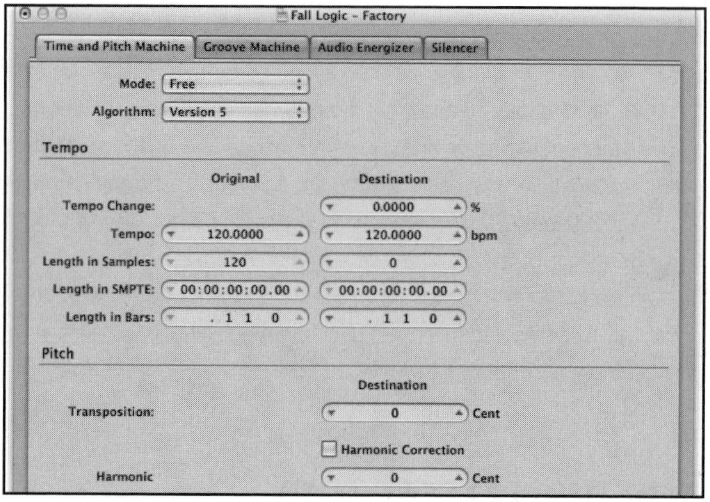

Fig. 7.54: The Time and Pitch Machine from the Factory menu in the Sample Editor.

MIDI EDITING

Now that we have a solid grasp of how to manipulate our audio regions in the Arrange window and in the Sample Editor, it is time to cover MIDI editing. Editing MIDI is very different from editing audio; however, many fundamentals still apply. You can edit MIDI regions in three different editors: the Piano Roll, Score Editor, and the Hyper Editor. The Piano Roll is the most common way to edit MIDI, as it presents a matrix-style way of editing individual events (see **Fig. 7.55**). When we talk about editing MIDI parameters, we will refer to them as *events*. There is much more to MIDI than just notes. For instance, when you press the sustain pedal on a keyboard, it is registered as a MIDI event. Changing any MIDI parameter creates an event; be sure to remember this when you start editing your MIDI performances.

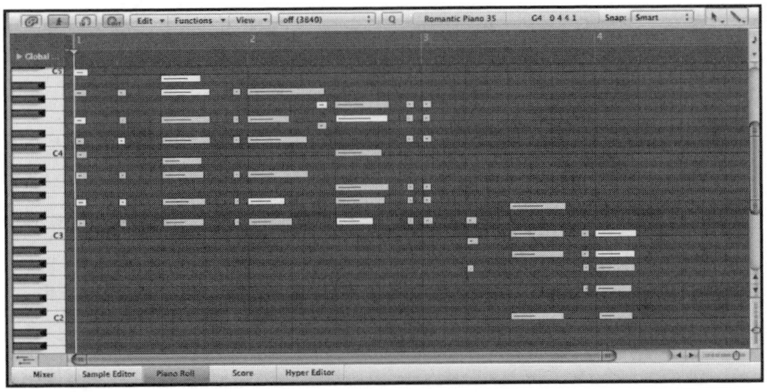

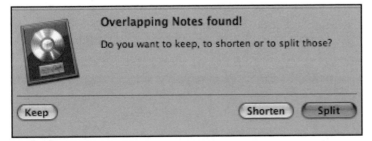

Fig. 7.55: A standard view of the Logic MIDI Piano Roll.

Let's revisit editing in the Arrange window. MIDI regions are similar to audio regions. Basic edit operations can be performed without leaving the Arrange window. Cut, Copy, and Paste are just a few examples of this. Be sure your zoom is set to an optimal level before performing edits. If you make an edit with overlapping notes, you'll be presented with a potentially confusing dialog (see **Fig. 7.56**). It is important to understand what your options are.

Overlapping Notes found!

Do you want to keep, to shorten or to split those?

Keep   Shorten   Split

Fig. 7.56: "Overlapping notes found!" message with option.

Keep. Performs the edit and leaves all notes unaltered. In this situation, the earlier of the two regions will keep the note. However, be aware that it will continue to play back even when the region ends. You can fix this by turning on Extended Region Parameters, which is located in the View menu of the Arrange window. When this option is enabled, you can see more info on a region in the Inspector. If you select "Clip Length," Logic will abruptly stop all MIDI events at the end of a region.

Shorten. This option will shorten the length of the note to where it was cut, and when the region ends the note will end.

Split. This will split the original note into two notes, one for each region. Each note will maintain its original length, pitch, and velocity. This is the default option. In some situations, you may have a MIDI event that needs to happen before the downbeat of your region. For example, a piano player might hold the sustain pedal down before playing. In **Fig. 7.57** we have a MIDI region. The white lines running vertically through the region represent the sustain pedal. If we drag the lower left-hand corner to the left, we can see more data (see **Fig. 7.58**). Notice that there is more information in this region than what we could previously see. The sustain pedal is hit earlier, and the first chord is actually played before the downbeat. To make life easier on you, Logic allows you to hide this data at the beginning of a region. It will still play back normally, though. This helps greatly when dragging to arrange your regions. It would be much harder to remember that the piano region starts a beat and a half before every other region. You can also drag the lower right-hand corner to see the full length of a note or event at the end of a region.

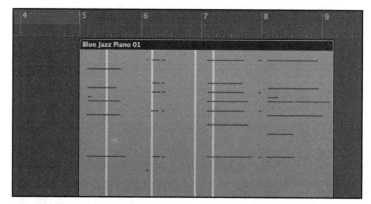

Fig. 7.57: Extended MIDI region view 1.

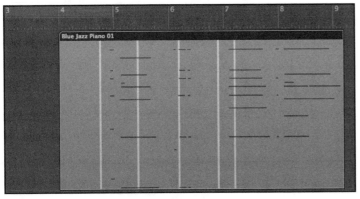

Fig. 7.58: Extended MIDI region view 2.

You'll primarily use the Piano Roll editor to edit MIDI events. You can open the Piano Roll editor within the Arrange window by selecting it from the bottom; however, just like the Sample Editor, it is a good idea to use a separate window that you can resize to suit your tastes. To bring up a separate window, use the keyboard shortcut Command + 6.

MIDI note events are represented by horizontal rectangles. The length of the rectangle determines the length of the note. The vertical placement of the note represents its pitch. Looking at the vertical piano strip on the left can serve as a quick reference. The horizontal placement of the note represents its place in time. It is easy to reference where you are because of the time grid drawn in the background. You'll notice the MIDI notes have different colors. This not only makes the MIDI regions nice to look at, but the colors also have a function: they represent the velocity of each note. The MIDI range runs from 0 to 127; a scale universal to MIDI. In the case of a knob, 0 represents the off position and 127 the on position. This scale also applies to the velocity of MIDI notes. Soft notes are bluish in tint while louder notes are red. Yellow and green lie in the middle.

Along the top of the Piano Roll Editor you will see a few familiar tools and some new indicators. The first new indicator is an info display that shows us the current selection. If you have opened up a single region and have no notes highlighted, this will read "1 region." Once you start selecting notes, it will represent the current number of highlighted notes. You can see the current location of your cursor in the info display window. This is a grid, so your cursor has an X and Y position. These are translated to Note for the X axis and Position in Time for the Y axis.

We also have our Tool selectors and Snap menu. By default, your primary tool is the Pointer. The default secondary tool is the Pencil tool. The Pencil tool can be used a few ways. For instance, you can use it to draw in new notes, or if you click-and-drag while creating a new note, you can change its length. A help tag will pop up to show you the length as it changes. Also, the Finger tool can be used similarly to the Pointer tool, but if a note's length is very short, it may be hard to resize with the Pointer. Use the Finger tool in this situation.

Remember that the same selection tools apply here as they do elsewhere. For example, rubber-banding a selection of notes, or pressing Shift while making a selection, will allow you to select multiple notes or add to your selection. To select all notes of the same pitch, click on the corresponding piano key, and all pitches in the selected region will be highlighted. All of the same basic edit functions also work with your MIDI selection. In addition to the basic cut, copy, and paste options, you can also move the selected events. Moving notes up and down will change their pitch, and moving notes left and right will affect their placement in the timeline. When moving notes, the selection will snap to the grid based on what you have chosen from the Snap menu. Remember, you can use the Pointer, Finger, or Pencil tool to click-and-drag to change the length of a note. To change the length of multiple notes, simply highlight the notes you wish to change, and all selected notes will change respectively.

Note that the sustain pedal changes the amount of time a note is played, but that amount of time is not reflected in the Piano Roll Editor. If you play a single 16th note and hold down the sustain pedal, the Piano Roll Editor will show a 16th note despite the fact that the note plays for much longer. To view the length of notes as the sustain pedal affects them, select the Sustain Pedal to Note Length option in the Note Events section of the Function menu. If you wish to view when the sustain pedal is used in this window, go to the View menu and under Hyper Draw, select Sustain Pedal (see **Fig. 7.59**). A value of 0 represents off and 127 represents on.

Fig. 7.59: MIDI controller event view of a sustain pedal.

If you need to make the same change to many notes, set the same endpoint for all selected notes by pressing and holding the Shift key while dragging a note; this sets all notes to end at the same time. To make all notes equal in length, make your selection and hold Option + Shift as you drag one note; this makes all notes the same length. This can speed up your workflow when cleaning up your MIDI performances.

One nice thing about editing MIDI is that there are more levels of undo than there are in the Sample Editor. Have a look at your undo history by pressing Option + Z. This list shows you the last 30 moves you've made. This number can be changed in Global Preferences under Editing (see **Fig. 7.60**). As you click through

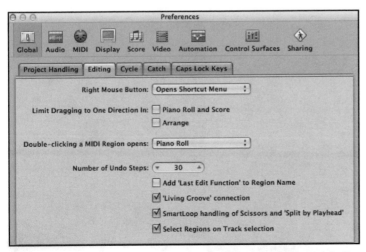

Fig. 7.60: MIDI undo preferences can be set from the Editing tab in the General Menu.

this list, all events below your selection appear grayed out, as they will be negated if you revert to that stage of undo. Be sure to use Undo/Redo carefully, and when in doubt, perform a Save As.

One of the most common features of MIDI editing is quantizing. Quantizing notes realigns them to a specific value. When you capture a MIDI performance, you have the ability to view your timing against the grid of the Piano Roll Editor. You can quantize your performance to line it up perfectly to the grid. Make a selection and pull down the Quantize window to select the level of quantization you would like (see **Fig. 7.61**). If your performance consisted of nothing shorter than an eighth note, there would be no reason to set the value to anything shorter than an eighth note; however, if your performance included 16th notes, they would be shifted to the nearest eighth note value on the grid. Quantization can really enhance a performance, but be sure to use it tastefully, as quantizing too much can remove some of the personality of your performance and make it sound too metronomic. You can undo a quantize without worrying about wasting your undo levels. Quantizing is nondestructive in Logic; you can change the level from eighth to 16th to tuplet without worrying that you are permanently editing your performance. If you quantize a performance and then decide you do not want it quantized, simply choose Off from the Quantize menu. Playing around with quantization and listening to how it affects your

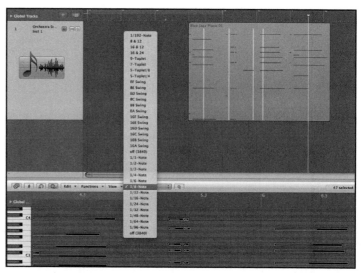

Fig. 7.61: Quantize selection menu.

MIDI performance is one of the quickest ways to get an idea of how it may or may not help you. You will probably find that using quantization will help in some situations, but not all of them.

Quantizing works best when aligning a performance to a strict grid. But sometimes, this doesn't work as well with syncopated and swung rhythms. For this reason, Logic offers a few swing presets. They may seem a bit confusing to understand at first, but simply put, an 8 represents an eighth note, and 16 represents a 16th note. The letters refer to the amount of "swing" in the preset. "A" represents a swing value of 50 percent, while "E" represents a more extreme swing at 71 percent. Again, trial and error and using your ears is the name of the game. Be careful when quantizing someone else's performance, as you may change their intended performance.

If you are really determined to enhance an average performance, there are a few more options you can try using. These options are found under the Transform section of the Functions window. These tools were designed to manipulate MIDI data to simulate human characteristics, and do a nice job of making a performance sound less like a machine. Let's have a look at a few of them, starting with the Crescendo tool. This will take your selection and generate a gradual increase in volume. **Fig. 7.62** shows the performance pre-crescendo and **Fig. 7.63**

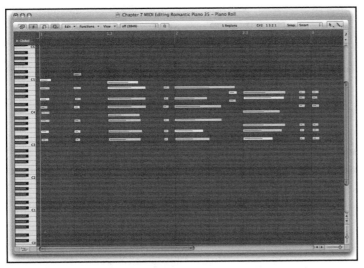

Fig. 7.62: MIDI notes view, pre-Crescendo tool.

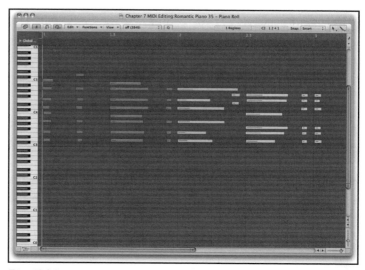

Fig. 7.63: MIDI notes view, post-Crescendo tool.

illustrates it post-crescendo. Another Transform tool is called "Humanize." This tool emulates how a human might play a part. For instance, when playing chords on a piano, you might not hit all the notes at exactly the same time or with the same velocity. Try hard-quantizing a part to the grid and then using some of these transformation tools. I've found that some of these tools work better when they are used on parts that have been quantized to the grid, rather than adding a "swing feel" on top of the "Humanize" function on a human performance.

Remember that music is art and can't always be fixed with the push of a button. Sometimes you may need to go with how the musician played the part or have them redo the part until everyone is happy. This is usually the best way to keep the natural "feel" of a performance that a computer just cannot produce.

Another fun, creative tool I'd like to mention before we move on is the Double Speed selection. Suppose you have an eighth-note arpeggio you like, but you would like to hear it as 16th notes. With a click of this button, you can audition your part in double time. If you think ahead, you can really get creative with this one.

SONG TO REGION LENGTH

This function is great for those of you who like to use audio loops as a source of inspiration. A common scenario when working this way is if you have an audio loop that is exactly four bars in length, but you aren't 100 percent sure what the tempo is. Now you want to build a song around this loop, and you know your project will go much more smoothly if you can figure out the tempo and lock it to the grid. Song to Region Length makes this possible, and it's a snap. Here is a quick example of how it works. Let's start with a new session. As usual, the default tempo is 120. Let's bring in our loop from the Loop browser. Look at **Fig. 7.64**, and notice that this region is roughly six bars long. If you look closely, the region doesn't stop exactly at six bars. This may appear confusing, but it will make sense in a moment. If we listen to the loop and disable the click track, we can clearly hear that it is a four-bar loop. But because we don't know the tempo, it is hard to set a cycle region accurately. Because we know this loop is perfectly edited to four bars, simply tell Logic to set the locators to the region's length by pressing Control + =. Now we can audition the loop and verify it is indeed four bars, and it is a clean edit.

Fig. 7.64: A new loop that is slightly more than six bars.

NOTE

In the event your loop isn't perfectly edited, you can open it in the Sample Editor and trim it so the region cycles flawlessly.

Once we know it's four bars for sure, we can readjust our locators to a four-bar selection (see **Fig. 7.65**). Now let's set Logic to the tempo of the loop. To do this, go to the Options menu, and under Tempo, select Adjust Tempo Using Region and Length

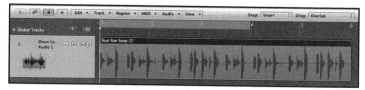

Fig. 7.65: A clean four-bar selection.

Locators. You can also use the keyboard shortcut Command + T. Logic will ask you if you wish to create a tempo change or if you want to change the global tempo. In our case we want to globally change the tempo. Notice our tempo is now set to 95 (see **Fig. 7.66**).

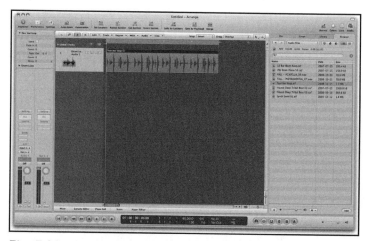

Fig. 7.66: A four-bar loop at the new tempo.

As you can see, this is very useful, but what if you need to do just the opposite? Let's say you would like to adjust the tempo of your imported region to match the tempo of your project. We can do that too.

REGION TO SONG TEMPO

Using the same example, let's say I have a great sampled bass line that I want to put over this drum loop. Again, you have a four-bar loop, but you are not sure of the tempo. In this case, you can't do what you did last time, as the drums will be out of time. In order to get this new loop to match the tempo, let's first import it and have a look. Turn off the metronome and set the locators to the region to verify it's a clean loop and is indeed four bars long. Remember, if it isn't exactly four bars, you can use the Sample Editor to edit the loop. Now that we know we have a perfect four-bar loop, we need to set it to the tempo of the rest of our project. Notice how it doesn't quite match up now (see **Fig. 7.67**). We know it's a four-bar loop, so let's set our locators to the same four-bar selection as our drums. Go to the Audio menu and select Adjust Region Length to Locators. Our loops will now be perfectly in sync with each other (see **Fig. 7.68**). Remember when applying time and pitch changes to audio, you shouldn't expect miracles. It is always easier to speed up audio than it is to slow it down. You'll notice more artifacts when you slow audio down because Logic has to create information that doesn't exist, whereas increasing the tempo removes samples and squeezes the file together.

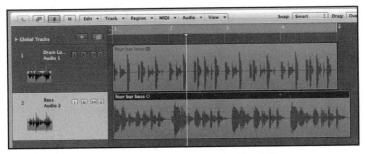

Fig. 7.67: Adding a four-bar bass loop and making it fit.

Fig. 7.68: Example of audio bin files after they have been stretched.

FINAL THOUGHTS

Once again, we've come to the end of a very extensive chapter. You are not expected to memorize everything in this book, but since you may end up referring to this particular chapter quite often, you should read it at least a few times while sitting at your computer and follow along. Remember that the QuickTime files that are included with this book will also help you a great deal. They include the techniques that are commonly used by skilled Logic operators, in practical, everyday-use situations.

Editing is a skill and an art. It requires a lot of practical application and creative experimentation. You may learn the basic functions of the tools rather quickly, but advanced editing skills will take countless hours of practice and a fair amount of real experience to acquire. Keep in mind that there are many ways to execute the same function in Logic. This book is designed to give you insight into some "Power Tools" that will instantly make you a better Logic 9 operator, and give you an awareness of several things that may have taken you a long time to figure out on your own. Awareness of these features is almost the most important thing. I suggest you use what works best for you, and develop your own method of working, but remember to be open to using other tools or workflows that might increase your proficiency too.

Don't forget: make sure you try to answer the Logic Tune-Up questions, review the Power Tips, and do your best to memorize the summary of keyboard shortcuts that are included at the end of each chapter.

POWER TIPS FOR CHAPTER 7

1. To quickly make several customized channels, start by creating one, exactly as you like. For instance create a new track, assign three separate bus sends on the channel, make one of them a pre-fader send for headphone mixes, and then select the desired output. Then, use the keyboard shortcut (Command + D) to duplicate the track as many times as needed. This will save you a lot of time once you get the hang of it.

2. When using Logic's comping features, you may wish to have a gap, or silence, between the individual phrases or audio. To make this happen, before resizing your selection, press

and hold Shift; this will allow you to resize your selection without constraining you to shuffle against other selections. You can shorten a region's selection to insert silence.

3. For maximum efficiency while Quick Swipe Comping, set a play range cycle that is the length of your comp. As playback loops you can make changes to your comp and hear them reflected in real time.

4. To make your Marquee selection as accurate as possible, hold down Shift + Control while making your selection. This will make your selection accurate to the sample or tick. This only works if the Marquee tool is the secondary tool.

5. To set your locators to your Marquee selection, go to the Region menu in the Arrange window and select Set Locators by Regions, or use the keyboard shortcut Control + =.

6. If you would like to scrub audio, click and hold on the Ruler and move the mouse. Playback will follow the speed and direction of the mouse. This is handy when you're trying to find a specific part quickly.

7. During loop playback, you can change your selection and the loop will update in real time. If you are trying to extrapolate a drum loop from an audio file, you can set the loop and keep changing your selection until it loops perfectly in time. Once you have made your selection, you can create a region from the selected area by going to the Sample Editor's Edit menu and under Selection choose the Region function.

8. You might notice that you can't edit Apple Loops in the Sample Editor. The files are locked to prevent destructive edits. To get around this, simply export the selected Apple Loop as an audio file of your choice (be sure to match your project's sample rate and bit depth), import the audio file, and edit away!

9. While editing MIDI, the Finger tool can be used similarly to the Pointer tool, but if a note's length is very short, it may be hard to resize with the Pointer. Try using the Finger tool in this situation.

10. Quantizing works best when aligning a performance to a strict grid. But this doesn't work as well with syncopated and swung rhythms. For this reason, Logic offers a few swing presets. The way these presets are labeled may look a bit confusing at first, but in simple terms, an 8 represents an eighth note, and 16 represents a 16th note. The letters refer to the amount of "swing" in the preset. "A" represents a swing value of 50 percent, while "E" represents a more extreme swing at 71 percent. Again, trial and error and using your ears is the name of the game.

KEYBOARD SHORTCUT SUMMARY

Here is a list of some keyboard shortcuts that are either mentioned in the text or used in the QuickTime tutorials that accompany this chapter. Try to memorize as many of these commands as quickly as you can. Knowing the menus is valuable, but knowing the shortcuts saves you time and is a real convenience once you get used to them.

KEYBOARD SHORTCUT	FUNCTION
Command + 1	Launches Arrange floating window
Command + 2	Launches Mixer floating window
Command + 0	Launches Event List floating window
Command + 3	Launches Score floating window
Command + 4	Launches Transform floating window
Command + 5	Launches Hyper Editor floating window
Command + 6	Launches Piano Roll floating window
Command + 7	Launches Transport floating window
Command + 8	Launches Environment floating window
Command + 9	Launches Audio Bin floating window
Command + A	Selects All

Command + D	Duplicates selected track
Command + T	Global tempo change using the selected region's tempo
Option + Command + I	Imports screenset data
Shift + Control-click-and-drag	Adjusts the curve of crossfades
Shift + P	Search Peak
Shift + S	Search Silence
Shift + Control + R	Reverses selection
Control + I	Fade In
Control + O	Fade Out
Control + Backspace	Adds Silence
Control + N	Normalizes selection
Control + P	Opens Time and Pitch Machine
Control + =	Set Locators to region length
Left Arrow key	Start of a selection in the Sample Editor
Right Arrow key	End of a selection in the Sample Editor
Down Arrow key	Selects the region's anchor

LOGIC 9 TUNE-UP

1. To save time when setting up multiple independent inputs on several tracks, be sure to select the _____ _____ option. Channel 1 will have Input 1, Channel 2 will have Input 2, and so on; this is limited to the number of inputs available on your interface.

2. A nice time saver when naming several tracks in one sitting is to double-click the first track and name it. After typing in the new name, advance to the next track-name box by simply pressing the _____ key.

3. To rename, duplicate, or delete screensets, you have to use the Screenset menu, as no keyboard shortcuts are assigned to these functions. You can, however, assign keyboard shortcuts to these commands from the _____ _____ window.

4. By default, the Pointer tool and the Marquee tool are the primary and secondary tools while in the Arrange window. However, you can also choose and assign a third tool for easy access. This third tool will be mapped to your _____ function. Right-clicking brings up a shortcut menu.

5. You can also access the zoom tool without making it one of your two or three default tools or by bringing up the Tools menu. Simply press _____ to temporarily use the zoom tool.

6. You can get really tight and mathematical with your fades by adjusting them in the Inspector's _____ _____ box. From this box, you can adjust the length in samples, as well as the curve for the fade-in and fade-out.

7. For more accurate and focused editing, open the Sample Editor in a floating window and stretch the window to maximize your _____ _____ _____. This will make your zoom and scroll settings seem less extreme, and easier on the eye. You should create a custom screenset to incorporate this feature into your standard workflow.

8. By default the settings for normalizing an audio track are set to peak at 100 percent, or 0 dB. This will give you maximum volume, but leaves you no headroom if you want to apply EQ or other dynamic processors. You should leave approximately 3 dB of headroom when normalizing if you plan on further processing. To bring the peak value down, choose Settings under the _____ menu and specify the desired peak settings.

9. While editing MIDI, if you need to set the same endpoint for all selected notes, press and hold the_____ key while dragging any one of the selected notes. This sets all notes to end at the same time.

10. To make all notes equal in length, make your selection and hold the _____ + _____ keys as you drag one note; this makes all notes the same length. This can speed up your workflow when cleaning up your MIDI performances.

Mixing and Mastering Essentials

A LITTLE PREPARATION GOES A LONG WAY

Here we are in the final chapter, and we still have plenty of information to cover. By this point, you probably realize the many hats a modern music artist has to wear. More than likely, you'll act as the computer tech, musician, audio engineer, and music producer all at the same time. In this book, we have already covered proper project setup and file management, gone over how to use the powerful and inspiring creative tools that come with Logic Pro 9, and learned some very helpful editing techniques. Hopefully, you have been following along with the book's examples and have created your own sample project along the way. If you have done so, you should have all of your parts recorded, submixed, and edited, and you probably have a decent-sounding rough mix, too. Now that the music is recorded and edited, and you are happy with all of its elements, it is time to learn some of the techniques that mix engineers use to make tracks really come alive.

It's nice that Logic allows us to produce and mix as we build our project. By doing so, it lets us get an idea of whether what we hear in our head is being presented properly. This used to be called pre-production. The original goal of pre-production was to capture the essence of the song, and the basic "sound" of the band, so that in the studio, the engineers and producers would have a better idea of how to record, produce, and mix the artists. These days, the line between pre-production and real production has been blurred. Some of the pre-production tracks you use in Logic (or any other DAW) may often end up in your final mix. This is amazing, if you think about it. Logic gives you the ability to go from the home or project studio computer to the store shelf, ready to sell your music to the world.

With that in mind, when you use great-sounding presets on a single track, take a step back and analyze what makes the track sound so good. Also, keep in mind that if you have a bunch of individual tracks that sound good on their own, that doesn't mean they will sound good when blended together. This is because the same frequency content will try to share the same space in the stereo field. If multiple tracks contain many of the same frequencies, it will be hard to get all of the instruments in your mix to both stand out clearly on their own and still be part of the mix. As you gain experience mixing, you'll learn how to make calculated compromises so that certain instruments "sit" better in the mix and don't just sound good on their own. Sometimes things may not even sound that good on their own but will sound great in the mix.

Logic Pro 9 comes bundled with a very nice assortment of professional-quality mixing tools. If used properly, these tools can make your mixes "radio ready" without your having to buy any third-party plug-ins. If you take the time to learn some of the fundamental principles behind mixing audio, your mixes will get a lot better—much faster than if you just used the factory presets and left it at that. The factory presets are great for initial inspiration, but they weren't designed for specific situations. If you don't mind your productions sounding a bit "generic," then by all means, use the presets; you will have a very nice-sounding "generic" mix. However, if you take the time to learn about what you are doing, you will have much more control over how your overall mix turns out. You may find that the preset settings are a great starting point and use them all the time, or you may discover that you have so much control over your mix that you will only use the custom settings that you've created and stored over time. Either way, both scenarios should inspire you to keep chasing the perfect mix. You'll more than likely never be totally satisfied, but you'll eventually develop a sense of when "it's as good as it's gonna get" and you'll be able to step away from your mix, and let your baby go.

With all this in mind, be assured that this chapter will continue to help you develop the necessary skills to achieve quality results. Optimizing your resources and being creative with your mixing techniques can often be overlooked out of haste. So be patient, practice good habits, and you will get the most out of your system. An optimized system means more creative freedom, which will greatly improve your mixes.

RESOURCES

Fig. 8.1a: Load Meters (CPU/HD usage meters) in the Transport.

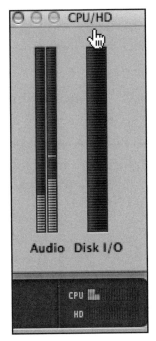

Fig. 8.1b: Load Meters as a floating window. (Double-click in the Transport.)

In earlier chapters, we learned that individual tracks eat up CPU power, as do software instruments and plug-ins, so it is a good idea to keep an eye on your computer's resources by monitoring the CPU display (see **Fig. 8.1a**). Another cool way to view this feature is to use the keyboard shortcut Option + X. This brings up a more precise floating-window CPU/HD usage meter (see **Fig. 8.1b**). The reason it is so important to know how much "power" you have left is because it will sometimes affect which plug-ins you use while mixing. Resource management plays a big role because the different individual plug-in components also take up resources. Look at this screenshot of the Channel EQ (see **Fig. 8.2**). You can quickly see which parameters of the EQ are active. This is easy to determine because the active EQ parameters are highlighted in blue. However, if you take a closer look, you will notice that 1440 Hz is the only frequency being affected on this EQ plug-in. If only one out of the eight bands is being used, but several of the bands are still active, you are wasting precious CPU resources. Therefore, you should either deselect the ones that are unused or simply choose an EQ with fewer bands. Also, don't forget that you can freeze your tracks or bounce them in place when you are done tweaking them. These are the most effective ways to free up resources on your computer and are employed quite often at this stage of production. If you have forgotten how to freeze your tracks or bounce them in place, be sure to go back through the book and refresh your memory.

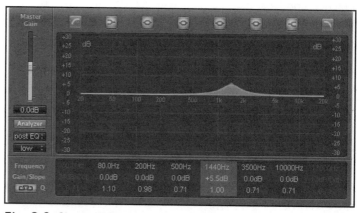

Fig. 8.2: Channel EQ with filters off. One of six enabled bands is being used. Bypassing unused EQ bands will save processing power.

You can also max out your I/O buffer size from the Core Audio tab, found under the Audio tab in the Preferences pane. Also, be sure you turn low-latency monitoring off to free up even more CPU for mixing. The button for this is on the Transport and is shaped like a mini speedometer; when active the button turns orange (see **Fig. 8.3**).

Fig. 8.3: Low Latency Monitoring button in the transport.

Mentioned above are some great ways to conserve and monitor your system resources, but if these aren't enough and you have an extra Mac at your disposal (or even a few), Logic has an awesome feature that allows you to offload some processing to your spare

Mac(s). Most audio enthusiasts have purchased a few different computers over the years, and it can be frustrating to buy a new computer and find within a matter of months that it is no longer the latest and greatest computer it once was. The options are to sell it and cut your losses, or keep it and reminisce about how much you paid for it not that long ago and what a great computer it used to be. However, one really cool thing about Logic is that it gives us the option of taking advantage of the processing power of these "spare computers." This resourceful way of making good use out of our old computers is referred to as distributed audio processing or "using nodes."

Nodes

Distributed processing, or chaining multiple computers, or nodes, together to pool their resources, has been used for many years in other professions. More recently, this technology has been made available for pro audio and video applications, and Apple has openly embraced it by allowing distributed processing to be done on Macintosh computers over an Ethernet cable.

To take advantage of this, you need to have the Logic Pro Node installed on all the Macs you plan to use. The Node installer is available on the Logic Studio install disc. You can also copy the Logic Node application to a flash drive or to your extra computers over a network. This brings us to the most important step: networking.

Note: These extra computers do not require individual licenses for Logic, nor do they need Logic or any other hardware or software to be installed; you only need the latest version of OS X and the Logic Node application.

Your Macs might be on a home network, but not all existing networks will be ideal for node-based processing. For example, you can't use nodes over a wireless network. You need to use Category-6 Ethernet cables for all of your node-based computers. If you only have one spare Mac, you can simply connect the cable between the two ports, and the Macs can do the network translation. If you plan on running more than one Mac, you'll need an Ethernet switch. Try to stay away from hubs, as they tend to run in serial. You need your data streamed in parallel. A small six-port gigabit switch will work just fine.

NOTE

Gigabit refers to 10/100/1000 speed, and requires Category-6 Ethernet cable, also sometimes referred to as "Cat-6" cable.

After installing the Node application, launch it on your nodes (other computers) before launching Logic Pro on your primary system. You may have to disable your software firewall. This is located in your System Preferences under Security. The default firewall settings should work fine. After the nodes are launched, open Logic Pro on your primary system and go to the Preferences menu. Under Audio, click on the Nodes tab (see **Fig. 8.4a**). Check the box to enable Logic Nodes. If done properly, you should see your computers listed. The name displayed is the share name of your computer. This can be found and changed in the System Preferences under Sharing. Be sure to select the checkboxes next to the nodes you wish to use. Also make sure that these node computers aren't engaging in any other network activity such as Internet browsing, as this will greatly affect performance.

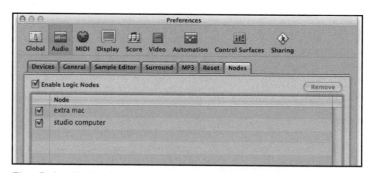

Fig. 8.4a: Node settings in the Preferences > Audio > Nodes window.

Now we're going to add another button to our track header. On your primary system, go to the View menu and select Configure Track Header. This button will allow us to enable and disable node processing for selected tracks (see **Fig. 8.4b**). Turn on the node for a track and it will turn green, indicating it is active.

So where do nodes really come in handy? The first thing that comes to mind is while using CPU-intensive software synthesizers and effects, such as Sculpture and Space Designer. Not all plug-ins work with nodes, however. Many third-party plug-ins work, but they require the plug-in to be installed on each machine. Sometimes this means paying for an additional license, and I wouldn't recommend it; just offload your other plug-ins to the nodes and keep the non-node-compatible plug-ins on your local system.

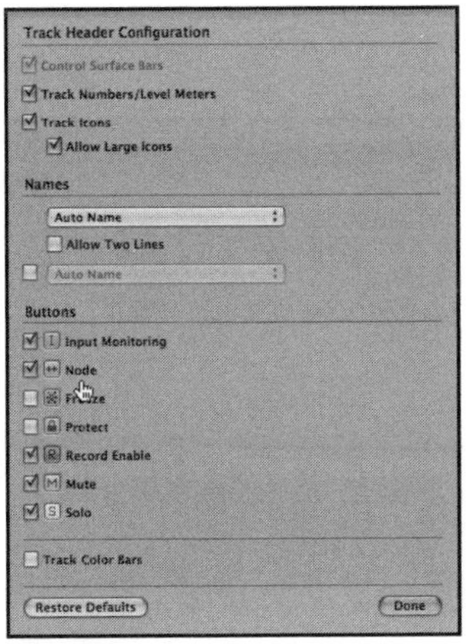

While nodes can do a lot of heavy lifting, telling them what to process and when to process it requires extra horsepower, and will cause massive latency. When mixing this is not an issue at all, but naturally this makes recording with active nodes impractical.

What can't nodes do? EXS instruments. The samples for EXS instruments are audio files, and these files would have to exist on your nodes. Since latency is already an issue, the amount of throughput needed to stream a sample library via Ethernet wouldn't make much sense; therefore EXS instruments and Ultrabeat must be processed on your local machine.

Tracks are dynamically assigned to nodes based on many variables. There isn't a great way to monitor how much is being offloaded to your nodes and how much performance gain you are getting. Naturally your mileage will vary based on the robustness of your network and the speed of the node's CPU. If you have an extra computer or three lying around, you should try this out. You will notice a nice improvement if Nodes is used properly.

Fig. 8.4b: Enable Node selector in the Track Header Configuration window.

MASTER FADER AND STEREO OUTPUT CHANNELS

Every new project automatically creates a Stereo Output channel fader as well as a Master fader. The Output channel represents the physical audio outputs available on your interface. If you have a two-channel interface, you will only see "Out 1-2," whereas if you have an interface with 16 outputs, you will also see "Out 3-4," "Out 5-6," etc. Output channels are just like any other channel in that they have the same number of inserts for adding plug-ins, they can be automated, and so on. Also in Logic 9 you have the option of selecting mono outputs. This is really nice if you are using an external analog console or a nice summing bus to sum your audio before printing your final mix prior to the mastering sessions. You also have the option of assigning all of your outputs in ascending order at the same time. To do this, simply hold down the Option key before you make your selection.

However, if you are merely using a few mastering plug-ins and bouncing your final mix from your Stereo Out 1-2 channels, then naturally you can select the Bounce option from the File menu, or you can use the "Bnce" button on your Output channel (see **Fig. 8.5**).

The Master fader allows you to bring the relative level of your mix up or down. This Master fader is linked to the volume slider on the Transport and serves as a quick and easy way to adjust the overall level of your mix, in a proportional fashion.

Fig. 8.5: Real-time Bounce button at the bottom of each channel strip.

When working with a rough mix or when you need to do a quick bounce, you'll probably load some mastering presets on the Output channel to boost your level to maximum without clipping. While this is a quick-and-easy way to get your mix's dynamics to even out, it is far from the most appropriate way to do a serious mastering session. If you do your mixing properly, on the individual channels, the Output channel's dynamics won't need to be doing all of the hard work to balance your mix. To get a good idea of how mixing and audio summing works, you should mix without a compressor/limiter on the Output channel. This will force you to get a decent mix without slamming the dynamics on the Output channel. It is not easier by any means, but in the end, your meticulous mixing will pay off.

EQUALIZATION

Equalization (EQ) gives you control over the frequency content of an audio signal. EQ allows us to shape our sound by adjusting various frequency parameters. The fundamental qualities of the waveform remain unchanged. EQ can be used to tweak and correct a signal to sound better, like cutting out some of the low mids of a kick drum to make it sound less muddy. EQ can also be used creatively, like boosting 1 kHz for a telephone/radio-like sound. Before we start applying EQ, however, we have to understand some theory.

Let's start with some of the basic terminology commonly used when dealing with EQ. These terms apply to outboard EQs as well as software-based EQs.

Frequency Spectrum

A frequency spectrum analyzer provides a visual representation of the frequencies in a given signal. The analyzer will react dynamically to the ever-changing incoming signal. You'll recognize the shapes; they should look similar to complex waveforms. By using a frequency spectrum analyzer, you'll be able to associate frequency with a visual source; in essence you'll be able to train your ears visually. Not every EQ has an analyzer built in. Most will only show you a graph-like representation of the changes you are making. The default Channel EQ for Logic has a powerful analyzer built in; to enable it, simply click on the Analyzer button during playback, and you'll see your EQ graph against the waveform of the audio track. You can then tweak and adjust your EQ and watch the signal change. You will be able to see what frequencies you are missing or have too much of, and adjust accordingly (see **Fig. 8.6**).

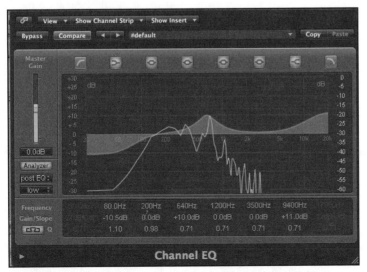

Fig. 8.6: The Frequency Analyzer on and off button is located just underneath the Master Gain control on the EQ plug-in.

Frequency Curve

The frequency curve of a signal is determined by the overall frequency content. In **Fig. 8.6** we can see which frequencies are most prevalent in our signal. This helps us to better decide what to boost and cut. When working with EQ you will discover early on that it is hard to mold the sound to match what you might hear in your head. This ability will come in time as you learn more about the fundamentals of how EQ works. Don't get too frustrated, though; it's still a good idea to adjust knobs and simply experiment.

Another method of ear training is visual. Sometimes it helps if you can see what it is you are listening for. I know it may sound strange, but mess around with the following options, and find out for yourself if they are of any help.

Just underneath the Analyzer button are two very important options for analyzing. There is a Pre or Post EQ option, so you can visualize the before, after, and during. Also there is a resolution meter with choices from low to high. Don't forget that each of these options, including the analyzer, use resources, so once you are done with analysis, turn the options off.

Do You Believe in Magic?

By now you have seen the countless presets available to us in Logic. Yet I can't stress enough that these should be used only as starting points. There is no such thing as a "magic setting" for an amazing sound. Some engineers will swear by certain settings, but those may not work so well for you. This is mostly because how the EQ will affect the sound depends on how the sound was captured, the musician's performance, the instrument, and so on. The same general rules of audio engineering will apply, which is why we can get away with sharing settings and using presets from time to time, but don't expect one magical setting to make your vocals sound amazing. Every voice or element is different, and therefore the EQ, dynamics settings, or time-based effects you apply should be just as unique.

Cutting vs. Boosting

A common habit when applying EQ is to lean more toward boosting a frequency rather than simply cutting one. For instance, you might be so focused on getting more "lows" out of your kick drum that you don't think about what frequencies should be taken out. My goal is to get you thinking about some of your options. You'll always have your "go to" settings, and those will eventually define your work, but it is the depth of your own knowledge that determines the quality and consistency of your mixes. I am not saying you should be some kind of walking audio engineering manual in order to have good mixes. What I am saying is, learn as much about the fundamentals as you can stand, and always be open to a "different" approach.

The next time you are about to EQ a source, try this. Set the bandwidth of your low mids to a very narrow setting. Crank up the gain a good 9–12 dB, and then slowly dial through the different frequencies until you hear the biggest offender. Once you have found this "ugly" frequency, change your bandwidth back to more of a bell shape, and then cut that "ugly" frequency by the desired amount. You may find that this style of corrective equalization will bring you closer to what you want without making huge changes to all of the other frequencies surrounding the biggest offender. It is certainly okay to boost frequencies, just be careful not to add so much gain that you are clipping the outputs. This is a common problem and I see this all too often with the hundreds of students I teach every year. Remember, sometimes less really is more. If you don't understand things like "set the bandwidth" or "boost 9–12 dB," that's okay. We will cover this type of thing in the next few sections of this chapter.

Frequency Interaction

You will notice that boosting or cutting the same frequency on different instruments will have different effects on the sound and frequency curve. This is because the fundamental frequencies of instruments differ, so when applying EQ you have to realize that your starting frequency curve will affect what you EQ. Every instrument or sound has a fundamental frequency range.

Applying EQ to an instrument's fundamental frequencies will yield more excitable results. Below is a table of frequencies and some descriptive terms that will help you when applying EQ to a mix.

General Descriptive Frequencies

Voice	Chest at 120 Hz; boom at 240 Hz; presence at 3–5 kHz; sibilance at 5–8 kHz; air at 10–15 kHz
Strings	Body at 240 Hz; scratchiness at 7–10 kHz
Bass Guitar	Bottom at 50–80 Hz; fullness at 120 Hz; attack at 800 Hz; slap at 2.5 kHz
Kick Drum	Thump at 65–90 Hz; boxiness at 350 Hz; beater at 3–5 kHz; pillow smack at 9–12 kHz
Conga	Tone at 200 Hz; smack at 3–5 kHz
Snare	Fatness at 120–240 Hz; shotgun pop at 800 Hz–1 kHz; crack at 3–5 kHz; snap at 9–12 kHz
Toms	Fullness at 180–360 Hz; attack at 5–7 kHz; snap at 8–10 kHz
Floor Tom	Fullness at 80–120 Hz; attack at 5 kHz; snap at 8–10 kHz
Hi-Hat and Cymbals	Clang at 200–350 Hz; harshness at 3–5 kHz; sparkle at 8–10 kHz
Electric Guitar	4×12 cabinet thump at 120 Hz; fullness at 240–600 Hz; presence at 1.5–2.5 kHz
Acoustic Guitar	Full body at 80–120 Hz; richness at 200–400 Hz; presence at 2–5 kHz; sparkle at 7–10 kHz
Organ	Fullness at 80–120 Hz; body at 240 Hz; presence at 2–5 kHz
Piano	Fullness at 80 Hz; boxiness at 200–360 Hz; presence at 2.5–5 kHz; sheen at 7–10 kHz
Horns	Fullness at 120–240 Hz; piercing at 5 kHz

COMMON EQ PARAMETERS

Bands. The frequency spectrum is divided into sections called bands. Each band spans a specific range of frequencies. By grouping frequencies into bands, we can more accurately apply EQ based on a range of frequencies.

Target Frequency. The target frequency is the frequency you are boosting or cutting. When you boost or cut, you are also affecting the surrounding frequencies. The target frequency is the center point, or starting point. In **Fig. 8.7**, the target frequency is 1000 Hz (1 kHz). You can see the center point of the curve is exactly 1000 Hz on the graph.

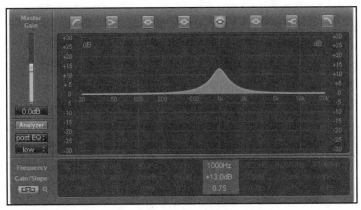

Fig. 8.7: A target frequency is indicated by the top number in the high-lighted box or in the center of the graphic band that has been boosted or cut.

Bandwidth. As previously mentioned, when we cut or boost we affect the surrounding frequencies. The range of affected frequencies is called the bandwidth, often abbreviated by the letter Q. **Fig. 8.8** the Q is represented by the number 4.30. To get a better idea of how Q works, look at **Fig. 8.8** and **Fig. 8.9**. Notice how a narrow Q and a wide Q affect the frequency curve.

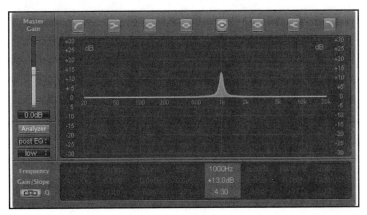

Fig. 8.8: Narrow Q, demonstrating how very few frequencies around the center (target) frequency are affected by the EQ boost.

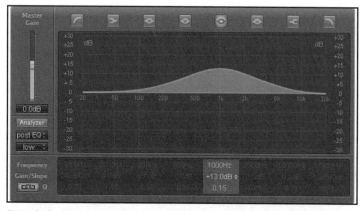

Fig. 8.9: Wide Q, demonstrating how a larger number of frequencies around the center (target) frequency are affected by the EQ boost.

Gain/Slope. This parameter determines how many decibels you are boosting or cutting from the signal. In **Fig. 8.10** the gain/slope is 18 dB. Keep in mind that these examples are only for a visual guide. Chances are you won't be boosting by 18 dB.

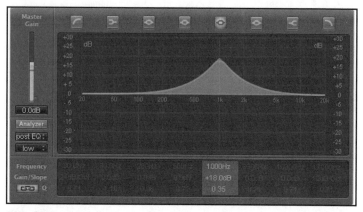

Fig. 8.10: The frequencies around the "target or center" frequency are often referred to as the gain slope.

Bell, Peak, and Notch. You won't see these terms listed in Logic, but they are used when referring to a combination of target frequency and bandwidth. A bell represents a broad curve and a wide bandwidth; the result is a smooth curve of affected frequencies that is more natural-sounding than its counterparts. Peak and Notch are similar in the sense that they both represent a clearly defined region with a sharp slope. Peak represents a sharp boost, while Notch represents a sharp cut. Think of them visually: a bell looks like a bell, a peak looks like a mountain, and a notch looks like a sharp cut notched out of the signal (see **Figs. 8.11**, **8.12**, and **8.13**).

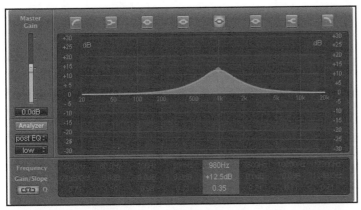

Fig. 8.11: This frequency curve or gain slope is known as a bell shape.

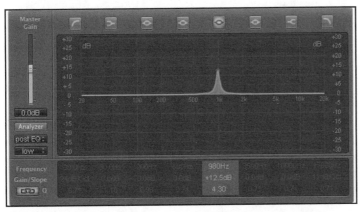

Fig. 8.12: This frequency curve or gain slope is known as a peak.

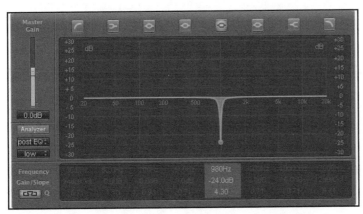

Fig. 8.13: This frequency curve or gain slope is known as a notch.

Active and Passive. An active EQ can add or remove the gain from a signal, whereas a passive EQ can only remove gain.

Graphic EQ. This is the type of EQ traditionally seen in home or car stereos. It consists of one or more vertical slots representing specific frequency bands, with individual sliders for boosting or cutting these specific frequencies. Each slot is labeled with the target frequency in Hz or kHz. The bandwidth of each band is predetermined and nonadjustable. You boost or cut the target frequency of each band by moving each slider up or down from the center position. A graphic EQ with multiple bands assigned to frequencies equally distributed across the spectrum is useful for smoothly shaping the contour of the entire range of frequencies present in a signal.

Parametric EQ. A parametric equalizer gives you full control over target frequency, bandwidth, and gain. This type of EQ was most commonly found on professional recording consoles and high-end outboard EQs. Most EQ plug-ins will also feature parametric EQs. The frequency spectrum is generally broken into four overlapping bands, designated as "lows," low mids," "high mids," and "highs."

Shelving EQ. Shelving EQ works by boosting or cutting all the frequencies above or below a target frequency by a certain amount, depending on if the EQ is a high shelf or a low shelf. For example, a high-shelf EQ with a target frequency of 4 kHz that is boosted 15 dB will apply 15 dB to 4 kHz and every frequency above 4 kHz up to 20 kHz. Notice how the "Q" affects the beginning of the shelf. You should also notice that the boosting begins slightly before 4 Hz, and adjusting the Q will makes changes to this curve that greatly affects its slope (see **Fig. 8.14**).

Similarly, a low-shelf EQ will boost or cut by a fixed amount the target frequency and all frequencies below the target all the way down to 20 Hz. If we apply a low-shelf EQ at 120 Hz with a gain of 15 dB, we will add 15 dB of gain to our target frequency and all frequencies below that (see **Fig. 8.15**).

High-Pass and Low-Pass Filters. Both high-pass and low-pass filters are passive EQs, as they remove, or filter out, selected

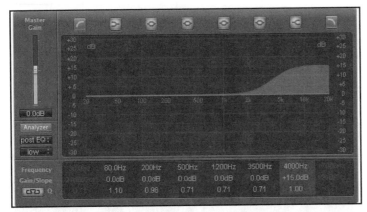

Fig. 8.14: This is an example of high shelving EQ.

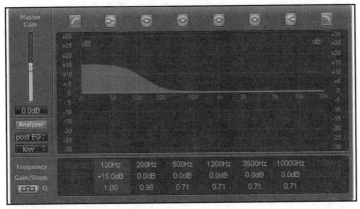

Fig. 8.15: This is an example of low shelving EQ.

frequencies. A high-pass filter does what it says: it allows high frequencies to pass through and remain in the signal, meaning it cuts, or filters out, the lows. A low-pass filter does the opposite: it allows the low frequencies to pass while filtering out the highs.

The frequencies above or below the target frequency are filtered out at a fixed rate, measured in decibels per octave, such as 6 or 12 dB per octave. The standard term for rating these filter slopes is known as the filter's "order." For example, a first-order filter will reduce a signal's amplitude by 6 dB for every octave above or below the target frequency; a second-order filter will reduce the signal's amplitude by 12 dB per octave; and so on. This "filtering" of the signal produces a spectrum shape, which tails off in a slanting line or "slope" from the target frequency to the end of the spectrum, in either direction. The severity of the slope is determined by which order of filter is being used. In Logic's Channel EQ, the first band is a high-pass filter and the eighth band is a low-pass filter. Notice that when active, the Gain field will allow you to see the slope. In **Fig. 8.16** and **Fig. 8.17** you can see the difference between first- and second-order filters; the same principle is reflected in the low-pass filters in **Fig. 8.18** and **Fig. 8.19**.

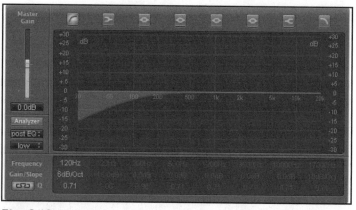

Fig. 8.16: This is an example of a first-order high-pass filter (6 dB per octave).

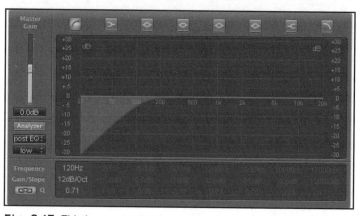

Fig. 8.17: This is an example of a second-order high-pass filter (12 dB per octave).

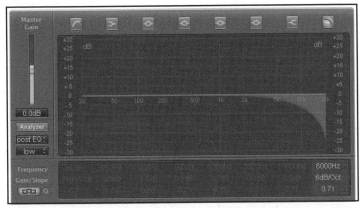

Fig. 8.18: This is an example of a first order low-pass filter (6 dB per octave).

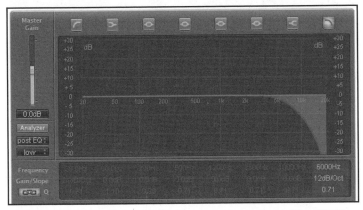

Fig. 8.19: This is an example of a second order low-pass filter (12 dB per octave).

COMPRESSION AND LIMITING

The use of compression on a track allows you to control its overall dynamic range. Compression is used to even out the varying levels of a performance, keeping it more consistent in volume overall. Compression will tame the louder portions of the signal and boost the volume of the less audible portions of the signal. Limiters, on the other hand, are used to stop or "limit" a signal from going over a certain volume level. This means that no matter how hard the signal hits the input of the dynamic processor, it will only pass through at a specific, predetermined level, and not 1/10th of a dB more. The use of these dynamic processors is very important in the mixing process, and they are commonly used on just about every professional mix you've ever heard. When you have more consistent signal levels, it is much easier to place instruments in your mix.

Let's take a look at a compressor in Logic (see **Fig. 8.20**). Just like with EQ, the parameters used in compressors tend to be universal.

Fig. 8.20: Logic's Platinum Compressor has all of the standard compression parameters.

Gain Reduction. This display lets us see how much compression is being applied to our signal.

Attack. This knob determines the amount of time it will take for the compressor to kick in and take effect. A fast attack will engage the compressor quickly; this is commonly used on sources with very fast transients, such as snare drums. A slower attack time may be more desirable for a bass guitar on a ballad.

Release. The release knob controls the amount of time it takes the compressor to get back to its starting point once the signal falls below the threshold.

Ratio. The ratio determines how much of the signal, measured in dB, is allowed to pass above the threshold. A four-to-one ratio is displayed as 4:1. This means that for every 4 dB the signal is above the threshold, only 1 dB will pass through. Here is a more specific example of a 4:1 ratio:

Threshold = 0 dB

Input = +4 dB (4 dB above the threshold)

Output = +1 dB (1 dB above the threshold)

The main difference between compressing and limiting is the ratio at which you are compressing. Compressing using a very high ratio, generally above 10:1, is considered limiting; above 20:1 it is known as brick-wall limiting.

Threshold. The threshold is a user-defined level. Any signal above this level will be compressed, or reduced in amplitude. Ratio has a direct effect on the level of gain reduction that will occur.

Gain. Also known as makeup gain, this allows you to bring the compressed signal back up to its original volume. If your gain reduction meter reads -5 dB, it is common to set the makeup gain at +5 dB, or maybe even a few decibels more than its original level. This is a preference and is usually determined by what kind of compressor is being used.

Knee. The knee feature adjusts how the compressor reacts when the signal is approaching the threshold. Lower values are for a *hard knee* style of compression, a more aggressive or immediate reaction, and higher values represent a *soft knee*, or smoother, and gentler type of compression.

There are many uses for compression, but as mentioned above, its main purpose is to control the dynamic range of any given source. However, there are other, more advanced methods of dynamic range manipulation. For instance, parallel compression, or "New York compression," is a typical method used for making rock drums more powerful. This type of compression is achieved when a compressor is placed on a parallel channel, is overcompressed and re-EQ'ed, and then blended in with the original drum mix. To do this, you bus the aux outputs of your drums to an auxiliary channel strip. Then you add heavy compression (10:1 or above with lots of gain reduction) to the auxiliary. Both the original drum mix and the new, heavily compressed signals will play back at the same time, in parallel. Start by bringing down the Aux fader and pressing Play, then slowly bring up the compressed drums and blend it with your original drum mix to your desired taste. You may have to experiment with the compression settings (attack/release), and maybe boost or cut certain frequencies to achieve the desired results. This is a great technique to add power to your drums, and has been used by professional audio engineers for decades.

GATING

A gate (see **Fig. 8.21**) is designed to block out unwanted background noise. For example, when you are recording with multiple microphones, you are likely to have "bleed," which is when another instrument leaks, or bleeds, into the primary signal. For instance, the kick mic will inevitably pick up the sound from the rest of the drum kit. Using a gate will block most of this unwanted bleed and leave you with just the sound of the kick drum. However, the end result may not sound anything like a kick drum if you don't spend time learning how to use a gate properly. We all have fun when we first learn how to use something, but I promise you, that doesn't mean you have to apply your new knowledge to every situation, all of the time. Remember, the ultimate gate is to edit your tracks individually and create good fade-ins and fade-outs so there are no clicks or

Fig. 8.2I: Logic's Silver Gate has all of the standard gate parameters.

pops. If you are trying to completely eliminate background noise from your primary source, a gate may not achieve the results you are looking for. I guess my point is, do not sacrifice the sound of the original source by trying to have the gate block out absolutely every bit of background noise on the track. Chances are, you will cut out some "ghost" notes, compromise the sound of the attack of the kick, and set the release so fast that there is no "drum" in your kick drum.

The parameters of Logic's Silver Gate are similar to those of a compressor. The attack and release determine how fast the gate will open and close. There is another parameter labeled "Hold." This determines how long the gate is held open after the signal has dipped below the threshold. The threshold sets the level at which the gate opens. Remember to be careful when setting your gate's threshold; it may not be high enough, and you could be gating more than you expected.

Gates can also be used for creative production enhancements. For instance, you can assign the key input of a gate so that it is triggered, or opened, by another audio signal that is being bused to it. Let's go through how to use a key input on a gate to fatten up a kick drum.

Fig. 8.22 shows the audio track of a generic kick drum. Notice that send 1 has been assigned to bus 1. In the example, I've set up the Aux track to have a Test Oscillator on the first insert and Silver Gate as the second insert. The Test Oscillator is a signal generator that will play back a tone or frequency of your choice. In this case we want a low sine wave that is very obvious and audible, around 120–240 Hz. Underneath the oscillator, the Silver Gate is set so that the gate is silencing or "gating" the 220 Hz oscillator tone. Then, I've set its sidechain input to bus 1, so it can receive the copy of the audio signal being sent from bus 1 of the kick drum. I then set a cycle range and play back my selection, and make adjustments to the gate's threshold so that it opens every time the kick is heard. When the kick triggers the gate to open, the sound of the oscillator is allowed to pass, and you'll hear the original kick and the sound of the oscillator. Once the oscillator is triggering properly, I go ahead and set the frequency to a tone that complements the kick drum.

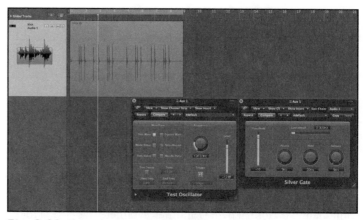

Fig. 8.22: Example setup of triggering a gated oscillator with the kick drum.

A 40 Hz oscillator is very common in hip-hop, and is a preset on many popular drum machines. It is what makes the car stereos go "boooom."

TIME-BASED EFFECTS

So far, we have covered dynamics processing, which affects the gain of the signal. Compressors, gates, and EQs are all dynamics based. Time-based effects, on the other hand, alter the signal by affecting its timing. These effects include reverbs, delays, choruses, flangers, phasers, and pitch shifters. All of these effects are generated by making a copy of the signal, altering the copy, and blending it with the original signal. For this reason you should use time-based effects on auxiliary tracks. If you do happen to apply a time-based effect directly to a signal, you will have to adjust the wet/dry parameters accordingly.

While these plug-ins tend to be more fun, they are generally only the icing on the cake that is your mix. A good mix is mainly based on adjusting faders and panning. EQ and dynamics are next in line. Time-based effects can make your mix sound amazing, but don't rely on them solely, as you still need to have a solid mix before applying these effects. Truth be told, they can be the icing on the cake, or the complete demise of your mix. Please use them sparingly. Most people can tell when someone just bought a new plug-in and are learning how to use it. Remember, sometimes less is more when mixing. When mixing, you are usually trying to create an illusion, a small space, a big space, a certain ambience, often times a "subtle effect," and that wont be achieved if the source is "drowning" in that effect.

Start by experimenting with channel strip settings on aux channels (see **Fig. 8.23**). You'll notice the available settings differ from the channel strip settings of audio channels and software instruments. Study the different settings and listen to the changes. Expose yourself to as many sounds as you can, and build your own mental effects library.

Next Channel Strip Setting	⇧]
Previous Channel Strip Setting	⇧[
Copy Channel Strip Setting	⌥⌘C
Paste Channel Strip Setting	⌥⌘V
Reset Channel Strip	
Save Channel Strip Setting as...	
Save as Performance...	
Delete Channel Strip Setting	
01 Spaces	▶
02 Imaging	▶
03 Delays	▶
04 Groups	▶
05 Warped	▶
06 Surround Spaces	▶
07 HD Surround Spaces	▶
08 Surround Delays	▶
09 Surround Groups	▶
10 Surround Multi-FX	▶
11 Surround Tools	▶
12 Warped Surround	▶
13 G4 Optimized	▶

Fig. 8.23: Options in channel-strip aux settings.

Space Designer

As you recall from a previous chapter, one of the more powerful effects included with Logic Pro 9 is the Space Designer plug-in (see **Fig. 8.24**). It has incredibly real-sounding reverb spaces for a very specific reason: it uses impulse responses. A really cool thing about Space Designer is that not only does it have a huge assortment of spaces to choose from, as well as the addition of the warped feature for enhanced creativity, but it also gives us the ability to create a convolution reverb or an "impulse response" ourselves. An impulse response, or IR, is a sampled reverb. Just as we can record a piano for sampling in a player like the EXS24, we can also sample the reverb of a given space. Each space will respond differently to the audio placed in it, based on the unique characteristics of the space. For example, a church with stone

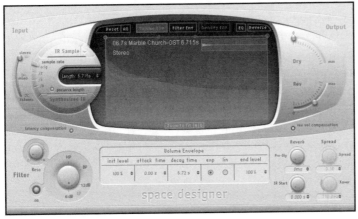

Fig. 8.24: The Logic Pro 9 Space Designer GUI.

walls will sound very different from a small room with carpet on the walls.

To sample your own space and create an IR from scratch, you must use the bundled Impulse Response Utility. When you install Logic this utility is placed in the following path: Applications/ Utilities/Impulse Response Utility. Navigate to the IR utility and open it up. Now, to create a custom impulse response, you must start by creating a New Project. Simply use the keyboard shortcut Command + N. The utility will ask you what format you would like to use. For this example, and to keep it simple, we'll just use mono. Set your input and output along the top. I suggest you just use the built-in settings for now, as it is more important to catch the steps and fundamentals of this process, and then let your imagination take over.

Once your I/O is set up, record-enable your track by pressing the square R button from the row of options just underneath where it says Empty Track. You'll notice that your choices are for Speaker Position, Mic Position, Input, Solo, Record, Lock, Peak, and Level. You should see the level jump if you make noise near the microphone. Leave the settings at their default for the sake of this example. When you are ready, press the Sweep button. This sends an oscillator tone into the room, sweeping in frequency from very low to very high; I would guess 20 Hz–20 kHz at least, as this is what represents the range of human hearing. While the sweep is played your microphones will pick up this tone and your IR is recorded. As soon as the sweep finishes, you are prompted to save. Now you need to select the Deconvolve option from the Process area of the utility (see **Fig. 8.25**). Let the computer crunch some numbers, do a little magic, and bam! You've created a usable IR. Nice! Once this process finishes, you can choose to audition your IR with some preset sources to immediately hear the result. Once you are finished auditioning, you must choose the Create Space Designer Setting option at the lower left corner of the utility. You will be asked to name it. Once named and saved, Logic will remind you of the save location (see **Fig. 8.26**). If you return to Logic and open Space Designer, your preset will now appear (see F**ig. 8.27**).

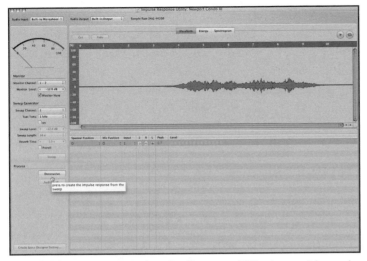

Fig. 8.25: Example of the Impulse Response Utility deconvolving and creating a custom impulse response.

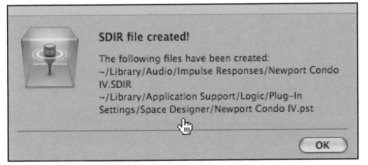

Fig. 8.26: Confirmation of a saved Space Designer Impulse Response file.

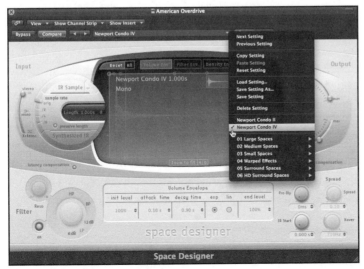

Fig. 8.27: Saved preset selected for use in Space Designer.

To create more specific and elaborate impulse responses, refer to the Impulse Response Utility Manual found within the application. This will also explain how to create custom IRs in multiple formats. Our example is just to show you what happens in a typical impulse response, and how reverb can be effectively sampled. If this doesn't inspire some creativity, I don't know what will.

Delay Designer

Delay Designer was a great addition to Logic 8, and it's still a great plug-in today (see **Fig. 8.28a**). This is a very versatile multi-tap delay where each "tap" is a unique delay. The Delay Designer is capable of up to 26 taps, so in essence one instance of Delay Designer is made up of 26 separate delay processors.

You can assign different parameters to each tap, including level and pan position, high-pass and low-pass filters, and pitch transposition. There are also global parameters that apply to all taps, such as synchronization, quantization, and feedback.

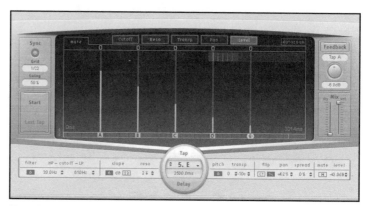

Fig. 8.28a: The Delay Designer GUI.

The main blue window is where you draw in taps, set levels, and adjust individual parameters. The five buttons that you can select along the top of this window are Level, Pan, Transposition, Resonance, and Cutoff. The taps are labeled alphabetically. You can draw in taps by placing your cursor over the ruler portion of the blue window. The cursor will turn into a Pencil tool. You can also reposition existing taps by grabbing them and dragging them along the ruler. By default, the ruler will be the same meter and tempo as your project. This is convenient as it allows you to easily create musically based taps such as eighth notes without having to do a lot of math. If you disable the Sync button, the ruler's grid disappears.

To adjust the individual components of a tap, click-and-drag vertically. For volume adjustments, a help tag appears to tell you the level. When Pan is selected, the taps turn purple, and the pan location is set by a dot. Dragging this shows the percentage of left and right panning. The Transposition tab turns the taps green, and the relative pitch of the tap is indicated by a dot. You can change this in semitones. Resonance and Cutoff act similarly. There are almost too many options available. You don't have to use all of them to make a great-sounding delay, but it is nice to have so many options for creativity.

Plug-in Settings

Finally, a few things to know about using the plug-ins. If you select the View menu, you have two choices for viewing the plug-in: Controls or Editor. Controls is for getting down to "brass tacks"—it's about the parameters available. If you want to use the plug-ins from a more aesthetically pleasing view, use the Editor view. Also, in Logic 9 you can resize most of the plug-ins from the View menu. Your choices are from 100 percent to 200 percent, so enjoy!

Also, remember that using the default presets for these plug-ins is a great starting point, but as you start to learn the plug-ins inside and out and can get the results you are listening for, you may want to start saving your own presets. Every plug-in gives you the ability to save and quickly recall your own presets. From the same drop-down menu where you load presets, you can select Save Setting As. Name your setting so you will recognize it. By default Logic will save it in the appropriate location: ~/Library/Application Support/Logic/Plug-In Settings/

The "~" represents your User folder. Logic will automatically choose the appropriate plug-in from within the plug-in settings folder.

A lesser-known, but very powerful feature is the ability to back up your plug-in settings, channel strip settings, and key commands to your Apple MobileMe (.Mac) account, if you have one. This creates a backup directory labeled MusicAudioData and is placed in your Public folder. You can also share the data using Bonjour, a local network-based service. If you have other Macs on your network that run Logic, as long as those computers are on, Logic will browse those computers for shared settings.

IMPORTING DATA AND SETTINGS FROM PREVIOUS PROJECTS

New in Logic Pro 9 is the ability to load important data from other sessions. This is a huge benefit in so many ways. The most obvious would be if you had a great vocal channel set up for a particular artist, with just the right dynamics, EQ settings, and effects. Now you can easily import the exact settings from the other project and don't have to set up this person's settings from scratch for each song and session. This capability is a huge time saver that has been around for years, so thank goodness it was added to Logic Pro 9.

There are three ways to import session data: go to File > Project Settings > Import Project Settings (or use the shortcut keys Option + Command + I); click the Settings button in the Arrange toolbar and choose Import Project Settings; or go to the Browser tab in the Media area. Next, navigate to the particular project that has the channel with the settings you would like to import, and click the Import option. From the Import Settings window (see **Fig. 8.28b**), select what you need from the available options checkboxes. Finally, click the Import button, and the settings will be imported into the current project. Simple as that!

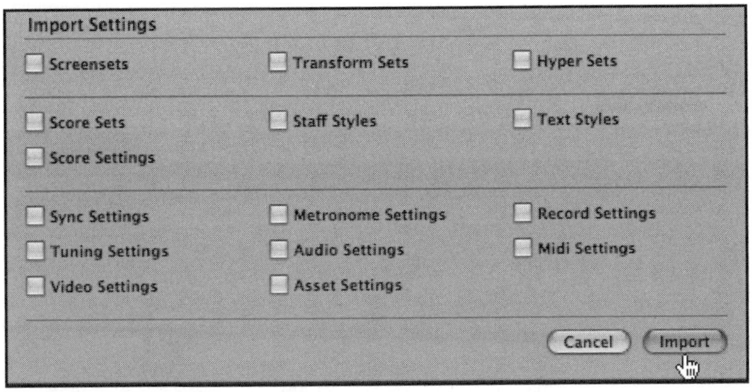

Fig. 8.28b: New Import Project Settings window.

AUTOMATION

Logic features an amazingly powerful yet simple automation system for mixing. Automation can control the playback movements of volume, pan, EQ, aux sends, and much more. There is even a new option to include the automation trail when moving or copying a region with automation. Plug-ins also are capable of being automated. Automation operates independently from audio and MIDI. It is also independent from the record and playback modes, so automation can be recorded at any time. Don't confuse recording audio and MIDI with recording automation.

To view the automation data, select Track Automation from the View menu, or simply press "A." Notice that your regions become transparent. This transparency allows you to keep the automation data in focus while still being able to reference the original region.

The automation data is shown as colored lines, curves, and dots known as nodes. Don't confuse these nodes with the distributed audio processing nodes we spoke about earlier; these nodes are simply points along the automation lines. Different automation data is represented by different colors (see **Figs. 8.29** and **8.30**).

Volume	Displayed in yellow
Pan	Displayed in green
Mute	Displayed in light blue
Solo	Also displayed in yellow
Sends and various plug-ins	Displayed in dark blue

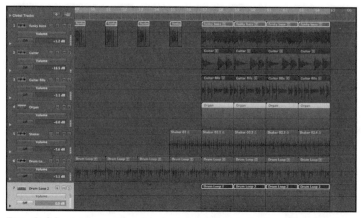

Fig. 8.29: Volume automation features shown in the track headers in the Arrange window.

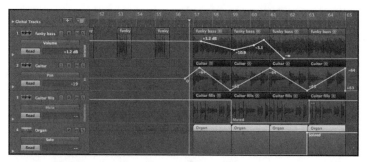

Fig. 8.30: Volume, pan, mute, and solo automation options shown in the track headers, and graphical examples in each of the audio and MIDI regions. Each automation feature is assigned specific colors for quick and easy recognition.

Fig. 8.31: Click on the Automation on/off parameter (or select the letter A), and then choose the desired parameter to automate from the automation-options drop-down menu.

These represent the automation parameters available for each track. To select them, click on the button below the name of the track, and choose them from the menu (see **Fig. 8.31**). You can also automate just about every parameter of every plug-in. If you have a plug-in inserted on a channel, those parameters will be displayed in the Automation menu. Every knob and fader is at your disposal. With so many options, the creative potential is unlimited.

Automation is a great way to even out the levels of your mix. Compression helps you maintain a more consistent level in your overall signal, but it still may be necessary to automate volume changes for a particular section of your song or for the entire track. Many engineers prefer using level automation to using compression for riding a vocal track. It's a bit more tedious, but it's really just a preference that yields different results. Anyway, automation allows you to record every fader move you make, and then play it back exactly as you entered it. You can automate a pan to have a signal move from left to right, or even create a "stutter"-type effect by quickly turning mutes on and off. You may have a great special effect for the vocal that only happens during the bridge of the song. This is when you would automate when plug-ins are active and inactive.

As you can see, pretty soon you'll want to add multiple levels of automation. On one track alone you may want to add volume, pan, mute, and plug-in automation. How can you do this? For each parameter you wish to automate, you will create a new automation lane. To create a new automation lane, simply click on the disclosure triangle next to the automation status button. A new lane drops down. This is similar to the lanes from when we did "comping." The lane looks like a duplicate of the track, when in fact it is just an alias. You can create many automation lanes to add as much automation data as you need. Notice in **Fig. 8.32** that we have added volume, pan, solo, and mute automation as well as a unique plug-in parameter and a bypass automation lane to temporarily disable a plug-in.

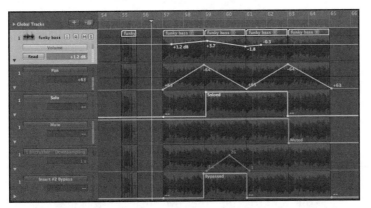

Fig. 8.32: Multiple visual aids for viewing and fine-tuning automation are called Automation Lanes. These lanes make it easy to have full control over all the automation possibilities for the channel.

All those automation lanes look pretty, but you can imagine that they can get out of hand when you are mixing a full project. Therefore, you can collapse the automation lanes into a single lane, and all the data will be retained and will play back. You can see all of the automation lines, but only the selected automation parameter will be highlighted. In **Fig. 8.33**, all of our automation from **Fig. 8.32** is still present, but the volume automation is highlighted.

Fig. 8.33: Collapsed lanes showing a "ghosted" visual aid for all automation on the track and on any given single channel.

Drawing in automation is a great way to accurately map the automation to your track, but just like everything else, it requires some fine-tuning and editing. To edit automation you will use a few tools. The regular Pointer tool is used to create nodes. When you create a node, you are creating a break in the line, after which you can drag up and down and the automation line will pivot from the node. The Pointer tool can also be used to adjust the position of nodes by clicking and dragging. To select automation, use the Automation Select Tool. This looks like the Pointer tool but has a squiggly tail on the end. When using this tool, you can rubber-band a section of automation for editing. Trimming automation maintains all the automation points, but brings the entire performance up or down. For example, you might have great volume automation, but the entire performance of the track is still too loud. To bring it down, select your automation data with the Automation Select Tool, click-and-drag on a selected node, and drag down. A help tag will display by how many decibels you are trimming your automation. Use the Automation Curve Tool to adjust the slope between two nodes. By default points are connected in a linear fashion. You can use this tool to sculpt the curve that controls how fast the change between nodes occurs (see **Fig. 8.34**).

Fig. 8.34: The curves or "slopes" for the automation move from breakpoint to breakpoint.

Now that we've had some fun automating in the Arrange window by drawing in automation, it's time to learn how to automate by making changes to the associated parameter. For instance, drawing in volume changes is great, but you may feel more comfortable grabbing the fader and making adjustments during playback. To make automation changes during playback, you need to select one of the automation modes. By default, a track's automation is set to "Off" until there is actual automation data. By drawing automation, the mode automatically changes to "Read," meaning the track will play back all the automation created. Let's go over the remaining automation modes and what they do.

Off. This will disable all automation without deleting it. No automation data is written, read, or played back.

Read. Reads all existing automation data. No automation data can be written.

Touch. Touch mode plays back automation similarly to Read mode; however, if a parameter is touched during playback in Touch mode, automation data will be written while that parameter is being touched. As soon as it is released it will return to its previously recorded value. Keep in mind that you can also adjust how quickly a parameter will return to its previously recorded value by adjusting the Ramp Time. This setting, and all other automate-able setting options, are available from Preferences > Automation (see **Fig. 8.35**).

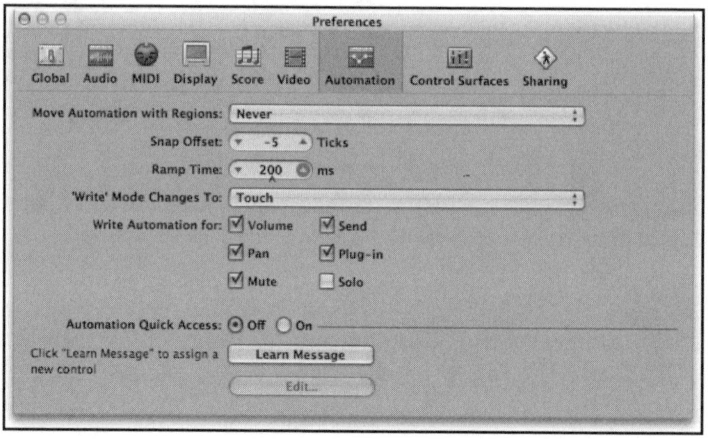

Fig. 8.35: Ramp Time settings can be customized from the Automation Preferences menu.

Touch mode is considered to be the most commonly used mode for automation, as it lets you audition automation as well as change it on the fly by "riding the fader." You can set a cycle range and make changes in one pass, audition them on the next pass, and then make more changes on the next pass.

Latch. Latch mode works like Touch mode, with the exception that when the parameter is released, automation data is written at the last value. This will overwrite existing automation. Essentially, the parameter is latched, and will not return to its previously recorded position when it is released. Automation is continually written even after the parameter is released.

Write. Write mode is very dangerous, as it is constantly writing automation, but will not read existing automation data. As the playhead moves, it will overwrite any automation. At some point, you may wish to overwrite volume automation with Write mode, but don't forget that *all* automation data is overwritten in this mode. To customize what is overwritten, go to the Automation preferences window and deselect the parameters you don't wish to overwrite in Write mode.

In Logic Pro 9, several automation tools have been moved, but they are available from the Track menu under Track Automation. One of the more useful options is to delete all track automation (see **Fig. 8.36**). You can do this quickly by using the keyboard shortcut Control + Shift + Command + Delete.

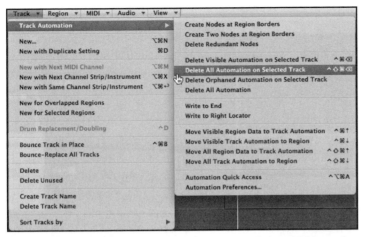

Fig. 8.36: Track Automation menu with the option Delete All Automation on Selected Track selected.

Automation Quick Access. You can also add automation data by using an external MIDI controller. This is great if you prefer to physically turn knobs and adjust faders. To set this up, go to the Automation preferences by pressing Option + A. Enable Quick Access Automation. A dialog prompts you to assign and learn a MIDI controller (see **Fig. 8.37**). Slowly move the knob or fader on your MIDI controller. Move it through its entire range. If it is a fader, start with the fader all the way down, so when you move it up you can take advantage of the fader's throw. Likewise, for knobs, start with the knob all the way down. For rotary encoders, make one full revolution. Confirm your selection by pressing the "Done" button. When finished, the MIDI controller will have control over the active automation parameter.

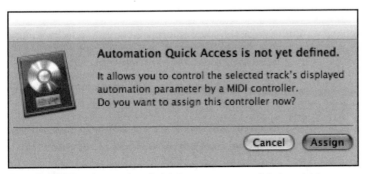

Fig. 8.37: The Automation Quick Access menu assists in quickly assigning MIDI controllers to specific parameters.

MASTERING

So now you've tracked every instrument, tirelessly edited each into a solid performance, and blended and automated everything so you have a nice stereo mix. Now it's time to master. What does this mean?

In the mixing stage you made certain that all of the instruments sit correctly in the mix, and you applied the proper amounts of EQ, compression, and time-based effects. The art of mastering usually consists of equalization, compression, multi-band compression, limiting, noise reduction, ambience creation, and dithering. The actual process of mastering will vary depending on the audio content. Logic Pro ships with a dedicated mastering application called WaveBurner, and I highly recommend that you learn how to use it if you are serious about mastering professional-quality CDs for mass duplication.

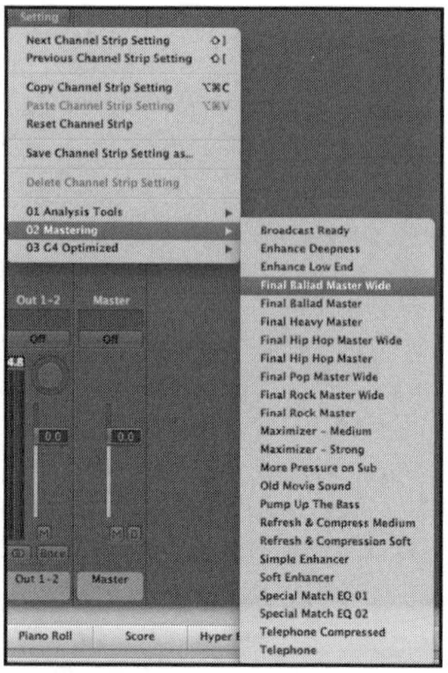

Fig. 8.38: Mastering presets to be used on the main channel outputs.

However, we can still master inside of Logic to maximize our mix. To do this, we can add some EQ and limiting to the main output. This will allow you to shape the overall frequency curve and overall volume levels of your mix to resemble the professional CDs you listen to every day. If you are unsure of the order for your inserts, you can start by loading some channel strip mastering presets on the main output (see **Fig. 8.38**). These are good starting points for getting an idea of what your final signal path may look like. However, I suggest you don't use a preset for mastering. In a commando-style mastering environment such as your bedroom or small home studio, where there aren't as many plug-in choices, try starting with a linear phase EQ on the first insert, followed by a nice limiter.

Listen carefully to a few professional CDs as a reference. You can even use a frequency analyzer as a visual aid to help you with frequency recognition. I highly suggest using a reference to help you achieve your goal. Remember, the goal here is to get the overall frequency curve of your entire mix to resemble professionally mastered songs that are played on the radio. If you have done a nice job of mixing, you will notice right away when you compare your mixes to professionally released CDs in the same music genre. If your mix is in the ballpark, you will only need to make very small boosts and cuts to your EQ along the frequency curve to resemble the professional reference you have chosen. The limiter at the end of the chain is only there to boost the overall output of your mix to make it "broadcast ready."

If the results are less than what you expected, that's okay. Mastering engineers are paid really well for good reason. They work in very controlled environments, use top-notch equipment, and usually have finely tuned ears and years of experience. However, you too can achieve great results if you take your time and have the right approach.

If you discover that mastering is just not for you, and you would like a professional audio engineer to master your music, be sure not to bounce your mix with any mastering plug-ins on your master outputs. In fact, it is important that you leave enough headroom in your mix so that a mastering engineer will have room to work. Somewhere between 3–5 dB below 0 dBfs is good.

If you aren't sending your mix to a mastering engineer, and you don't plan on mastering it in WaveBurner, then go ahead and apply the final EQ and limiting to your mix as discussed earlier. When you feel that you've achieved a well-balanced mix overall, your frequency curve is in check, and you've brought your mix up to within 0.1 dB of clipping, you can finally "bounce" your final mastered mix.

You can access the bounce dialog from the File menu by pressing the "Bnce" button on the "Out 1-2" fader, or by using the keyboard shortcut Command + B. By default, bouncing will create a stereo mixdown from the start and end markers of your project. If a cycle range is selected, only that range will be bounced. Make sure your selection captures the entire song. Also, allow room at the end of your song for reverb tails and delays to end without being cut off.

When the Bounce dialog comes up (see **Fig. 8.39**), you will have many destinations to choose from. First of all, name and choose the Save location. Next, choose the destination. You can select more than one, which is convenient if you plan to deliver your song in multiple formats. You can burn directly to a CD by using the CDDA option, but if you wish to burn a disc later from your audio files, use the PCM option. Select WAV or AIFF, and be sure to choose 16-bit resolution, Interleaved as the file type, and 44.1 as the sampling rate. This is the consumer standard. If you wish to add this song to your iTunes library, you have the option to do so from the PCM, MP3, and M4A bounce destinations. I recommend using the M4A for iTunes export, as it is the compression scheme that Apple uses for music in the iTunes Music Store. If you bounce using the MP3 option, you can add ID3 tag information, which allows you to add metadata to the track, including artist, album year, etc.

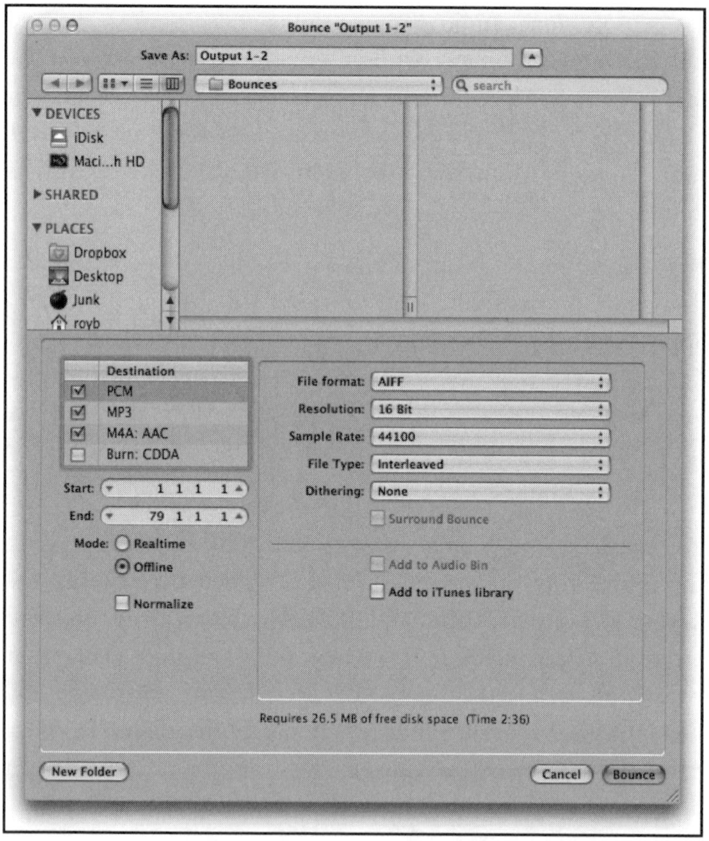

Fig. 8.39: The Bounce menu allows several audio formats to be selected and created in one pass. It also includes settings for dithering, normalizing, and start and end times.

You can select as many destinations as you like from here so you can do an all-encompassing bounce to handle all of your delivery needs. You also have the option to normalize your mix. This is one last gain stage to ensure that your mix is at an optimum level. Yet if you have created a great mix and mastered it well, you should not need to normalize when you burn. You also have the option for a real-time bounce or an offline bounce. A real-time bounce will play the length of the song as it bounces. An Offline bounce will utilize your CPU power to quickly process a bounce. Generally, you will use Offline as your bounce of choice. Many professional audio engineers will do a real-time bounce, as they typically use external outboard gear.

FINAL THOUGHTS

Congratulations—you have made it through a thorough music creation and production process from beginning to end. In this final chapter, you learned how to create a well-balanced mix and a mastered final product. Remember as you go through the entire production process that your product will only be as good as the previous stage. This is one of the most important things to realize if you are serious about obtaining professional results. If your computer is not set up properly and you don't have the right hardware and software combinations, you are limited from the start. If you don't have a fundamental knowledge base regarding the platform on which you are working, you can't expect a manageable, well-organized project or session. If you don't start the recording project with a good source to begin with, do not expect to "fix it in the mix." And if you don't use solid fundamental mixing techniques while mixing, don't expect the mastering process to magically make your mix come alive. You will find that some steps are more fun than others, but you must remember that they are all equally important. In this book, I've tried to at least touch on every stage of the music production process, and open your eyes to the many different aspects of audio engineering.

Many students attend audio engineering schools or buy books to teach them how to make their music sound like what they hear on the radio. Often they believe they simply need to learn how to push a few buttons and twist a few knobs, and the computer will take care of the rest. In reality, the process is nothing close to that. It takes years of dedication for someone to learn on their own or to gain experience and wisdom from professionals in the field.

As a professional music and audio engineering instructor for over 20 years, I can only hope to instill in you the basic and sometimes not-so-basic aspects of audio engineering, and share with you some of the many things I've learned from my own personal experience. Trying to condense this knowledge down into one digestible book that isn't too intimidating in size has been a rather tall order. However, after reading this book, I hope you will have developed some good habits for project organization and setup, as well as learned several Logic Power Tips that will help you streamline your workflow.

There are always many ways to accomplish a given task, so be sure to constantly seek better ways to get from point A to point B. At times Logic, or any DAW platform can get a little technical, but make sure it doesn't interfere with your creativity. Remember, the ultimate goal of recording music is to create your own unique masterpiece. The computer is only there to help you in this process. You'll soon come to know Logic as an instrument unto itself, and as with any instrument, a lot of practice will help you get better. With all of the powerful new features, and software instruments bundled with Logic Pro 9, you should always be able to find new ways to sculpt sounds and shape your creations the way you hear them in your head. If you ever need an inspirational jump-start, create a new track with a few random plug-ins on it and start playing around. Logic 9 is true inspiration in a box. Knowing the information in this book will show you how to open that box and create something new every time.

Be sure to continuously review what you have learned, not only in this chapter, but also in the entire book. Watch the QuickTime videos and review the end-of-chapter Power Tip summaries and the Logic 9 Tune-Up questions.

I sincerely thank you for taking the time to read this book. Hopefully you've learned a lot, and I wish you the very best of luck in your musical adventures with Logic Pro 9.

POWER TIPS FOR CHAPTER 8

1. When mixing, you should max out your I/O buffer size from the Core Audio tab. Also be sure to turn off low-latency monitoring. This will optimize your CPU power, and allow more plug-ins, automation, track count, and anything else that requires CPU processing.

2. Apple's built-in Activity Monitor will provide a good visual representation of exactly how much RAM you have available. You will find this feature in the Applications/Utilities folder on your main OS drive. Once you have it open, select the System Memory tab to see your RAM information.

3. If you have a few extra computers lying around, Apple has embraced the process of distributed audio processing, or chaining multiple computers together so you can pool their resources to take care of CPU-intensive activities. Make sure you go over the Nodes section in this chapter to take advantage of this process.

4. Try mixing all of your audio without using any compression or limiting on your main output channel. It may be a bit more difficult not to slam the main output channel, but it will be worth your careful efforts when it comes time to master your mixes.

5. Remember to use dynamics processing directly on the track via inserts, but use aux tracks for your time-based effects.

6. When using the automation features that return to their original position when you let go of them, remember that you can set the amount of time it takes for them to return to their original position by adjusting the Ramp Time from the Preferences/Automation menu.

7. Write mode can be very destructive if not used properly, because it overwrites all automation data by default. However you can customize what is overwritten by going to the Automation preferences window and deselecting the parameters you do not wish to overwrite.

8. When mastering, it is crucial to carefully listen to professional CDs as a reference. You can also use a frequency spectrum analyzer to visualize the frequency curve of your reference and help you match the frequency curve of your mix to the reference.

9. If you are sending your mixes to a professional mastering house, be sure to leave the mastering engineer approximately 3 dB of headroom so that they can do their job properly. Try to be accurate and consistent with the amount of headroom you leave. It will let them know that you are serious and consistent, and that you expect the same level of professionalism and consistency from them.

10. Logic is very cool when it comes time to bounce your final mixes. You can select as many bounce formats as you like so you can do an all-encompassing bounce to handle all of your delivery needs at once. If you have done your mixing and mastering properly, be sure to deselect the Normalize function from the Bounce dialog.

KEYBOARD SHORTCUT

Here is a list of some keyboard shortcuts that are either mentioned in the text or used in the QuickTime tutorials that accompany this book. Try to memorize as many of these commands as soon as possible. Knowing the menus is very important, but knowing shortcuts saves you time and is a real convenience once you get them under your command.

KEYBOARD SHORTCUT	FUNCTION
Option + X	Show CPU Usage Meters
Option + Click	Sets ascending outputs for channels
Option + Command + I	Import Session Data
Option + A	Show Automation Preferences Pane
Control + Shift + Command + Delete	Clear all automation
Command + B	Bounce outputs 1-2

LOGIC 9 TUNE-UP

1. When using plug-ins while mixing, please remember that the _____ _____ are great for inspiration, and are a great place to start, but they weren't designed for specific situations.

2. _____ _____ is probably the most effective way to free up resources on your computer and is used quite often during the mixing stage.

3. If you are using Nodes for distributed audio processing, the Logic Pro Node software must be _____ on every spare Mac you wish to use. You can find the Node installer on the Logic Studio install disk.

4. Nodes can be used on a wireless network. True or False?

5. The Node application much be launched _____ launching Logic Pro on your primary system.

6. Nodes are best utilized when mixing. If you are using Nodes while recording, the amount of _____ will make using it impractical.

7. You can select the Bounce option from the File menu, but the most convenient way to quickly access the Bounce dialog is by pressing the _____ button on your Output channel.

8. Logic's powerful delay plug-in is called _____
_____.

9. You can save your custom plug-in settings by using the
_____ _____ option from the drop-down menu
where you load the factory presets.

10. Different automation data is represented by various colors.
Please list the color of the corresponding automation feature.
automation feature.

Volume _____

Panning _____

Mute _____

Solo _____

11. To create a new automation lane, simply click on the
_____ _____ next to the Automation
Status button.

12. There are four modes of automation: Read, Touch, Latch,
and _____

13. _____ mode is the most commonly used and is
considered by many to be the most powerful.

14. To delete all track automation, use the keyboard shortcut
_____+_____+_____
+_____

15. When you choose the Bounce option, the stereo mixdown
will include everything in between the start and end
markers. To be more specific with your "bounces," set the
_____ _____ to be exactly the length
you would like your stereo mixdown to be.

16. The consumer standard for audio CDs is _____-bit and
_____ kHz.

17. The compression scheme Apple uses for music in the iTunes
Music Store is _____.

18. If you bounce using the _____ option, you can include ID3 tag information, which allows you to add metadata to the track, such as artist, album, year, etc.

19. A _____ bounce is typically used by professional audio engineers, as it is common for them to use external outboard gear when mixing or mastering.

20. An _____ bounce will utilize your CPU power to quickly process the bounce.

Answer Key for Logic 9 Tune-ups

CHAPTER 2
1. amplitude, frequency, and waveform
2. decibels
3. 120 dB
4. frequencies
5. hertz
6. kilohertz
7. 20 Hz–20 kHz
8. lower
9. one octave
10. waveform
11. simple and complex
12. complex
13. microphones
14. condenser
15. frequency response
16. frequency curve
17. analog to digital conversion
18. 44.1kHz
19. two times
20. 96 dB, 144 dB
21. plug-in
22. Audio Units
23. delay

CHAPTER 3
1. Explore, Compose, Produce
2. music/logic
3. 24, 16
4. dynamic range
5. 4 GB
6. Save As
7. Core Audio
8. transport

9. Klopfgeist
10. Command + Option + N
11. audio, software instrument, external MIDI
12. Scroll in Play
13. early, often

CHAPTER 4
1. signal flow
2. 44.1
3. name
4. Arrange
5. Arrange, Mix
6. Track Names to Regions
7. green, blue, mustard
8. H
9. audio, MIDI
10. C Major, 120 bpm, 4/4

CHAPTER 5
1. seconds
2. playback
3. Replace
4. lanes
5. red, green
6. feedback
7. aux sends
8. pre-fader
9. merge
10. phantom power
11. dynamic processing
12. Time-Based Effects
13. wet/dry
14. 100 percent
15. convolution

CHAPTER 6
1. CPU power
2. aux sends, panning, fader levels
3. group
4. group clutch
5. optimizing
6. 40
7. Ultrabeat
8. synthesizer
9. Alter Existing Randomly
10. EXS24 mkII
11. RAM
12. Tune, fine tuning
13. attack, decay, sustain, release
14. 5.1 surround
15. sidechain input

CHAPTER 7
1. Ascending Inputs option
2. tab
3. Key Commands
4. right-click
5. Control + Option
6. Inspector's Region Parameter
7. maximize your screen real estate
8. Shift + Control + R.
9. functions
10. shift

CHAPTER 8
1. factory presets
2. Freezing Tracks
3. installed

4. False
5. before
6. latency
7. "Bnce"
8. Delay Designer
9. Save As
10. Volume—Yellow, Panning—Green, Mute—Blue
11. Disclosure triangle
12. Write
13. Touch
14. Control + Shift + Command + Delete
15. cycle range
16. 16-bit and 44.1 kHz
17. M4A
18. MP3
19. real-time
20. offline

Index

ABOUT THE AUTHOR

Rick Silva is the owner of Mixed Emotions Productions, a mixing and mastering facility in Studio City, California, and a veteran pro-audio instructor for the Recording Institute of Technology at the Musicians Institute in Hollywood, California. He is also a member of the Program Advisory Committee for the Bachelor of Science program in audio engineering at the Art Institute of California – Los Angeles in Santa Monica. His specialties include musicianship, practical recording technique, console theory, Waves Certification training and all aspects of DAWs.